THE TREE OF LIFE AND DEATH

THE TREE OF LIFE AND DEATH

Transforming the Qliphoth

Ian Rees

AEON

First published in 2022 by
Aeon Books

Copyright © 2022 by Ian Rees

The right of Ian Rees to be identified as the author of this work has been asserted in accordance with §§ 77 and 78 of the Copyright Design and Patents Act 1988.

All rights reserved. No part of this publication may be reproduced, stored in a retrieval system, or transmitted, in any form or by any means, electronic, mechanical, photocopying, recording, or otherwise, without the prior written permission of the publisher.

British Library Cataloguing in Publication Data

A C.I.P. for this book is available from the British Library

ISBN-13: 978-1-80152-006-5

Typeset by Medlar Publishing Solutions Pvt Ltd, India

www.aeonbooks.co.uk

DEDICATION

*This book is dedicated to
Aly who above all people on Earth
keeps me connected to the Tree of Life.*

*To the memory of
Thomas Walter Oloman (1914–1995).
My teacher, friend, and a hidden saint.*

*And to Will Parfitt, Kabbalist, psychotherapist,
companion on the way.*

CONTENTS

INTRODUCTION ix

PART 1: THE FOUNDATIONS
1. Beginnings 3
2. The Egyptian background—the principles of Maat and Apep 13
3. Engaging with the Tree of Life 23
4. Contemplating the sephiroth 43
5. The paths of light and shadow 61
6. The dynamics of creation and the nature of evil 79
7. The linen-clad priest 87
8. Holy Mountain, Holy City, Holy Temple, and Holy of Holies 93
9. The living image and the body of glory 99

PART 2: THE TRAINING
10. Becoming the Eloquent Peasant 107
11. The work of the Good Shepherd 125
12. The *Geru Maa*—the silent one 135

PART 3: THE PRACTICE OF TRANSFORMING THE QLIPHOTH

13. The art of mirroring 149
14. The principal practice 159
15. The sanctum sanctorum 169
16. Contemplating the Qliphoth 177
17. Baptising demons and freeing prisoners 187

PART 4: APPLYING THE PRACTICE

18. The serpent is the saviour 197
19. The collective dybbuk—the egregore 205
20. Exorcising places and persons, the living and the dead 213
21. Radical innocence—becoming Simple Simon 219

REFERENCES 225

INDEX 227

INTRODUCTION

Some thirty-five years ago when I was very much a fledgling qabalist, my wife and I visited a small church in the depths of Suffolk. It was a sunny day; the village was a classic English village with a duckpond—a haven of peace and tranquillity—and an eleventh-century Norman church that looked beautiful in the afternoon sun.

We anticipated a pleasant visit, looking at stained glass windows, tombs, and learning a little about the history of the church. When we entered, we found what we would have expected to find: a plain, well-proportioned country church, but the psychic atmosphere hit us between the eyes. There was a sense of coldness, airlessness, and what I can only describe as *fouled* air. I recall stumbling in shock and surprise. I was near to the baptismal font, so I reached out in order to stabilise myself. As I did so I was suddenly aware of the presence of a medieval priest. holding me up and overshadowing me. I was given a strong impression that this place had been desecrated and rather than a place of peace was now a fountain of despair and anti-life. I found myself repeating the Name YHShVH יהשוה which, in our tradition, is called the Healing Name and, as I did so, it was as if a fountain of pure water burst out of the font and flowed through the church.

My wife stood with me and repeated the Name with me. I don't know how long we stood there, as I was not in an ordinary state of mind, but gradually the sense of oppression lessened. However, rather than the experience fading away it intensified; it was as if the priest stepped more deeply into me, and I leaned back into him and into the Name. I found myself walking up the nave to a twelfth century tomb in the north chancel and, as I did so, there was a sense of another presence as if rising out of the tomb. There was a different quality in the church now, an active will which engaged with and resisted the will that was coming through me. I found myself laying hands upon the tomb in a gesture of contact and blessing even though what was coming from the tomb was what I can only describe as pure antagonism.

Again, I do not know how long I stood there; it was like standing in the epicentre of a great storm as the light and presence of the Healing Name, coming from the priest and what seemed to be a great line of figures behind him, moved through me to be met by a dark shape of resistance. Gradually the resistance seemed to fade and, for a moment, I caught a glimpse of a human being. Something gave way and the figure and I came together, were embraced by the light, and it was as if he passed through me into the light. In the aftermath I was exhausted, although at peace, and certainly the church was an easier place to be in. The experience, although challenging and tiring was, in a strange way, a profound demonstration of the nature of love and embracing even that which rejects love. This book is my attempt to make sense of this experience and of many others over the last thirty years, and has taken me into a contemplation of human purpose and the nature of evil.

The nature of evil is a perennial human contemplation; it has been addressed by all religions and spiritual systems. In some ways it has never been more important to understand its nature and our relationship to it. We live in times where there is great division between and within nations, generations, belief systems, households, and even within our own psyches. The default setting for dealing with the experience of difference is to label some part of it as other, alien, dangerous, and to seek ways to cast it out. Western culture has an established track record of dealing with difference in just this way, from marginalizing and exiling the other to actually killing them. That same violence can be applied when we find that same difference existing in our psyche and is responsible for much human pathology. Indeed, our inability to deal with the splits and divisions within ourselves supports and amplifies the external processes of driving away the evildoer.

That sense of exile and driving out is right at the heart of the Abrahamic religions. In the Book of Genesis we find the archetypal human beings being driven out of the Garden of Eden because of disobedience and listening to the serpent rather than the divine presence. Their son, Cain, kills his brother and is driven out. Esau, the son of Isaac, sells his inheritance for a bowl of stew and is sent into exile in Edom. The act of disobedience that sets all this in motion is the eating of the fruit from the tree of the knowledge of good and evil, which takes us from a place of union and communion with the divine into a place of separation in which we become ashamed of our nakedness and cover ourselves with fig leaves. We are then driven out into a hostile universe where we must fight tooth and claw to survive. Orthodoxy in Judaism, Christianity, and Islam would say that in order to remedy this situation we must obey God and follow a set of religious rules so that we may be purged of our intrinsic evil and return into the goodness and holiness of the divine presence.

The Qabalah, the inner tradition of both Judaism and Christianity, takes a different view and points our attention to the other tree found in the centre of the garden—the Tree of Life. This tradition appears in Europe in the twelfth century CE and gives us a way of working with self and world so that what is perceived as evil or wrong, instead of being driven away or slain, is brought into the heart and there undergoes an alchemical transformation in which the disturbed feelings, thoughts, and beliefs undergo a process of death and resurrection which, instead of dividing the energies of life, unites and magnifies them. The Qabalah is a practice of prayer, contemplation, and way of life that has its heart in this way of being and is organized around this image of the Tree of Life, simultaneously the image of the true human being and the universe in which we find ourselves. In place of institutionalizing separation and division, the Qabalah gives us paradoxes to contemplate, such as "the serpent is the saviour", in Hebrew משיח הוא הנחש. As each Hebrew letter is also a number, the qabalists believe that if two words have the same number then there is a relationship between them. The word for serpent, *NChSh* and the word for messiah, *MShICh*, have the same number as each other and, in the contemplative process called gematria, qabalists would be invited to meditate on both words to discover their

xii   INTRODUCTION

identity. Another such example is found in the phrase, "one is the spirit of the living God", אחת רוח אלהים חיים. This has the same number as *olam ha qliphoth* or "the world of shells", עולם הקליפות (Crowley, 1973, p. 61).

"The world of shells", or *Qliphoth*, is seen as the abode of fragmentation and the denial of life. So, in this contemplation, qabalists would be invited to discover the relationship between it and the unity of the divine living spirit.

This approach was described as "the return to the garden", experiencing the mysteries of the Tree of Life through working with the Tree of the Knowledge of Good and Evil, which might more truly be named the Tree of Death. This requires a capacity to work with opposition and paradox until the deeper unity underneath apparently irreconcilable positions is revealed. This led to the qabalists considering evil as an obstruction or covering that restricts or occludes the energy of life, linked to the notion of shame and Adam and Eve's need to cover themselves with fig leaves. In essence this covers and obscures their and our sense of our true being, so the word they gave to "evil" is the Qliphoth, a word that means "shells" or "husks", forms without true life whose function it is to resist and stop the full expression of life.

An accomplished qabalist is one who can unite the Tree of Life with the Tree of Death and assist others both individually and collectively to do likewise. The Judaic term for such a person is the *tsaddik* or "righteous one"; in the Christian Hermetic Qabalah, which arose during the Renaissance, they would be called an "adept". In both cases these terms are applied to one who has embodied the true image of the human being, which is in turn the reflection or image of the divine—the *tselem*, צלם.

This *tselem* serves as a touchstone and an ideal image that both inspires and orients our work in this territory. The Qliphoth are forms, energies, or beings that have become separated and self-referential and whose function it is to block or divert the divine life so that it is at the service of a part, not the whole, and constitutes a shadow tree that blocks and entraps life so there is no growth. The work that we will be exploring in this book is the embracing of the Qliphoth within ourselves and within the greater world, binding them into the warmth of the heart and restoring them to the great bundle of the living. Central to our consideration will be the relation between intention and will, imagination and embodiment, looking in particular how these functions are freed as we work with the divine life flowing within the Tree of Life, but become bound and entrapped as we become entangled in the Tree of Death.

We will consider also how we affect each other and the world depending on whether we are aligned with the Tree of Life or the Tree of Death.

The twentieth-century qabalist Violet Firth, who wrote under the pen name "Dion Fortune" and set up a group called the Society of the Inner Light, addresses this area in her book *Psychic Self-Defence*. She describes three situations that give us some insight into her approach to this territory: in the first she shows us the way in which qliphothic energy can manifest between two people; in the second example she describes the internal dynamics that create such a form and in the third she shows an adept or *tsaddik* working with the divine life and enabling lost and separated forms to return to the bosom of the Tree of Life.

She begins by telling us about her life as a young girl working in Studley Hall Agricultural College in Warwickshire for a woman called Lillias Hamilton, the warden of the college, whom she believed to have a considerable knowledge of occultism and whose will she had crossed. She had decided to leave the college as she felt the warden was not ethical, but had to meet with her to terminate her employment. This resulted in a session where the warden constantly repeated two phrases at her: "You are incompetent and you know it. You have no self-confidence and you have to admit it" (Fortune, 1970, p. 14). This went on for four hours and ended only when Dion pretended to have come to agreement with the warden. Shortly afterwards she went into a stupor and had no conscious memory of the interview, and it was only much later that she was able recall what had happened to her. This experience was pivotal in propelling her to study both psychology and occultism and opened her eyes to the ways in which the will and imagination can be used to destructive effect.

If we consider what happened to Dion in this encounter, we see the focused will of the warden projecting images of incompetence and absence of confidence and insisting that Dion agree and, in so doing, aligning her will with that of the warden. Dion's saving grace in this encounter was, in a ju jitsu type move, to pretend to surrender her will (thus keeping some part of her intact) but even in doing this she had a powerful somatic reaction and a blanking out of awareness followed by a collapse as the subversive images penetrated her soma and psyche. Her recovery from this collapse caused her to have to remember the images and to consciously engage with them, in the process re-experiencing the emotional charge and intentions held in the images. She described her body as being like a run-down battery and as if she had a leak in her energy body so that she could no longer hold a charge. It was only when she recovered the images and worked consciously to nullify them that her energy recovered.

Another key story in *Psychic Self-Defence* casts Dion Fortune in the position of one who is projecting unbalanced qliphothic energy. In this case she had been injured by someone and was brooding on the situation, getting more and more angry while she was also drifting on the borders of sleep, and so focusing her will and engaging her imagination. She found herself imagining the Nordic myths and Fenris, the ancient wolf spirit. As her rage and imagination combined, she felt an extrusion of energy from her solar plexus and had the sense of a wolf form taking shape from her. On consulting her teacher, she was told that she had manifested a form of rage and hatred and needed to recall it and—at the same time—she would have to renounce her desire for revenge. Interestingly, just at this point she had an opportunity to take her revenge but chose to pass it by. She then described using her will and imagination to draw the wolf form to her, and then to draw the life out of it into her body. As she did this, she re-experienced the feelings of rage and hatred she had put into the form. These she had to contain within herself until they dissipated.

In contrast to the preceding stories, she describes the work an adept would do in working with the Qliphoth. She describes the adept, whom she called "Z" (most likely her teacher, Theodore Moriarty) dealing with a troubled young man, D, who was sharing a flat with someone she knew. Around him various poltergeist type activities would manifest, as well as an unpleasant, deadening coldness that sucked all sense of life and light from all present. D felt that he was under attack from a ghost. When Z visited, he perceived the presence of a disturbed entity, which he saw as a dull glow in the corner of the room. Z engaged with it and cast a circle of containment around it before absorbing it into himself through compassion. Z later reported that the entity was an earthbound soul that had attached itself to D, and it seemed that from then onwards the young man's life took a much more constructive course.

Dion Fortune describes what Z did as aligning with the divine, linking his will with the divine will and becoming a channel through which the divine life can flow. Then he used his inner perception to identify the form that needed to be dissolved, the earthbound spirit attaching itself to D. His next step was to discern the quality that enabled this form to persist—in this case, fear, leading to a refusal to pass through the death process, and the attempt to vampirize the living. Having established this he then contemplated compassion as the antidote to fear, embodying this quality so that any manifestation of aggression or attack towards him only provoked more compassion. The combination of alignment with the divine pressure and the embodiment of the compassion created a field of awareness that embraced the earthbound soul. Z then drew the soul into his body, letting it be the alchemical container within which the light and dark energies mixed together. There was then a moment of transformation in which the fear dissolved, and the soul and D were freed from their unholy attachment. At this point Z appears to have fallen over unconscious, as a result of the stress of the operation.

Another key twentieth-century qabalist who addressed this area was Aleister Crowley. Described as both the wickedest man on Earth, and as the prophet of the new age of Horus, he was an advanced exponent of working with unbalanced energies. He drew on an Egyptianized form of Qabalah based around a twenty-sixth dynasty funeral stela of the priest Ankh af na Khonsu whom he believed to be his prior incarnation. When Crowley and his wife were on honeymoon in Egypt she went into trance and dictated an inspirational text that he called *The Book of the Law*, which was based around the figures on the stela that he later called "The Stele of Revealing". This stela, and the inspirational book, describe a cosmology and set of practices that have strong links with the Egyptian traditions of working with the unbalanced energies of Apep, the serpent demon of chaos, and bringing into being a new creation. Crowley's novel *Moonchild* deals with both the creation of a literal magical child and the manifestation of our own creative life. It addresses the question of absorbing unbalanced force, though perhaps in a less dramatic way than Dion Fortune's examples.

Simon Iff, an adept, is with two companions in a garden, when he perceives a patch of murk that on closer attention takes the shape of a large wolf-like demon. He chants some lines from another inspirational book written by Crowley, "The Book of the Heart Girt with the Serpent":

> I me and mine were sitting with lutes in the market place of the great city, the city of the violets and roses.
> The night fell and the music of the lutes was stilled.
> The tempest arose, and the music of the lutes was stilled.
> The hour passed and the music of the lutes was stilled.

> But Thou art eternity and space, Thou are Matter and Motion; and Thou art the Negation of all these things. For there is no symbol of Thee. (Crowley, 2015, p. 111)

Having aligned himself with his deeper self, he steps into the wolf-demon, letting the demon enter his body while he speaks the Crowleyan formula: "Do what thou wilt is the whole of the Law. Love is the Law love under Will." As he speaks, at the heart of his body is an oval form of light into which the demon form dissolves.

Crowley then takes us through a discussion of working with deep will and has Simon Iff explain that if unbalanced forms or forces come into his sphere of awareness, he absorbs them as quietly as possible so that the whole balance of the universe is restored. He goes on to explain that the reason he can do this is because he works with the principles of love and will beyond duality, so that love has no object and will no aim. In the doing of this he has become one with everything and nothing, and hence there is no resistance in him to disturbance. Love enables him to connect to all and thus all can pass through him into a similar state of alignment with the universe. This he describes as the way of the Tao.

The work Simon Iff describes, done as quietly as possible to restore the balance of the universe, is a daily activity of meeting the qliphothic aspects of the universe as they present themselves to us. This can take the form of noticing a patch of murk (as with Simon Iff) or a disturbed energy, or feeling a disturbance between yourself and somebody else, or, on rare occasions, encounters with the Qliphoth themselves as active malevolent presences.

PART 1

THE FOUNDATIONS

CHAPTER 1

Beginnings

I have worked with this tradition for nearly fifty years. It has demanded that I be continually attentive to the ways in which I either act in the service of light or become an obstacle to it. It has asked me to take seriously the reality of the inner worlds and subtle beings and the ways in which the outer and inner worlds affect each other. I have stood in old churches that have become dormant or despoiled; in older sacred sites that have somehow become detached from their original purpose; on old battlefields; in the back streets and alleys of Jerusalem and the Drakensberg mountains of South Africa. I have also worked with it in the middle of cities, on trains and buses, in council estates and cottages, in gatherings of powerful people, in great cities and with powerless and despairing people in small towns. In all these places and occasions, the choice has been whether to find a way to affirm unity and the mystery of the indivisible nature of love and will, or to divide will and refuse love; to align with the *tselem*, the true human image, or to set up an idol in its place.

I was taught this art by two remarkable people, Walter Ernest Butler and Tom Oloman, both, in my view, *tsaddikim* or adept qabalists in their capacity to enhance life and transform disturbance.

Walter Ernest Butler (1898–1978) was taught the Qabalah by Dion Fortune and was part of the Society of the Inner Light that she founded. He was also a priest of the Liberal Catholic Church. I encountered him in 1973 when I joined the Helios Course on the Practical Qabalah. His training was focused on the development of the will and imagination while retaining the capacity to be grounded and embodied. A particular feature of his work was the development of the image or *tselem* of the true human being; this he called "the magical personality" and he worked with it so as to enable a sense of ourselves as centres of light and life through which the practice of effective prayer and blessing manifested. This work involves descent into and emergence from what he described as "the inner sea at the foundation of our psyche". In the act of dissolving into the inner waters he would be receptive to the deep prompting of his own soul and inner guidance, letting go of his customary self-image and, as he emerged, would take whatever form was needed to meet the conditions of the moment. His teachings infuse this book as he continues to be one of my major influences but, as I write this, what I most remember is his clarity, kindness, and no-nonsense simplicity—no frills or elaboration.

I worked with Ernest Butler for only a short time, but I went on to work with his disciple Tom Oloman (1914–1995) for over twenty years. His work too was centred in a practice of blessing and prayer and, like Ernest, he used a process of dissolving and arising, but his approach was less precise and more mystical than Ernest's. Like Ernest he followed the same process of aligning with light and embracing disturbance. Tom had great clarity and stillness, a similar sense of ground and embodiment to Ernest, and a capacity to go beyond form to identify the heart of whatever he was confronted by.

For both of these teachers working with the Qliphoth was an everyday matter; the quiet rebalancing of the universe. Ernest would routinely bring whatever he encountered into the presence of Christ through prayer whilst Tom would bring everything into stillness. Both regularly blessed everyone and everything they came across.

Ernest Butler had two principal teachers, the first and probably most significant in terms of this work was Robert King (1869–1954), a psychic, occultist, and a bishop in the Liberal Catholic Church. He had been a prominent medium working with Sir William Crookes and W.T. Stead and for four years was at the centre of a series of sittings called "Julia's Bureau", which met daily. He was also active in the Theosophical

Society, acting as a medium for prominent members such as A.P. Sinnett. At the time Ernest Butler met him, he was principally working with a small group of personal students. Robert King taught Ernest the basics of the practice of Qabalistic occultism, the development of the body of light, and the practice of exorcism, and whilst Ernest later worked with Dion Fortune it was to Robert King and the teacher behind Robert King that he always returned. As a medium, Robert King was used to making contact with and communing with spirits of many different kinds and, in particular, beings who came to help, teach, and to guide esoteric development. His central teacher was a spirit being, a man who presented himself as an Egyptian priest wearing the mask of Anubis, the jackal god who is the guide of the dead and whose title is "the opener of the ways". He would also appear in the form of a Gnostic Christian teacher and would refer to the ancient city of Alexandria as an archetypal place existing in the inner worlds as the fountainhead of these teachings. Ernest Butler was introduced to this figure through Robert King as a young man, and went on to work with this inner guide for the rest of his life and through its inspiration set up the Servants of the Light School for the Practical Qabalah.

Ernest described this early training in an article entitled "What We Are":

> Many years ago, more than half a century, I came into contact with the man whom I regard as my first teacher in esoteric matters: Robert King, or "R.K." as we used to call him. During the time that I was working with him in those early days, I was introduced to one person who was his particular teacher. And before very long I was working with R.K. on various esoteric work, under the guidance and influence of this particular teacher. When, later on, circumstances moved me away from R.K., and I was on my own, this teacher informed me that I, too, was one of his pupils; and for all the time which has elapsed since then, he has been my guide, philosopher, and friend in the background.
>
> Now I am not going to say who he is—or whom I think he is—neither am I going into any esoteric explanations concerning him; whether he is a master or an adept or what he is. These titles mean very little. The proof of this pudding is always in the eating. Many people can say "master" and at the same time they are simply telling a lie. Many people can claim to be gurus, to be teachers, but

their teachings are very poor; there is very little in them. Those who really know, do not shout about it; and those who shout about it, do not really know.

However, it is from this man that I derive my contact. He has given me a certain work to perform, and during the last fifty years I have been doing that work. Not only in speaking, in lecturing to various bodies of people, not only in writing, but in other ways. For occultism is not a theoretical thing; it must by its very nature be practical. And so every occultist, worthy of the name, is constantly engaged in practical occult work […]

The contact, upon which our course is built, is an Egyptian contact. We do not say much about that. That is something which the student grows into in the course of his work. But it is generally an Egyptian school. That does not mean to say we all float about wearing the robes of Osiris or the robes of Isis. We do not make of it a silly mythological thing. But we do say, that the forces which are working in our course, are the forces which were also working in the old schools of Alexandria at the time when the Mysteries were just drawing to their close and the new teaching of Christianity was emerging as a power in the land. The teaching which was given in Alexandria in those days, was a composite teaching. Alexandria was a city which faced upon the world; East and West met in Alexandria. There the great schools were formed. And it is with that contact that we are concerned.

We work in the spirit of the old Mysteries of Egypt. Which, incidentally, does not conflict with what we also say about working in the spirit of the Rose-Cross, for the Rose-Cross Mysteries stem very largely from pre-Christian Egypt. But Christianity gave them a particular slant; it "baptised them into Christ" as they said in the old days: they were taken up into the very fabric of the new religion. And therefore, they are there in the Mysteries of the Rose-Cross; they are there as the fundamental teachings of both the pagan Mysteries and Christianity. (Butler, 2022)

I first encountered Ernest and Tom and what was then The Helios Course on the Practical Qabalah in 1973. The course was and is seen as the teaching vehicle for this inner teacher and my first direct encounter with him occurred when I was midway through the training. I had a particular affection for the figure of Merlin and used to begin my meditations by contemplating a little statue of him, seeing him as the master or archetype of magic, and myself as Merlin's apprentice. This is my record of the encounter, which happened in a small bedsit in Nottingham on the morning of Saturday 16 October 1976:

> Morning Meditation Record.
>
> Began by contemplating Merlin seeing myself as Merlin's apprentice but found that my concentration kept wavering and the figure of Merlin kept turning into the figure of an Egyptian Priest wearing the mask of the Jackal God Anubis who said he was the Priest who wears the Mask of Anubis and is the Opener of the Ways. I brought my mind away from this image and returned to the image of Merlin. I then received a strong impression from the image of Merlin that I was behaving like an oaf and to bring my attention back to the Egyptian figure. As I did so I had a sense of a strong but incredibly gentle and kind presence who was also stern and clear. There was a depth of silence and a smell of myrrh and frankincense, his presence surrounded me and he seemed to be showing me a way forward for my inner work.

I still remember the power of that stillness and deep, deep kindness; it was a brief encounter but timeless and I didn't know it, but it was the beginning of a relationship that persists to this day. This book is the fruit of this collaborative relationship. Like Ernest Butler, he has been my teacher, friend, and colleague; very much a living man existing in a subtle dimension who has taught me so much about the nature of life and love as well as esoteric practice. At the heart of his teaching is the capacity of the human heart to bless and curse, to trap and to free.

Ernest Butler in this context would often quote a poem, "The Rabbi's Song" by Rudyard Kipling, as an illustration of this capacity. This poem is derived from a verse in the Book of Samuel:

> Like water spilled on the ground, which cannot be recovered, so we must die. But that is not what God desires; rather, he devises ways so that a banished person does not remain banished from him. (2 Samuel 14: 14)

The Rabbi's Song

If Thought can reach to Heaven,
    On Heaven let it dwell,
For fear the Thought be given
    Like power to reach to Hell.
For fear the desolation
    And darkness of thy mind
Perplex an habitation
    Which thou hast left behind.

Let nothing linger after—
    No whimpering ghost remain,
In wall, or beam, or rafter,
    Of any hate or pain.
Cleans and call home thy spirit,
    Deny her leave to cast,
On aught thy heirs inherit,
    The shadow of her past.
For think, in all thy sadness,
    What road our griefs may take;
Whose brain reflect our madness,
    Or whom our terrors shake:
For think, lest any languish
    By cause of thy distress—
The arrows of our anguish
    Fly farther than we guess.

Our lives, our tears, as water,
    Are spilled upon the ground;
God giveth no man quarter,
    Yet God a means hath found,
Though Faith and Hope have vanished,
    And even Love grows dim—
A means whereby His banished
    Be not expelled from Him! (Kipling, 1909)

The biblical verse and poem speak of the human capacity to generate life so that our thoughts can bless and bring a sense of heaven to earth, but can also create a hell on earth. The poem is part of a Kipling story called "The House Surgeon", which describes a house that appears perfectly normal on the outside but that has an inner atmosphere of depression and hopelessness that makes people want to kill themselves. This is described as a dark cloud that at intervals descends on everyone in the house and is discovered to be caused by a previous owner brooding on what she believed to be her sister's suicide in the house and imagining her sister's state of mind. She is concentrating her thoughts upon the place like black light passing through a burning glass and is projecting her presence into it. The situation is resolved by the narrator entering the house, experiencing the black light, and tracing the story back until he finds the previous owner. He brings her back to the house and proves to her that her sister died as a result of an accident. She then withdraws her projected energy, much as we find Dion Fortune doing with her wolf form. This is thought to have been based on an actual experience of Kipling while living in a house in Torquay. J.M.S. Tomkins, in her study of Kipling's works, tells us regarding this story,

> In the House Surgeon the grim conception of damnation by a vindictive God and the consequent blackness of despair are evoked precisely that they be melted, dispersed, dissolved utterly out of the lives, not only of those who have suffered innocently under the curse, but of those who with passionate stern grief have imposed it. When Kipling fused his experience in the unhappy house at Torquay, of which he has told us, with the still living experience of the spiritual climate of the House of Desolation, and cleansed the site, not as by fire but as by the water of grace, he performed an act of imaginative charity. Moreover, he put the "I" into the story, subjected him to the reflected agony of despair, and used him to remove the barriers that obstructed the renewal of love and hope. (Tompkins, 1959, p. 130)

Ernest Butler felt that the Samuel quotation, the story, and the poem spoke very directly to the practice of transforming the Qliphoth and used to recommend the poem as a subject for meditation to assist us to see that the power of the mind and imagination is such that we can create energies and forms which remain attached to physical locations and can infect them with sour and bleak intentions. The work of "imaginative charity" and the insertion of the "I" into the story he saw as a description of the work of transformation in which the worker in the service of the light enters into the disturbed conditions or series of events that have given rise to the creation of the disturbance and, through an act of will and imagination, brings what Tompkins poetically describes as the "water of grace" to cleanse and renew the place. Ernest Butler felt that the sense of infection of a place could be at any level of scale from an immediate environment and situation to a collective, national, or planet-wide infection. Further, this sense of overshadowing by disturbance did not apply just to places but also to persons, whether living or dead, passive recipients of disturbance or active collaborators and generators of it. The final lines of the poem "The means whereby his banished, / Be not expelled from Him" Ernest took to mean this particular work of prayer and blessing, which restores the lost and disturbed beings and energies back into communion with the life of the universe.

The Gospel of John formed the basis of much of his thinking in this area, as we can see from the following quotation from the "What We Are" lecture:

> In the beginning of the Gospel of St John, it says, "the Light shines in the darkness, and the darkness cannot overcome it." Imagine a million and million of miles of space. Dark, dark space. But in that million of miles of dark space you light one small candle. And it shines in the darkness. And all the millions and millions of cubic miles of space cannot extinguish that one little candle. The darkness cannot overcome the Light, but the Light always will overcome the darkness. And that is the promise for us for the future; the Light shines in the darkness of this world, as it always has been shining throughout the Ages. It is within us and without us, and we have to work upon ourselves in order that that Light may shine forth and so reinforce the Light which shines around us, until everyone is aware that the inner Light in ourselves and the outer Light around us are aspects of the One Light in which the whole universe is bathed; of which indeed the whole universe is a manifestation. (Butler, 2022)

The symbolism of the light was so important to him that he used the image of a servant of the light as the basis for his own magical personality, and gave the name Servants of the Light to the organisation he founded. Being a servant of the light for him was to be an esoteric priest overshadowed by the Christ, and the work of exorcism was not an act of banishment but an act of inclusion and surrender in which the living Christ did the work through him, generating light where there was darkness, hope where there was fear, joy where there was sorrow. In this work, he would align with the figure of the crucified Christ and reach into the presence of the resurrected Christ, becoming a vessel for the radiant Christ Light. This light he would then bring into relationship with whatever needed blessing, healing, or releasing.

Tom Oloman, on the other hand, had a more abstract, zen-like approach based upon the unity of light and silence, seeing himself as a contemplative monk in a white habit whose task it was to bring the deep, silent music of heaven into the cacophony of the Qliphoth. He similarly would link into the sense of the divine as the Christ, but this was less linked to biblical forms and he would symbolise this presence by the image of an equal-armed cross of gold with a red rose blooming at its centre. This was linked to the name YHShVH יהשוה having the letter *shin* at the centre of the rose and the letters of YHVH aligned with the four arms of the cross thus:

Tom would align with the golden cross and the rose, experiencing the balance and radiance of the golden cross and the fragrance and beauty of the flowering red rose. This he linked with the healing and harmonising quality of the Name, which he would bring into the sense of discordance and lack of balance. He would simply sit with the disturbance until the inner cacophony subsided, leaving behind a stillness that would hover in the air like the fragrance of the rose.

As might be imagined, my own approach reflects the influences from both my teachers in that the *tselem* that I formed has its roots in the image of being an apprentice of Merlin, but expanded to being a servant of the light, much as Ernest used. However, over time this has become much more like the shape that Tom used: an image of deep stillness that connects with an ancient Egyptian form of the *geru maa*, the man or woman of silence and truth. The form of my imaginal body is very like that of the tarot card the Hermit while at my heart is an image of a gold-circled cross with a small bowl that holds the image of the Egyptian goddess Maat at its centre.

The adept or *tsaddik* whose task it is to work with the Qliphoth is a *tselem*, a living image, an expression of an ideal that we sometimes fail to live up to but continue to aspire to. It is formed from the actions of our will, imagination, and embodied awareness, and then acts like a strange attractor bending the flow of inner and outer events so that we (like Simon Iff) increasingly work with will and love, step by step, and balance the world. To understand more about the nature of this *tselem* and the practices that arise from it we must investigate the history of Qabalah and, in particular, its roots in Egypt.

CHAPTER 2

The Egyptian background—the principles of Maat and Apep

At the root of this esoteric art is a principle that goes back into ancient Egypt—the principle of Maat: justice, order, balance. This principle is found everywhere in ancient Egypt and is envisaged as a goddess crowned with a single feather bearing the *ankh*, the symbol of life. It is this principle that is asserted when unbalanced forms are absorbed and transformed.

Hieroglyph of Maat

It was an important function of the priesthood to assert Maat, or balance and good order, which defends against Isfet, or chaos. The New Kingdom books of the netherworld show the nightly journey of Ra, the sun god, who descends to Osiris in order to be made young and new again. In this process his enemy is Apep, the great serpent of chaos, who seeks to stop this nightly journey and overthrow the balanced movement of the universe. One of the primary concerns of those who worked with those books was to become an embodied and dynamic centre of balance, responsible for binding and restraining the power of Apep. This early tradition shows very clearly some of the main features of our subject. Apep is not destroyed; it is the resistance or friction against which the creative energy of life pushes and, in that act of struggle, discovers its own deeper potentials. Egyptian tradition was founded on the emergence of Maat from the undifferentiated chaos, a continual act of creation in which the life and light of the new day arises out of the chaos of the night. In each daily cycle Ra, the creator, is born at sunrise, achieves maturity at noon, and becomes old by sunset. As the sun sets, Ra descends into the *duat*, the underworld, returns to the waters of the beginning and is renewed.

This place of beginning is called Zep Tepi, "the first time", and it links each moment of present time with the myth of the beginning. In one important myth found in the temple walls of Esna, the goddess Neith, the weaver goddess, is described as a personification of this first time. She, arising from the chaos of the beginning, brings the primal mound out of the waters and causes the Ished Tree, the first tree, to appear. She then on the one hand creates Ra, the creator god, who manifests as the bennu bird, the solar phoenix, whose function it is to bring the world into being and, on the other, by spitting some of the primal waters of chaos out of her mouth, she creates Apep, the coiling serpent seeking to bring all back into the waters of chaos. She is depicted as a woman with a crown of two crossed arrows, or a loom representing working with dualities to create life. She is seen at times as androgynous and depicted with a phallus and as the mother of the gods, the *neteru* or living, generative images. She is also depicted as having three heads, again showing opposites and the balance between opposites. Her identification as the most powerful creative force in the universe is noted by Plutarch (c.50–120CE) who writes that the temple of Neith at Sais held this inscription: "I Am All That Has Been, That Is, and That Will Be. No Mortal Has Yet Been Able to Lift the Veil that Covers Me" (Plutarch, 1936, p. 23). One of her key functions in *The Book of the Contendings of Horus and Seth* is to affirm that Horus should be king after the death of his father Osiris, and become the first pharaoh ruling over the fertile Nile valley, the black land, while to Set should be apportioned the red infertile desert.

One of the earliest images of the human being who embodies Maat is that of the peasant—the human being who tills the land and enables crops to grow and flourish and who works creatively with the cycles of the seasons and the flow of the Nile. This figure is linked with the hieroglyph taa, which shows us the fertile land with seeds buried in it waiting to sprout, or this variant form the irrigated land, the combination of the solidity and straightness of the earth with canals of Nile water. The Middle Kingdom poem, "The Tale of the Eloquent Peasant", gives us the image of such a man who is cheated and has his possessions stolen by a nobleman. Taking his stand upon the solidity and fertility of the earth, he takes his case before the Chief Steward of Egypt and in nine remarkable speeches challenges the entire Egyptian political system in phrases like this:

> Goodness is annihilated for there is no fidelity to it,
> No desire to fling deceit backwards upon the earth.
> If the ferry has been beached how can one cross the river,
> Success can be attained only in abomination,
> To cross the river on foot is this a feasible way to cross?
> Such cannot be done … (Simpson, 2003, p. 36)

> Let your eyes see, Let your heart be instructed!
> Do not be tyrannical in your power,
> That evil may not overtake you.
> If you ignore one incident it will become two.
> It is the eater who tastes,
> It is he who is questioned who answers,
> And it is the sleeper who sees the dream.
> As for the judge who merits punishment,
> He is an archetype for him who does wrong.
> Idiot! Behold you are struck!
> You know nothing! And Behold you are questioned!
> You are an empty vessel and behold you are exposed!
> Helmsman do not let your ship veer off course;
> Giver of Life do not let men die;
> Provider do not let men perish;
> Sunshade do not attract the heat of the sun;

> Refuge do not let the crocodile carry me off.
> This is the fourth time I appeal to you,
> Must I spend all my time at it. (Simpson, 2003, p. 37)

Here we see the peasant telling us that the absence of *maat* violates the natural order and asserting the primacy of *maat* in seeking to have order restored. He is rejected each time by the Chief Steward, but through both his eloquence and persistence he is sent to Pharaoh who confirms the truth and balance of his story and rules in his favour, giving the nobleman's possessions to him as an act of restitution. The peasant is showing an important quality called *maat kheru*, "speaking with a just voice", which later becomes central to Egyptian funerary literature in which, in the judging of the soul before Osiris, the god of the dead, the heart of the deceased is called upon to show that it has spoken *maat kheru* upon the earth when alive.

It is significant that it is only when the peasant comes before Pharaoh that *maat* is re-established, for Pharaoh is seen as the true human being, the living image of the divine, the incarnate Horus who is given a Horus name that indicates their identity with the god. Hence, Seti I is called "The good divine one, the image of Ra, who causes the Two Lands to live through his rays." Thutmoses III is called, "the image of Ra on earth", and Shepenewen II, the sister of the twenty-fifth dynasty Pharaoh Taharqa, who served as the Divine Wife of Amun, is called "the image of Ra."

The scarab of Amenophis

Above, we see a scarab of Amenophis III, bearing the throne name of *Neb Maat Re-Neb,* consisting of the offering bowl at the base of the cartouche; *maat*, the middle image; and the solar disc of Re at the top. It has the meaning "The Upholder of Truth" and it is this image that I use in my own work with the Qliphoth.

The image of Pharaoh as the incarnate divine being is linked intimately to Pharaoh's role as the promoter and protector of Maat. One of the key priestly rituals is the Maat offering in which Pharaoh makes offering of a small bowl that contains a small statue of Maat as the goddess with the single feather, holding the *ankh* symbol. This vignette is the incarnate god offering the quality of Maat, which he has enabled to exist and flourish back to the source of life itself. Maat is regarded here as a cosmic quality that feeds the gods and develops life, strength, and stability, and its offering back into the source of life enables that source to manifest more fully on earth so that the creative energies of the first time renew the time in which the offering is being made. The offering formula speaks of the god giving life in response to the offering of Maat, pointing us to the circular nature of the communion that ultimately speaks of the union between the divine and the human and the continual generation of life and order that emerges from this union.

The model for the righteous ruler who acts like Ra is the Good Shepherd and, in a praise hymn found in one of the hieratic ostraca of the New Kingdom, we find the verse:

> O Amen Ra, you shepherd who cares for your flock in early morning, and leads the hungry to pasture. As the shepherd leads the flock to green meadows, Amen do you lead me, the hungry one, to food. For Amen is indeed a shepherd, a shepherd who is not neglectful. (Karenga, 2004, p. 224)

Ra is also called "Great Shepherd" and "Beloved Shepherd", and we find pharaohs styling themselves as the shepherd of Kemet, as the protector of the *maat* of the land. The hieroglyph for "shepherd king" ancient Egypt is a seated man holding the crook and the sceptre of authority combining, therefore, the authority of the sovereign and the protective and guiding nature of the shepherd.

This ancient image of the sacred king who is the good shepherd and protector of Maat echoes down through western tradition, particularly in the psalms of David, the Shepherd King of Israel This is shown most vividly in Psalm 23, "The Lord is my shepherd", in which there is a journey through the valley of the shadow of death. Its other key appearance is in Jesus' parable of the good shepherd, which again speaks directly to the work of recovery of the lost sparks of light under the symbol of the lost sheep.

The sense of Pharaoh as the sacred king is linked also to the ancient Egyptian Tree of Life. This was called the Ished Tree. We find this illustrated in the Ramesseum, the mortuary temple built by Ramses II where we find him seated in the midst of this tree while the god Atum and the goddess Seshat inscribe his throne name upon its leaves: *User-Maat Ra, Setepen Ra*, "The Chosen One of Ra who brings the balance and Truth of Ra." In some of the royal tombs we also find images of the Tree of Life with a goddess standing in the midst of it, suckling Pharaoh.

Working with the Tree of Life brings us to a place where, like the Pharaoh, our names are inscribed upon it even as its pattern is inscribed upon our nature. We will discover that it will feed us and guide us through a process in which we discover ourselves as an upholder of Maat and aligned with the divine creative presence.

The idea of the human being who is the image of the divine and who is the keeper and transmitter of the qualities of Maat, which in early tradition was attributed to Pharaoh, expanded to include all of humankind in some of the Egyptian wisdom literature. In *The Instructions for Merikare*, a Middle Kingdom wisdom text, we find the verse:

> Well cared for is humankind who are the flocks of God
> He made the earth and the sky for their sakes,
> He destroyed the danger of the waters for them
> He gave the breath of life for their noses
> They are his images and came from his person. (Karenga, 2012, p. 226)

Another image of the embodiment of Maat is given in a genre of writings in which a wise sage describes the qualities of the true human being as being the *geru maa*, the self-mastered human being wholly infused with the quality of *maat*. In *The Book of Amenope* written during the twentieth dynasty the *geru maa* is described as one who is shade and fruit to those who he or she meets and who abides in peace in the garden where he or she belongs. She or he is one who destroys Isfet or chaos and brings Maat into being. The root of the word *gr* suggests silence, control, self-mastery, and is suggestive that this act of promoting Maat and destroying Isfet is a function of the being or nature of the person who generates the field of balance and peace called "the garden".

In the Middle Kingdom sanctuary at Karnak there is a hidden chamber offset from the sanctuary of Amoun orientated north-south. It is called the botanical garden, containing many images of plants, and it is thought to be a place where the higher priests—the *geru maa* were made. In it is the image of the ancient garden, the generating ground of the *neteru*, later known as the Garden of Eden. The priests and priestesses who work here are in a way the gardeners of Amoun, the hidden god, whose secret image is a human being, and who points back to us the truth that the secret image of the human being is the hidden generative field. It is this quality that is being described in the image of *geru maa* who cultivates their garden and the circularity that is being shown in the Maat offering. The higher esoteric priesthood is responsible for embodying Maat and expressing it in their lives and within the world.

In the nineteenth dynasty the scribe Neferhotep said, in a prayer to Ra: "You placed Maat within my heart, that I may raise her up to your ka" (Karenga, 2012, p. 93). This is an example of the internalisation of the presentation of the Maat ritual, bringing it from ritual action to an internal process of intention and prayer. It also points us towards the

20   THE TREE OF LIFE AND DEATH

importance of the *ab* or heart in Egyptian tradition. This sense of heart as a centre of awareness and as the seat of Maat within us is emphasised in *The Maxims of Ptahotep* in which he tells us: "But he who obeys his heart will set everything in order" (Simpson, 2003, p. 141), and again: "It is the heart which causes its possessor to be One who hears or who does not hear. The 'life, prosperity and health' of a man are his heart" (Simpson, 2003, p. 146). The heart was seen as the centre of will, intelligence, and love, and the seat of the *ba* or soul. The Middle Kingdom mayor, Paheri, speaks of the heart as the dwelling place of the *ntr*—the god who is your personal god. In the mummification process it is linked with the scarab amulet, which depicts the beetle god, Khephera, whose particular quality is the ability to create and manifest. This creative ability was seen as being able to create order, or Maat, by aligning with the will of the gods for life, prosperity, and health to be extended or, alternatively, our heart's creative power could be aligned with the will of Apep in order to disrupt or obstruct the unfolding of the universe. It is for this reason that in the judgement scene from *The Book of the Dead* the heart is weighed against the feather of Maat.

The presence of one whose heart is aligned with Maat was in itself seen as generative in that just by being still, and aligned with those deeper principles, one becomes *geru maa*—the very silent being who is infused with Maat, who is seen as the tree in the midst of the garden who gives shade and refreshment. The hieroglyph of the silent one is this:

The implication here is that we have the human being who takes their seat in silence, and in silence transmits the quality of Maat. It is this quality we see in Crowley's depiction of Simon Iff who, through the cultivation of his heart and his capacity to remain centred in Maat, can simply absorb the unbalanced form. It is no accident that later in the novel he is referred to as "Simple Simon" for this capacity to be still and to work with the simplicity of the principles of love and will are key to this whole subject.

These principles of love and will are shown in Egyptian tradition in a series of stelae from the twenty-fifth dynasty in which we see tomb owners making an offering to the falcon headed god, Ra Horakhty, who is surrounded by the goddess Nuit, the goddess of infinite space and the winged sun disk. Here the sun disk represents will, movement, and the single point of view. The goddess Nuit stands for the principle of love that unites opposites and infinite points of view. Ra Horakhty is the principle of the new and arising sun that brings these principles into manifestation—he is also Horus of the Horizon, the transition point between the invisible and the visible. His twin is the silent child *Hr Paa Hrd*, Horus the Child, normally depicted as holding a finger to his lips in the sign for silence. The offering formulae in these stelae recall the Maat offering and the union between the divine and the human. The total formula combines therefore infinite possibilities and the single point, silence and speech, will and love.

If we consider the Egyptian background as a whole, we will see that these basic principles have been transmitted across time and retain their relevance even now. At the heart of Egyptian practice is the generation of Maat, the binding of Isfet, and the creation of the living image that promotes the qualities of life, stability, and strength. The embodiment of the living image in the form of the Pharaoh, the priesthood, and—later—in the sense of the *geru maa*, the human being of silence who is infused by Maat, is the fundamental process that underpins the practice of working with the Qliphoth.

This is linked to the return to the first time and the immersion in the waters of the beginning, and it is interesting to see how the practice of the descent into the inner waters and the arising of the creative form is still a central practice in the Qabalah. The centrality of the Tree of life, the image of the garden, the presence of the divine in the heart and the communion between the human and the divine in the Maat offering also remain important as does the cosmology of practice we find in the Ra Horakhty stelae.

Above all, there are three images used to indicate the Maat-infused human being, which remain patent in qabalistic tradition. Firstly, the peasant—a man or woman of the land who speaks out of the firmness and fertility of the land to assert Maat; secondly, the Shepherd King or Queen who protects and cares for the life of the land; and thirdly, the Silent Sage, the *geru maa*—the keeper of the garden of life. We still find these stages in the Qabalah in the sense of the three transition points of Malkuth, Tiphareth, and Da'ath. In more recent Qabalah these transition points are described as the experience of the Neophyte, Adeptus Minor, and Master of the Temple. Aleister Crowley described them as the grades of Man of Earth, Kingly Lover, and the Hermit.

CHAPTER 3

Engaging with the Tree of Life

This tradition developed in Egypt was carried on in an underground way as Egyptian civilisation came to an end. We then see it manifesting in the Judeo-Christian Gnostic and Hermetic groups that proliferated in the Middle East during the Graeco-Roman period and early Christian era, in particular the city of Alexandria. This city was founded in 331BCE by Alexander the Great as the ideal city that combines cultures and promotes the growth of the human spirit. It persists as a potent archetype within the collective human consciousness as the city that unites the East and the West, the place that holds the lost tomb of the sun king Alexander and the lost mausoleum of Cleopatra, the dark queen. It is the place of the great lighthouse that shines across the world and the library that contains all the knowledge of the world. Here the ancient Egyptian teachings come together with the wisdom of Greece, from the pre-Socratic philosophers such as Parmenides and Empedocles, to Socrates, Plato, Aristotle, and the neo-platonic teacher Ammonius Saccas, the teacher of Plotinus. Alexandria was home also to the largest urban Jewish community in the world and the place where the Septuagint, the Greek version of Hebrew scriptures, was composed. One of the great Jewish teachers of that city was Philo of Alexandria who, in applying neo-platonic ideas to the Torah, laid down the foundations of the Qabalah which would later manifest in the Middle Ages.

Alexandria became a melting pot of spiritual and philosophical thought and practice and developed new and creative ways of fusing the ancient Egyptian teachings with Greek Neoplatonism. As the Christian era came into existence, the Graeco-Egyptian synthesis was augmented by thoughts and practice from Judeo-Christian sources. Initially, Christianity co-existed with the older traditions, but as Christianity became the official religion of the Roman Empire this changed and in 361CE the Roman Emperor Constantius II closed all the pagan temples by decree. This had the effect of dispossessing the Egyptian priesthood from the temples, many of whom become itinerant spiritual teachers and, in the early part of the Christian era, formed part of the heterodox mixture of the spiritual landscape of Alexandria.

The closing and destruction of the pagan temples had a number of powerful effects on the expression of spirituality over the next 200 years or so. In the fifth century CE the neo-platonic philosopher Proclus, the last of the publicly known neo-platonic philosophers trained in Alexandria, moved to Athens where he initially attached himself to the temple of Socrates before becoming a devotee of Athena. When the temple of Athena was despoiled and closed, he had a dream in which the goddess appeared to him and asked if she could now live in his home and his heart as she had no temple to dwell in. This created a new pattern of underground worship and practice in which small groups met in private homes, in desolate places, and in literally underground locations such as the catacombs of Kom El Shoqafa in Alexandria (see below).

The catacombs of Kom El Shofaqa, Alexandria

Here, the ancient traditions and increasingly Christian and Jewish Gnostic traditions began to find common accord and created a style of house or private practice that continues to this day.

Out of this time of transition, confusion, and recreation many different traditions arose in new forms. In particular, a series of texts emerged, the hermetic literature, organised around the Graeco-Egyptian figure of Hermes Trismegistus or "Thrice Great Hermes" who is derived from the ancient Egyptian deity *Djehudty*, called "Thoth" by the Greeks. This being is the archetype of priesthood and the patron of the magical art of creating images, and of the arts of measurement and geometry—needed for the building of temples in ancient Egypt. These much later texts are a continuation of the teachings that would have been found in the House of Life in ancient Hermopolis. The cosmology of Hermopolis (originally called *Khmenu* or "City of Eight") is based around eight archetypal beings who arise from the primeval waters, or *Nun*, as masculine and feminine couples:

> Nun and Nunet (fluidity and water)
> Heh and Hehet (infinity and air)
> Kek and Keket (darkness and fire)
> Amen and Amenet (hiddenness and earth)

The sense of the balancing of opposites, both of male and female and of the elements, is emphasised by the fact that the key deities of Hermopolis are Thoth and Maat. As we already know, Maat is the principle or order and balance and Thoth, or *Djehudty*, is seen as the lord of divine words who, through speech and word, enables all the forms and images of the universe to arise. He is said to have written *The Book of Thoth,* which contains all the secrets of the universe. As the moon god he is the reflection of Ra and the measurer of time and cycle, the scribe who records all; he was also seen as the master of balance and the judge of the living and the dead. The art of constructing inner temples and living images which indwell them and working with the divine word that stems from this ancient teaching centre remain central to Qabalistic tradition even to this day, as does the practice of working with the interplay of opposites to enable creation.

The Hermetica begin with the dialogue called "Poimandres" in which we witness a teaching given by Poimandres—the personified divine mind, the *nous*—to Hermes Trismegistus. Poimandres appears as a vast human being and his name is translated as "the shepherd", which reminds us both of the hidden god Amoun Ra, whose secret image is that of the human being, and that sense of the pharaoh who, as Ra's vice-regent, is the Good Shepherd. Hermes Trismegistus is shown a gentle and joyous light, and a downward-moving, fearful, and loathsome darkness with a twisting and enfolding motion. This is very similar to ancient Egyptian descriptions of the life-giving qualities of Ra and the life-denying energies of Apep. The dialogue goes on to describe the creation of the cosmos, which contains both the joyous light and the enfolding darkness, much as ancient Egyptians describe the goddess Neith weaving the world into existence, working with the principles of Ra and Apep as the warp and weft of the universe. It goes on to describe the arising of the holy word that enters the primal substance and awakens the qualities of the elements. It then shows us human beings as the bearers of the image of the divine who, like the divine, have the power to create. We are then shown a process in which the abuse of this power breaks the balance between the joyous light and the twisting darkness and people become mired in the darkness and ignorant and unconscious of the divine mind within them. Poimandres has come to Hermes Trismegistus to restore him to his true estate and to assist him to awaken others to these riches which may be found within. Hermes Trismegistus accepts his mission and concludes,

> I engraved in myself the beneficent kindness of Poimandres and having been filled with what I desired I was delighted. For the sleep of the body became the sobriety of the soul, the closing of the eyes became true vision, my silence became pregnant with the Supreme Good, and the utterance of the Word became the generation of riches. (Salaman, 2004, p. 24)

In the eleventh book of the *Corpus Hermeticum* we find *nous*, the divine mind, telling Hermes Trismegistus about the nature of time as consisting of the sense of eternity and repeating cycles. This arises directly out of the ancient Egyptian notions of *djet* time and *neheh* time, and the nature of Thoth, as we saw earlier. We are told that the active power of divinity is in the mind and soul, and that all of the cosmos can be found within the divine mind and its reflection within the soul. The image of that divine mind and creative presence is presented as the Sun, and Hermes Trismegistus is invited to practise a bodiless imagination through which his consciousness can be as vast as the cosmos or as small as an atom and can, through projecting his presence through time and space, act as a shepherd of souls.

> See what power you have and what speed! You can do all these things and yet God cannot? Reflect on God in this way as having all within Himself as ideas: the cosmos, Himself, the whole. If you do not make yourself equal to God you cannot understand Him. Like is understood by like. Grow to immeasurable size. Be free from every body, transcend all time. Become eternity and thus you will understand God. Suppose nothing to be impossible for yourself. Consider yourself immortal and able to understand everything: all arts, sciences and the nature of every living creature. Become higher than all heights and lower than all depths. Sense as one within yourself the entire creation: fire, water, the dry and the moist. Conceive yourself to be in all places at the same time: in earth, in the sea, in heaven; that you are not yet born, that you are within the womb, that you are young, old, dead; that you are beyond death. Conceive all things at once: times, places, actions, qualities and quantities; then you can understand God. (Salaman, 2004, p. 57)

Alexandria functions as a nexus point between the distant past of Egypt and the present day, and a place from which the inner teachings spread.

Proclus initially trained in Alexandria and then moved to Athens. The Hermetica moved to the ancient city of Harran, situated between the contemporary states of Turkey and Iraq. In its day, Harran was the city state of the Sabeans and a place to which many unreformed pagans went in order to be able to freely practise their religion. From there the Hermetica went to Baghdad and became one of the influences behind the development of Sufi tradition in Islam.

These teachings, pagan, unorthodox Christian, and Jewish, eventually become known as "gnostic teachings", the word *gnosis* meaning "knowing", referencing the inner knowing that is delivered through these practices as an expanded sense of self and universe combined with a role similar to that found in the Egyptian priesthood of being responsible for maintaining balance, order, and blessing in the world. One of the particular consequences of this melting pot was the fusion of the traditions of Judaism with the geometric and number mysticism of the school of Hermopolis, a fusion that was heightened and deepened by Greek Pythagorean thought and practice. In Philo of Alexandria we see the way in which the stories of the Torah become allegorised. He has a particular interest in the numbers one, two, seven, and ten, seeing the one as representing the divine unity, the two as representing the duality of creation—the separation of light and darkness; the seven as representing the seven days of creation of Genesis and the mystery of shabbat, and ten as the number of completion (Lévy 2018). Previously, Jewish mysticism had mainly focused on the visions of Ezekiel and was called "throne mysticism" because it involved a visionary ascent to the divine throne. However, the effect of the Alexandrian synthesis was to bring in a new approach to the tradition.

In the second or third century CE a key text, the Sefer Yetzirah ("The Book of Creation") emerges, which begins:

> By thirty-two mysterious paths of wisdom Yah has engraved [all things], [who is] the Lord of hosts, the God of Israel, the living God, the Almighty God, He that is uplifted and exalted, He that Dwells forever, and whose Name is holy; having created His world by three [derivatives] of [the Hebrew root-word] s^ef^ar: namely, *sefer* (a book), *sefor* (a count) and *sippur* (a story), along with ten calibrations of empty space, twenty-two letters [of the Hebrew alphabet], [of which] three are principal [letters] (i.e. א מ ש), seven are double-sounding [consonants] (i.e. בג"ד כפר"ת) and twelve are ordinary [letters] (i.e. ה ו ז ח ט י ל נ ס ע צ ק). (Qafih, 1972, p. 35)

This is the beginning of the Qabalah as we now know it: the prototypical Tree of Life found in ancient Egypt and in the Book of Genesis becomes a geometric mandala linked to the Hebrew alphabet in which each letter is a number and a hieroglyphic image. As Christianity became increasingly orthodox and militant gnostic teachings were driven underground, many of the ancient texts became lost. In the case of the Hermetica it is known that there were many more texts than the handful we now have and most of the unorthodox Christian texts and teachings have been completely expunged, known only because they are referenced through early Church attacks upon them, such as *Against Heresies* by Iranaeus. The survival of much of the Greek wisdom is most likely due to the transmission through Harran to Baghdad so that they were preserved through the cultural influences of the Middle East, which later appear as Islam. So highly regarded are these teachings that some of the early Sufi orders acknowledge Empedocles and Plato as *sheikhs* or great spiritual teachers.

As Islam entered its golden age in the eighth century CE it became a dominant culture that preserved and developed the Greek, Egyptian, and Jewish wisdom. Meanwhile in Europe, the Dark Ages had descended and the Christian Church took considerable control over the permitted directions of spiritual thought and practice. For centuries, therefore, gnostic practice was carried out in small groups, before emerging in a recognisable form at about the tenth century CE in the case of those working with the *Sefer Yetzirah*. There were significant practitioners and groups in Provence and Northern Spain, the city of Girona in particular, and in North Africa the city of Fez became an important centre. It is likely that groups continued to work in both Egypt and in Israel, but no independent trace has been found and all the extant qabalistic manuscripts date from the twelfth century CE and later.

One of the first such manuscripts to appear in Provence was the *Sefer Bahir* or "Book of Brilliance", a series of discourses attributed to the first-century sage Nehunya ben HaKanah, based upon the story of Genesis, it concerns the "Tree of Life" planted in the heart of the Garden of Eden. This is the antidote to the Tree of the Knowledge of Good and Evil that Adam and Eve have eaten of, and which causes them to be exiled them from the garden. In a sense, the Tree of the Knowledge of Good and Evil is the Tree of Death of our title, as it brings Adam and Eve from the deeply interconnected growth and life of the garden and the experience of union with the divine into an experience of being separate from and struggling with the universe. It is connected also with a sense of badness and shame, as one of the first experiences of Adam and Eve after they have eaten the fruit is the sense of sexual shame and the need to cover themselves with fig leaves. This sense of covering nakedness, badness, and needing to hide, is right at the heart of the sense of the Qliphoth—they are literally shells that cover and hide, just like the fig leaves, and contain within them therefore the impulse to separate from the sense of the divine.

As these teachings emerge into the light, we are given ideas and practices with which we can begin this task of removing the shells that obstruct the light of our own creativity and the creativity of the divine. The root idea behind these teachings is the identity of the world of the soul with the soul of the universe, much as we find described in the Hermetic dialogues where the *nous*, the divine mind assists Hermes Trismegistus to find the reflection of the divine mind within the soul and to project the presence of the soul throughout the universe.

The Tree of Life, then, is the tree that leads us back into the heart of the garden, away from shame and hiding and into the light of discovery and connection. In the early Qabalah, the exploration of the tree with the intention to return to the garden was said to be perilous. There is a legend of four rabbis who entered the garden: one died, one went mad, one sought to destroy the garden, and one was able to come and go in peace. The peril arose out of the inability to remain balanced in the midst of powerful experiences and to continue the inner inquiry to its conclusion. The rabbi who was simply able to come and go like Simon Iff, Ernest Butler, and Tom Oloman could perform the quiet, daily work of restoration and balance without disturbance.

The word for "garden" in Hebrew is *pardes*, פרדס, or *PRDS*. There is a rabbinic commentary that considers this word as an acronym for the fundamental qabalistic contemplative approach. This practice of is one in which we increasingly discover that which is hidden or concealed. It is sometimes described as eating the nuts that grow in paradise, breaking through the shell of the nut to find the sweetness at the kernel of the nut. The acronym describes four levels of contemplation:

    פ *Peshat* (פשט) this word means "surface", "direct", or "literal".

    ר *Remez* (רמז) this means "hint", or the suggestion of a symbolic meaning beneath the surface.

    ד *Derash* (דרש) this means "to inquire" and to seek to penetrate the symbolic hint.

    ס *Sod* (סוד) this means "mystery", or a secret revealed through inspiration and revelation.

This meditative process is begun by firstly paying attention to ourselves, using our body and five senses as anchors to create a sense of presence. We then focus on the object of contemplation, beginning with the surface or literal meaning, letting our mind and senses circle around the object and listening to what emerges in response to our inquiry. What emerges is the hint, which may present itself as thought, image, feeling, or even physical sensation. As we catch the hint we become more deeply engaged; we become the seeker and it becomes the sought. As we pass through the doorway of *derash*, it becomes part of our inner process, connecting with our psyche and inner and outer world. As we pursue this quest we remain attentive, sitting in silence and waiting for the mystical insight that shows us the hidden or secret meaning, the *sod*.

It is this fundamental process that is at the heart of the practice of transforming the Qliphoth, leading us from the shell-like outer rind of things, in which the world is experienced as filled with separated objects, through the fluidity and creativity of the world of symbols, into the sense of oneness and unity at the core of each and every being. In this way we reach into and embody the Tree of Life.

Ernest Butler described the Tree of Life thus: "the key glyph around which all the other associated symbolism of the western training is centred, the mighty all embracing glyph of the universe and the soul of man" (Butler, 1978, p. 17). He goes on to say: "For the Qabalah is not only a body received from the 'Masters in Israel' it is a method of using the mind in a practical and constantly widening consideration of the nature of the universe and the soul of man" (Butler, 1978, p. 22). He saw it as a guide, map, and method through which we explore ourselves and universe.

The key point being made here is that the tree enables us to create relationship between the deep places of our soul and the depths of the universe. The diagram of the tree gives us a skeleton, which we work with to bring it to life within us, so that ultimately it becomes a living presence in our heart. This practice of working with the tree is referred to in the Book of Ezekiel, in his vision of the valley of dry bones. The prophet is asked to prophesy over the dry bones and, as he does so, breath enters them and they come to life. In effect we sit with the diagram of the tree and place our breath and vision upon it so that it comes to life. The pattern, described below, is the bare bones which, using the contemplative process of *PRDS*, we breathe into and bring to life within us by taking the surface meaning of the words and working with them through each of the four levels until the mystic secret, the sweetness at the heart of the nut, is revealed.

The root image of the Tree of Life is of a tree growing from the earth, embracing the moon, planets, sun, and stars. It is depicted in abstract terms by ten circles called *sephiroth* (singular: *sephirah*).

The sephiroth are arranged in the geometric shape of the Tree of Life thus:

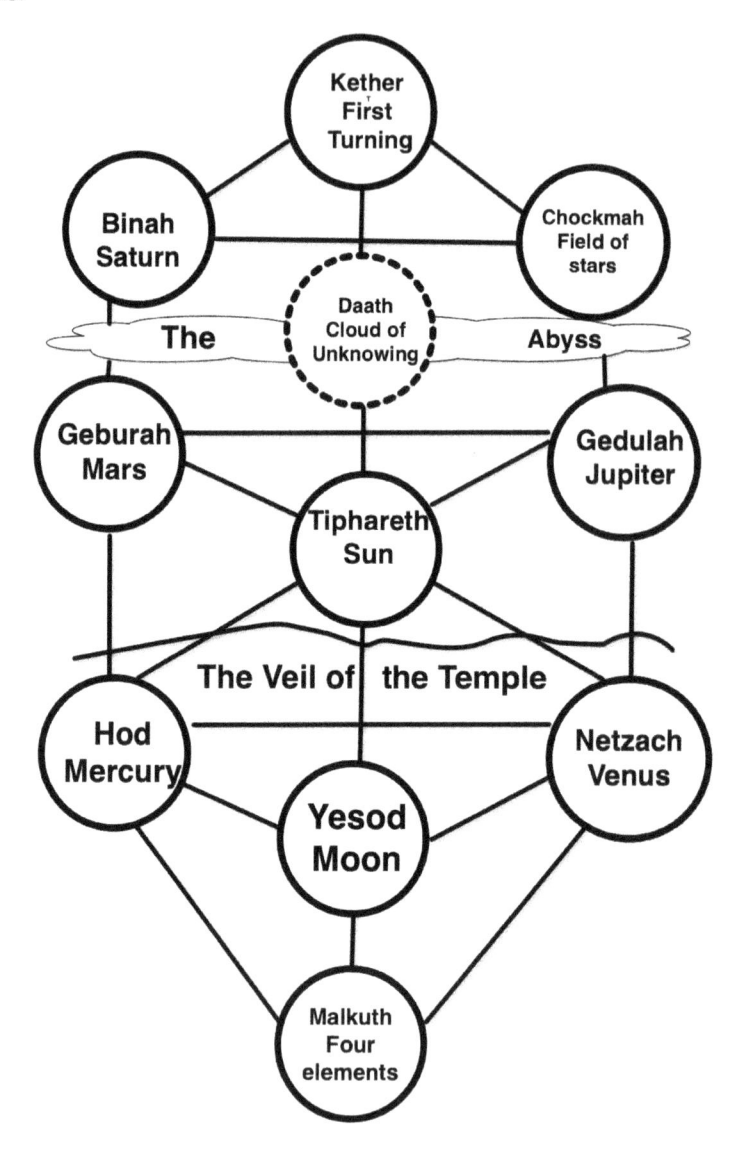

The Tree of Life

As we explore the Tree of Life and its shadow, the Tree of Death, we must know that there is only one tree—the tree in balance and communion is the Tree of Life; the tree out of balance and in separation is the Tree of Death. Our journey, like the rabbis, will at times involve experiences that may feel like madness, inner death, and apostasy as we digest and resolve the Qliphoth that we carry and encounter, until—like the fourth rabbi—we are simply able to go and return in peace. The exploration of the tree can be considered in three stages, based on the ancient Egyptian forms of the Eloquent Peasant, the Shepherd King or Queen, and the Silent Sage, which lead to the fourth stage of returning to the non-dual roots of the tree.

Stage one—the Eloquent Peasant, or the man or woman of earth

The creation of our tree begins in a place of experiencing the Qliphoth—the world without meaning and centre, the world of "shells". In his seminal poem *The Wasteland*, T.S. Eliot describes this state as being in a dry land without water, being hollow, and holding only a heap of broken images. To consciously experience this is very difficult, but knowing it as a *felt* experience, of aridity and lostness, is the beginning of connection with the living tree. It is the starting point. Engaging with this is the task of what, following the Egyptians, we might call "becoming the Eloquent Peasant, the speaker of truth" or, in Aleister Crowley's thinking, the man or woman of earth. As we have seen, the image of the peasant comes from the very earliest sense of Maat, which is of a rectangular block representing the firm ground on which the peasant stands. Connected with this idea is the cultivation of the fertile land that must be irrigated and managed so that the crops flourish. Central to this task is the establishment and maintenance of clear boundaries, the nourishment of the crops and defending them against enemies. Applying this to the Tree of Life, we enter into the first stage of engaging with the tree.

This is as simple and as complex as paying attention to our body and our senses in present time. This act of embodiment opens us to the Janus-like mystery of our senses, which point both outwards and inwards if we develop the capacity to stay present. What we will discover is that the apparently simple act of remaining present is continually interrupted by distractions that manifest as trains of thought, uprushes of feeling, memory, and associative images. This sense of distraction and inability to maintain consistent presence is an aspect of what the Egyptians would have called Apep, the presence that seeks to disrupt the order of the world. The Qabalists envisaged this (like the Egyptians) as a serpent that coils around the Tree of Life, entangling the spheres and the paths so that the harmony of the tree is disrupted. The task of the initiate at the peasant level is therefore to begin the task of disentangling the spheres and paths of the Tree of Life from the coils of the serpent.

As we enter the tree in this way, we step into Malkuth, the Kingdom. This is the first archetype at the base of the tree. It is linked to the earth and the body; a place of rooting and grounding and the anchor for all that follows. This first step is important as we start to develop a sense of inner sovereignty and capacity to take possession of both our inner kingdom and our place in the world. As we connect to our body and senses we create a vessel of containment within which the rest of the work can arise. From this place of presence and containment we look inwards, relating to mind, and feelings, and start to enter the sphere of Yesod, which is the pool of life and memory at the foundations of our psyche.

The path that connects Malkuth to Yesod is called "the underworld path". It is both a descent into our own subconscious and our own subjective universe, and into the inner side of the objective universe. As we pass along this path we contemplate the internal and external worlds and the relationship between them. We start to relate to interiority, dream, and memory, to image and to the flow of our life force and sexuality, and come into relationship with our unconscious and preconscious self. Yesod is also called "the treasure house of images". It is the storehouse of all our memories and contains the image of ourselves and the image of the world we live in. It is often imagined as a pool that can be still or turbulent, clear or filled with imagery.

As we deepen this awareness we notice the effect of our mind and feeling on both our body and our subjectivity. We enter into relationship with the archetypes of Mercury and Venus, or Hod ("Glory") and Netzach ("Victory"). These are experienced as a pair of opposites, one set either side of the central line above Yesod, the Moon. As we become more proficient in relating to these aspects of life and being, we start to notice their interplay in the world. We gradually notice when there is a feeling of ground or anchor in the world around us, and the flow of life energy and sexuality or the power of images. We notice the power of ideas and emotions. As we do this inwardly and outwardly, we create paths of connection between these aspects of our nature and start to grow our tree. Until we do that, however, these energies of Mercury, Venus and the Moon—or thought, emotion, and unconscious memory—form a spinning wheel that keeps our attention trapped in past need, resentment, and future fear. These entangled energies over the course of a life develop considerable momentum and are a major barrier to the process of transformation, and constitute the *prima materia* or matter that needs to be transformed.

This barrier is described as Paroketh ("the veil of the temple") seen as created from the inner dialogue of Yesod, Hod, and Netzach; a confluence of thought, feeling or desire, and the subliminal images of self and universe that are housed in the inner sea of Yesod. This reflects down into Malkuth and maintains our sense of self and universe as the momentum of this spinning wheel overrides any fresh input, whether from the outside world or from the deeper parts of the psyche. Any insight or understanding that does not fit with the pre-existing sense of self and world is taken into the inner dialogue and assimilated, so that its overall stability is maintained. Say, for example, you have a deeply held sense that you are an unlucky, uncared-for person. You suddenly win a prize. There is an opening, a moment of choice in which that part of the inner dialogue responsible for that belief has the opportunity to dissolve. If we are careful and attentive that is indeed what might happen but, if not, the experience is covered over and made part of the dialogue, perhaps by us deciding that this was a one-off random occurrence that will never happen again, or by deciding that the prize is not very good and if the universe really cared about us then the prize would be more significant.

As we deepen our understanding of Malkuth, Yesod, Hod, and Netzach we enter into conscious awareness of the dynamic of the inner dialogue, noticing its automatic nature and the strength of its flow. In particular we can notice how the vices of each sephirah increase the automatic flow and the virtues disrupt it. The vice of Malkuth, for example, is inertia and when it is active gives a sense of the solidity of the dialogue and the impossibility of transforming it. By contrast, the sense of sovereignty that is the virtue of Malkuth reminds us that we have power over all the contents of our inner world. Similarly, the independence or indolence of Yesod, the commitment to truth or lies of Hod, the unselfishness or lust of Netzach, either dissolve the dialogue or reify it.

36   THE TREE OF LIFE AND DEATH

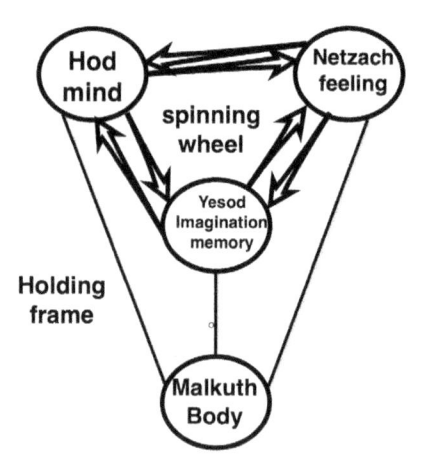

Diagram: Triangle with Hod (mind) at top-left, Netzach (feeling) at top-right, Malkuth (Body) at bottom, and Yesod (Imagination, memory) in the center. Arrows connect Hod and Netzach through Yesod, labeled "spinning wheel". The triangle itself is labeled "Holding frame".

The inner dialogue

As we become more proficient in feeling and working with the interplay of these archetypes and their patterns, we will discover a sense of depth and connection between our different states and our perception of the world. At times we will touch a sense of stillness or presence behind the flow of feeling, thought, image, and body sensation. At this point we touch on the archetype of the Sun, Tiphareth, the beauty of presence whose quality of stillness starts to interact with the whirl of energy we are becoming used to. This is positioned in the central line above Hod and Netzach. Experiencing this sphere is sometimes called "the knowledge and conversation of the holy guardian angel" as what is experienced here is a deepening sense of immersion in stillness and a dialogue with a presence that is both intimate with us and yet standing behind our everyday self.

Stage two—the Shepherd King or Queen

This is the place where the work of the peasant or man or woman of earth concludes and we enter a new stage which the Egyptians described as "the path of the Shepherd King or Queen". Aleister Crowley called this "the path of the lover" or "the minor adept" who learns to balance and unite the principles of love and will, expanding their capacity and functioning as an alchemist. This is the active engagement of the deeper aspect of our soul with the established patterns of our life to create a new, active, and embodied presence that has the capacity to generate truth, balance, and beauty. The word "alchemy" is an Arab word meaning "the Egyptian art", and the work that we now carry out calls upon us to transform the entangled material of the inner dialogue, to work with the energy of opposites and cooperate with the sense of presence and guidance emanating from the part of us that is the angel of Tiphareth. Another way of looking at this is to see the descending presence as the Good Shepherd whose function it is to gather the split and lost portions of our life and energy back into our bundle of life.

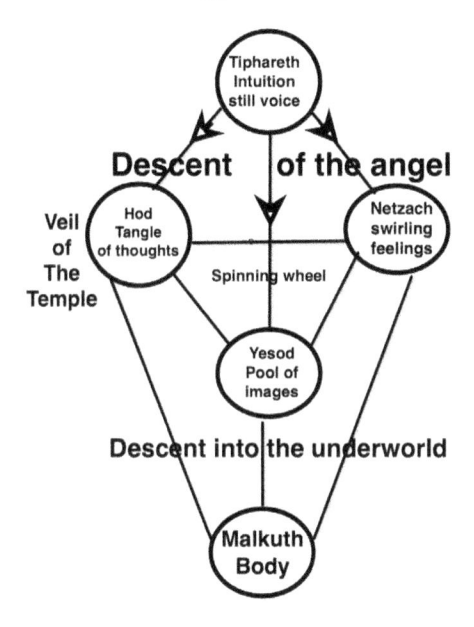

```
                    Tiphareth
                    Intuition
                    still voice

            Descent    of the angel

    Veil     Hod              Netzach
    of      Tangle             swirling
    The    of thoughts         feelings
    Temple       Spinning wheel

                    Yesod
                    Pool of
                    images

            Descent into the underworld

                    Malkuth
                    Body
```

This diagram shows us the presence of Tiphareth descending into the inner dialogue of Netzach, Hod, and Yesod, untangling thought, calming feeling, and working with the disturbed and concrete subliminal images of Yesod so that they become less and less opaque and more permeable to the inner light shining from Tiphareth. The subliminal images that sustain the inner dialogue are formed from the resolution of the dilemmas of our lives. Our commitment to these past choices has meant that, moment by moment, we affirm the truth of our past and therefore intensify the dialogue. This spinning wheel veils us from other possibilities. It is only bringing awareness into this wheel that enables us to start piercing the veil and coming into direct relationship with the Tiphareth.

As we become more centred in Tiphareth we start to become aware of greater depth and lucidity in both thought and feeling. This is the inclusion of the deeper archetypes of Geburah (which corresponds to Mars) and Gedulah (which corresponds to Jupiter), representing respectively the principles of will and love. Our minds become more focused, disciplined, and clear, and our emotional nature more loving and compassionate. This creates a new wheel of stillness, acceptance, and clarity that deepens our connection to our interior life.

These spheres are positioned on either side of the central line above Tiphareth, so that Geburah is above Hod, and Gedulah above Netzach, thus:

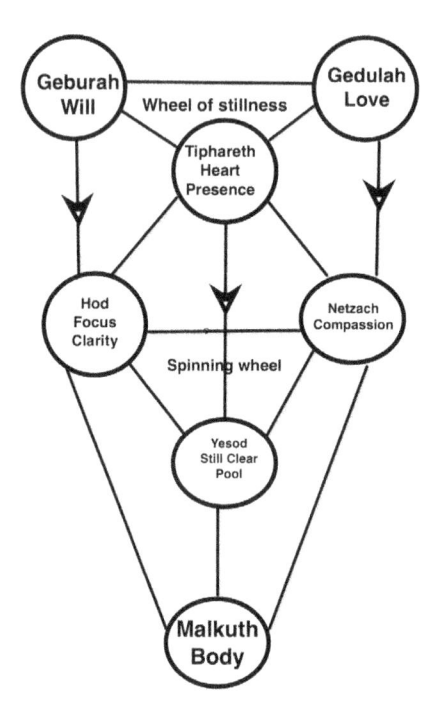

The wheel of stillness

Stage three—the Silent Sage, Da'ath, and the abyss

As this new triumvirate of Tiphareth, Geburah, and Gedulah comes into play, there is a much greater sense of depth and possibility. Through this we sense the mysterious aspect of ourselves and the greater universe, the sphere of Da'ath, mystical knowledge, or the knowing of not knowing. It is the gateway to the deepest parts of our being. It is also called "the bridge across the abyss" as it asks us to surrender our old ways of thinking, feeling, and doing in favour of surrender to the unknown. It is placed on the central line above Tiphareth, Geburah, and Gedulah, and depicted as a dotted circle to indicate the sense of mystery it conveys. As we pursue this path we become more responsive to its sense of mystery and more focussed on this oddly tangible but unknown ground. This path between Tiphareth and Kether, which leads through Da'ath, is called "the desert path" and represents the leaving or stripping away of all we have previously known. It is also called "the crossing" or "bridging the abyss". It is the main transition point of the inner process, though it is prefigured in the movement from the fragmented world of the Qliphoth into the sovereignty of Malkuth and the journey between Yesod and Tiphareth. The active alchemical presence of Tiphareth, Geburah, and Gedulah here lays down its guardianship as we enter into the mystery of Da'ath and come into relationship with the Silent Sage or the *geru maa* at the heart of our being. Here the groundedness and discriminating intelligence of the peasant, and the active compassion and presence of the Shepherd King, is surrendered into the hands of the deeper soul—the true contemplative.

This place of transition is also called "the abyss", and it is a place of profound choice—or rather, a place where previous choices become visible and can be affirmed or rejected. If we have cultivated the virtues of devotion to the great work, courage, and obedience (the virtues of Tiphareth, Geburah, and Gedulah), then the deep surrender demanded in Da'ath, while no less challenging, will be resonant with our inner trajectory. If, however, we have cultivated the corresponding qliphothic vices of pride, cruelty, and tyranny, then without a herculean rejection of our past choices and cultivation we will not be able to make this transition and, in qabalistic terms, we will fall into the abyss, creating there the shadow of the three supernal sephiroth.

The step that is required here is to become what is called "a babe of the abyss": to give up all previous skill and mastery, and to wait in stillness.

40 THE TREE OF LIFE AND DEATH

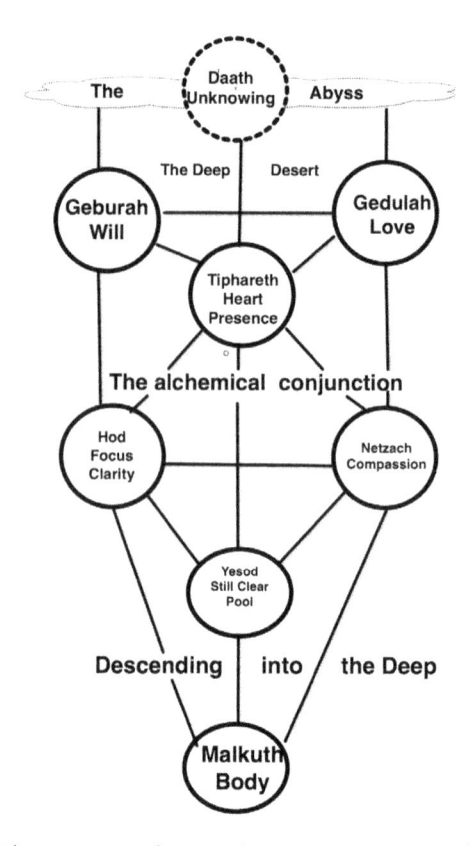

```
                    Daath
        The      Unknowing    Abyss
              
              The Deep    Desert
        Geburah                Gedulah
         Will                   Love
                  Tiphareth
                    Heart
                   Presence
              The alchemical conjunction
          Hod
         Focus                Netzach
         Clarity             Compassion
                    Yesod
                  Still Clear
                     Pool
        Descending   into    the Deep
                    Malkuth
                     Body
```

The return to the garden—entertering Da'ath

As we pass the gate of Da'ath we enter the deepest places of the tree: a pair of spheres called Binah ("Understanding") and Chockmah ("Wisdom"), corresponding respectively to Saturn and the field of stars. At the time the tree was developed, Saturn was the outermost planet, the container of all the inner planets, and here it represents the archetypal mother and the womb of space while the sphere of the stars, as the great fertilising principle, is the archetypal father. These arise from Kether, the central point at the crown of tree, called the *primum mobile*—the first movement. These three are depicted in a triangle at the top of the tree and represent our deepest connection to spirit and the energies of creation. Kether is our own deepest self, Chockmah the deep will that arises from it, and Binah the deep love that births the image of that will through the rest of the sephiroth of the Tree of Life. The world of the supernals is a non-dual world in which each of the three is intimately part of the other two; this is the world of the garden, our true home.

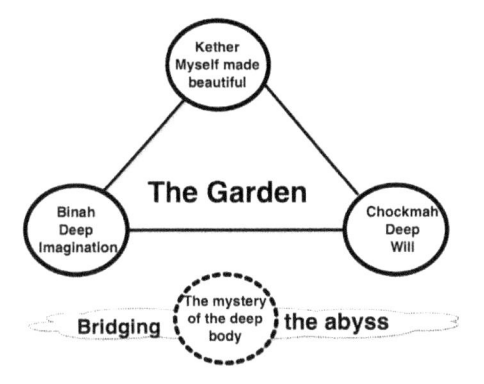

The garden—the supernal sephiroth

To summarise the journey of the tree:

1. We begin by becoming present in our body and senses. As the Eloquent Peasant we investigate the complexity of the inner dialogue that obstructs our capacity to grow and change. Through contemplation of breath and body and working with the tree we learn to slow and stop that dialogue.
2. As we do this, we start to pierce the veil of the temple and increasingly commune with the intuitive presence of Tiphareth.
3. As we follow the intuitive guidance that comes from the silent voice, our thinking and feeling nature transforms and our imagination becomes lucid.
4. Our centre of awareness shifts from the spinning wheel of the inner dialogue to the more expansive wheel of stillness, and we learn to work with the principles of love and will and the alchemical conjunction.
5. As the alchemical work proceeds, and as we increasingly embody the principles of love and will, we are guided to the major transition point of the tree: the abyss. Here we enter the desert way, in which we surrender our mastery into unknowing, becoming a babe of the abyss or, conversely, if we refuse to surrender then we risk falling into the abyss, walling ourselves up in our sense of knowing and accomplishment and creating a shadow tree.

6. As we bridge the abyss we enter into non-dual communion with deep will, deep love, the source of our being, discovering the mysterious aspect of our bodies as the living vessel for these great principles. Here we become the *geru maa*, so steeped in stillness that we are infused in Maat, becoming at last the living tree in the midst of the garden, perpetually fruiting and offering shade to all who seek shelter with us.

CHAPTER 4

Contemplating the sephiroth

Having considered the major structures of the Tree of Life, we will now consider the nature of the sephiroth; the word *sephirah* ספירה means "counting" or "enumeration" and is linked to *sefer* ספר, the word for "book" or "text", *sippur* סיפור the word for "recounting a story", the word *sappir* ספר meaning "sapphire" and "brilliance", the word *sfar* ספר meaning "boundary", and the word *sofar* סיפר "scribe". As we contemplate the sephiroth we encounter the sense of living numbers that tell a story, that have many facets of brilliance, and that are inscribed into both our nature and the nature of the universe.

The roots of the sephiroth are found in number as the archetypal order of the universe. It begins with the numeral 0 that represents the unmanifest and unconditioned ground from which all else arises. This is similar to the ancient Egyptian conception of the waters of the Nun, or the sense of the body of the goddess Nuit that represents the field of space within which every form arises. This was called by the qabalists *ain* or "negation". This they went on to develop as the sense of space containing infinite viewpoints and infinite forms comparable to the ancient Egyptian sense of the body of Nuit as the field of stars. This they called *ain soph*, "the infinite". They went on to consider that field of viewpoints as infinitely luminous, and so added the word *aur* to their description of the 0 state, thus: *ain soph aur*, "the infinite light". These they called the three negative veils, as they point at a phenomenon rather than describing it, just as for the ancient Egyptians the image of Nuit is not a literal image but an icon that points to an uncreated reality. This sense of negative existence enters into manifest existence by the uncreated light concentrating around a central point—the number 1.

This numeral for the Egyptians indicates the sense of singularity of a position in space around which all else takes form. This numeral is in itself a paradox, being simply one, but if we position a point we invoke the sense of twoness as there is the point and the background of the point. This is the sphere Kether, the monad complete in itself, but also the beginning point of a whole series of numbers through addition, thus bringing in the whole principle of reflection and the image of the line that extends itself, potentially infinitely, by continued reflection—the second sphere, Chockmah. This line is contained and formed by the dimension of surface as we contemplate the number 3, the addition of 1, introducing a new factor that produces the triangle which encloses the sephirah Binah. This first triad of position, extension by reflection and bounding and enclosing all, continually arising out of and returning to the field of negative existence, holds the fundamental dynamic of the roots of self and universe.

The next step, via what is variously called "the abyss" or "the sephirah that is not a sephirah" of Da'ath, is experienced as a step of discontinuity, a leap or prismatic refraction into the dimension of solidity or fourness and the appearance of the second triad of the tree as the sephirah Gedulah comes into being. This fourness, being a reflection or doubling of twoness, contains within itself the impulse of extension, thus bringing into being the sense of both motion and time; the sense of change and therefore of death and birth—the number 5 and the sephirah Geburah. This is followed by the appearance of the number 6, which represents the doubling of the triangle and the conjunction of 2 and 3 and therefore the principle of extension by reflection and the principle of boundness and enclosure. This is the self-conscious, self-reflective point occupying the centre ground of balance, mediating between the deeper spheres and the outer, and between stability and change—the sphere of Tiphareth.

This sense of balance is overset by the extension of Tiphareth into the multiplicity of desires or forces and thoughts or forms represented by the numbers 7 and 8, Netzach and Hod. Odd numbers represent the addition of the initiating energy of Kether to a stable form and the beginning of a new series. Thus here we find the self-reflective stability of Tiphareth manifesting a new, multiple dynamic of change in the number 7 and Netzach. This is met by the sephirah Hod, the number 8, or two times four, which takes the reflective capacity of Chockmah and marries it to the expansiveness of Gedulah, which is itself a reflection of Chockmah. The meeting of Netzach and Hod therefore forms a mutually reinforcing field of resonance, of generation and reflection. This then finds stability again through the number 9, Yesod, "the foundation of things", which is created out of the multiplication of three times three and, therefore, the multiplication of the formative and enclosing energies of Binah. The final step is coming into full manifestation and action; the number 10 and Malkuth, "the kingdom", formed by the multiplication of two and five and Chockmah and Geburah conjoining the principle of infinite reflection and constant change and uniting the numerals 1 and 0.

Beneath and around all of these arising shapes is the unmanifest ground, the zero. Aleister Crowley summed up this whole process by the equation $0 = 2$ that he explained by seeing it as $0 = +1 -1$. This is the dynamic that emerges when the first point arises out of the unmanifest and then expresses itself as the arising will to be causing the principle of reflection or twoness to come into activity. This creates a triad of $0, +1$, and -1, which reflects itself through the rest of the tree. The forms that then arise remain equal with the unmanifest base, if they are a true reflection and they remain in relationship. Should the arising forms separate and break apart then then the relationship between the unmanifest and manifest similarly breaks down. This process of distortion and separation breaks the chain of reflection as the spheres, instead of functioning as transmitters of life, become opaque and their generative function splits into fragments. It is this splitting and distortion that brings the Tree of Death into being. When Simon Iff deals with the thing in the garden he is reasserting the pre-eminence of the $0 = 2$ equation, connecting his $+1$ with the -1 of the thing and through the act of conjunction returning all into balance.

Our contemplations of the sephiroth begin and return here, but as we continue we will find that each of the sephiroth has four levels or aspects: its divine or essential nature, its creative nature, its formative nature, and its expressive and action-orientated nature. These are traditionally called the four "worlds" or "universes" and are derived from Isaiah 43:7: "Every one that is called by My Name and for My glory, I have created, I have formed, even I have made."

- "My Name and for My glory" is the essential level of *Atziluth*—the nature of divinity.

46 THE TREE OF LIFE AND DEATH

- "I have created" is the world of *Beriah*, the world of creation—being in movement.
- "I have formed", the world of *Yetzirah*—movement expressing itself in individual shape and form.
- "I have made", the world of *Assiah*—shape and form taking incarnation and acting.

These are envisaged as the name of God that expresses the essential nature of the sephirah in Atziluth; in Beriah, the world of creation, as an archangel whose will it is to express the being of the God Name. This act of creation becomes formed and shaped in Yetzirah through the mediation of a choir of angels that arises out of the archangel to form and shape the luminous image which, in the world of Assiah, appears in concrete physical form and action denoted by the planetary form that shows its function. We will consider also the virtue and vice of the sephirah that show it operating, respectively, in a balanced and unbalanced form.

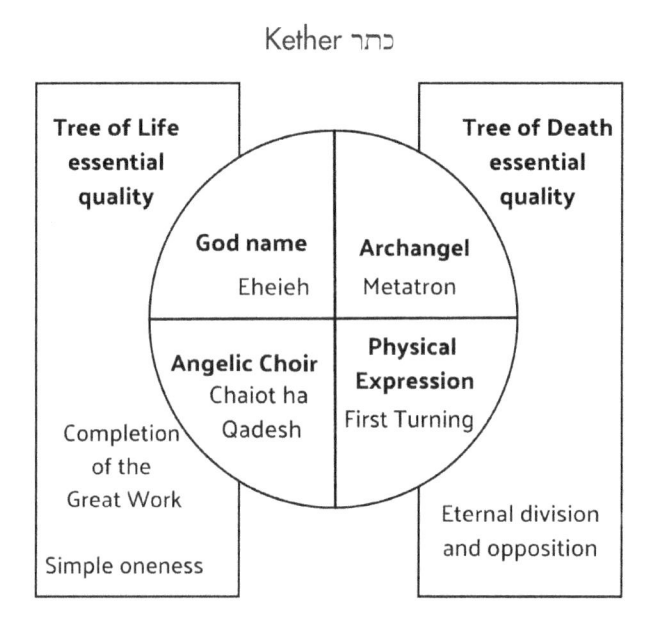

Kether כתר

Tree of Life essential quality	Tree of Death essential quality
God name Eheieh	**Archangel** Metatron
Angelic Choir Chaiot ha Qadesh	**Physical Expression** First Turning
Completion of the Great Work	
Simple oneness	Eternal division and opposition

We begin at Kether כתר, the crown and source of creation, visualized as a field of crystal white light. The physical manifestation of Kether is called the *rashith ha gilgalim* רשית ה גלגלים or "first movement or turning". Here we contemplate the very first movement upon which all the rest of the universe is based. The angelic choir that enables this movement is the *chaiot ha qadesh* חיות ה קדש, the "holy living creatures". These can be visualized as multi-winged figures of white and crystal light having four faces: human, bull, lion, and eagle. These beings are constantly in motion and entirely still; they are said to go and return and, when they are contemplated, we may feel both energized and stilled. Their archangel is Metatron מטטרן, the angel closest to God who once was Enoch, the first qabalistic initiate. "And Enoch walked with God and was not. For God took him" (Genesis 5: 24). Metatron is the root teacher of the Qabalah and can be visualized as a hooded form of incandescent white light holding in his hands a single point of light that is brighter than all. The God Name of this sephiroth is *Eheieh* אהיה, "I am and I will be", sometimes expanded to *Eheieh Asher Eheieh* אהיה אשר אהיה, "I am that I am, I will be that which I will be". Here we enter directly into the divine presence, becoming one with the divine. It is the deepest of surrenders which, in its depths, affirms the deep nature of our being. It is a negation that is the ultimate affirmation and is the completion of the Great Work: simple, pure non-duality and no separation.

The experience of this sephirah is the return to the beginning of life, to the first movement, to the essence of being a holy living creature, to being one who has walked with God and was not, to the declaration: "I am the ever existent one". This is the place where 0 and 2 reflect each other. In contrast, the one who is committed to the Tree of Death here asserts eternal opposition, division, and separation, breaking apart the components of the equation. Such a one is (we could say) a saint of evil, dedicated and devoted to the principles of positive evil. The magical image of this sephirah is that of the spiral nebula, and the qliphothic image is Thaumiel תאומיאל: two quarrelling heads joined together in opposition.

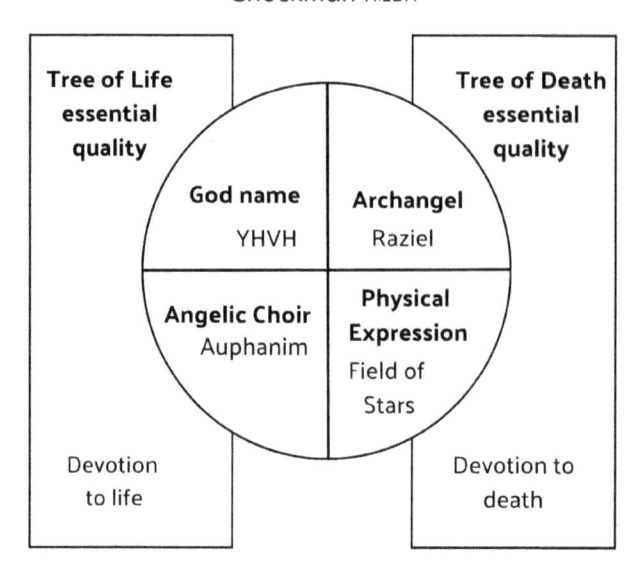

Chockmah חכמה

Tree of Life essential quality	**Tree of Death** essential quality
God name YHVH	**Archangel** Raziel
Angelic Choir Auphanim	**Physical Expression** Field of Stars
Devotion to life	Devotion to death

Chockmah חכמה is the archetype of twoness, of the act of reflection itself. It is envisaged as masculine. Its physical expression is the field of stars and can be visualized as a cloud of translucent starlight. Its key image is of a star burning in space, sending out light and warmth and impacting and enabling the emergence of life. The choir of angels that enable this are the Auphanim אופנים, "the wheels"; they can be envisaged as interlocking wheels of rainbow light with many eyes and wings that are constantly in motion and whose proximity generates movement and life. Their archangel is Ratziel רזיאל, the angel who holds all the wisdom of creation and who each day speaks that deep wisdom for those who can hear. He can be visualized as a hooded form in a luminous grey robe against a background of the night sky holding an eternal flame in which the Hebrew letters for ABBA אבבא spiral around. The God Name of this sphere is YHVH יהוה, the unique and particular name of creation and divine will.

The Tree of Life quality of Chockmah is devotion to all life; the commitment to the flourishing of the created universe. The Tree of Death quality is the devotion to death; the opposition to the cosmic scheme and the will and wish to hinder and obstruct life wherever and whenever it manifests. The magical image of Chockmah is the generative star; the qliphothic image, *Augiel* עוגיאל, a chaotic, cancerous growth.

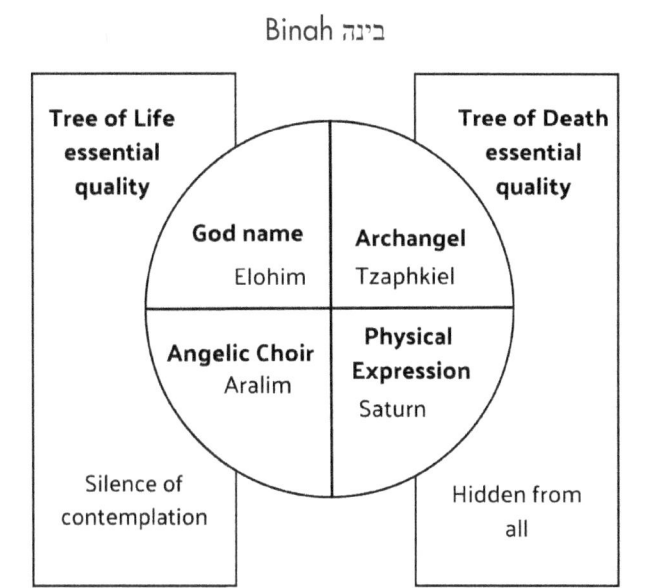

Binah בינה

Tree of Life essential quality	**Tree of Death** essential quality
God name Elohim	**Archangel** Tzaphkiel
Angelic Choir Aralim	**Physical Expression** Saturn
Silence of contemplation	Hidden from all

Binah בינה ("Understanding") is the archetypal feminine power. Its physical manifestation is Saturn, regarded as the outermost of the planets at the time the Tree of Life was devised. Binah can be visualized as black light. She is the container of life, the womb of all form, the deep imagination that brings all into expression. The choir of angels that enable this are the *aralim* אראלים, the thrones. These are the primal containers that create the forms and patterns that enable the divine will to pass into manifestation. They can be envisaged as multi-winged, cup-like forms of shining blackness with many eyes. Their archangel is Tzaphkiel צפכיאל who holds the archetype of the temple, and who teaches the art of contemplation. She can be envisaged as a hooded woman contemplating a sphere formed of interlocking rings with the Hebrew words *ama* אמא, *aima* אימא, *amen* אמן spiralling inside the form. The God Name of Binah is *Elohim* אלהים. This is the feminine creative power, the great sea, of which the inner sea of Yesod is a reflection.

Here in Binah, the essential quality of this sphere of the Tree of Life is the silence of contemplation within which the universe emerges and is seen by all. Her Tree of Death quality is hiddenness so that none can see, the root of all subterfuge and lies. The magical image of Binah is the field of space filled with stars; the qliphothic image, Satariel סאתריאל, is a stifling, airless darkness.

Da'ath דעת

Da'ath דעת is not a sephirah in the normal sense and does not have the same attributions as the other spheres. It can be visualised as a field of incandescent violet-grey light and as a series of images: the abyss, the condemned cell, the upper room, the prism, a grain of wheat, the cloud of unknowing, and the name of God *YHVH ELOHIM* יהוה אלהים. It is the mystery of transition.

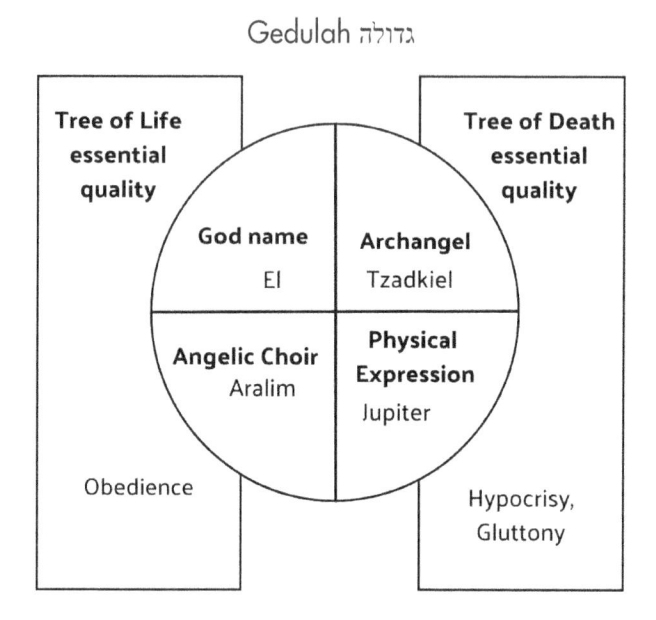

Gedulah גדולה

Tree of Life essential quality	Tree of Death essential quality
God name El	**Archangel** Tzadkiel
Angelic Choir Aralim	**Physical Expression** Jupiter
Obedience	Hypocrisy, Gluttony

Gedulah גדולה or "Love" is the sephirah of growth and expansion, of divine mercy, and can be visualised as a field of sapphire-blue light. Its physical expression is Jupiter, and the angelic choir is the *chasmalim* חשמלים, "the brilliant ones", who generate life, light, laughter, and who hold the universe together. They can be envisaged as multi-winged spheres of sapphire and purple light. The archangel is Tzadkiel צדקיאל—the righteous one who presides over the energies of growth and expansion and ensures that that the arising structures conform to the divine will. Tzadkiel can be visualized as a hooded form in sapphire and purple holding a shepherd's crook. The God Name of Gedulah is *El* אל, one of the oldest middle eastern names for the divine. The letter *aleph* is the ox and *lamed* the oxgoad, so the name gives us the image of power under control, directed movement, ploughing and enabling new growth. The name *El* is the expansive compassion of the divine enabling all life to grow and flourish. The Tree of Life quality of this sphere is obedience to the divine will and the unfolding pattern that emerges here. The Tree of Death quality is hypocrisy, gluttony, and tyranny that comes about from taking these energies of life and growth into ourselves, consuming more than we should in gluttony; pretending to follow the will of God in hypocrisy; and setting ourselves up as the source of creative life in tyranny. It is the quality of love turned inward into self-love and seeking to possess all. The magical image of Gedulah is a throned king in blue and purple robes holding an orb and crook. The qliphothic image Gamchicoth גמחיכת, is a ravenous mouth like a black hole consuming all.

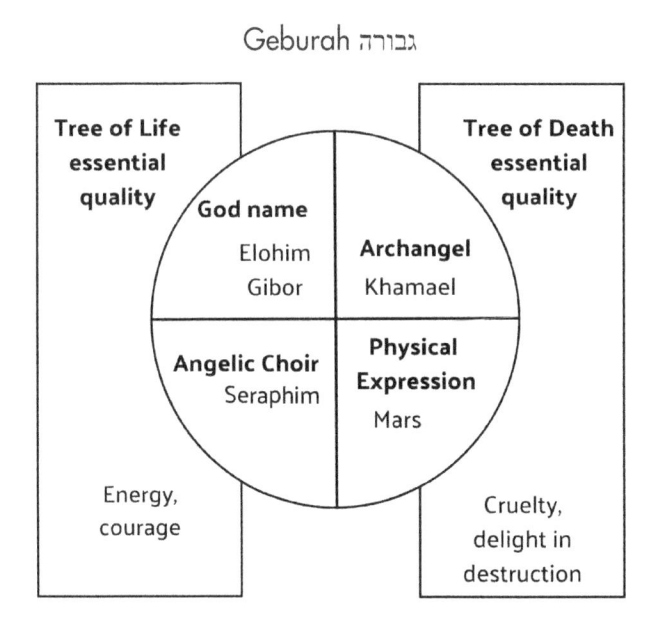

Geburah גבורה

Tree of Life essential quality

- God name: Elohim Gibor
- Archangel: Khamael
- Angelic Choir: Seraphim
- Physical Expression: Mars

Energy, courage

Tree of Death essential quality

Cruelty, delight in destruction

Geburah גבורה or "Strength". Its physical expression is Mars and this sephirah holds all the martial qualities of will, clarity, and discipline, and can be seen as a field of bright red light. Its choir of angels are the *seraphim* שרפים, "the burning ones", and they can be visualized as winged, scarlet, fiery serpents like the Egyptian *uraeus* that protected Pharaoh. They are said to continually proclaim *qodesh, qodesh, qodesh*, or "holy, holy, holy" and are perpetually purifying all they come into contact with.

The archangel of this sephirah is Khamael חמואל, the archangel of war, who embodies the wrath of God. He can be envisaged as a towering figure in bright red robes holding a sword of iron and an iron chain. The God Name of the sephirah is *Elohim Gibor* אלהים גיבור—"God who is almighty", God the warrior. The Tree of Life quality of this sphere is energy and courage as here we have to take upon ourselves the qualities of the warrior who wields power in the service of the light and who can bring about destruction in that service. The Tree of Death quality is cruelty and delighting in destruction, and here the powerful energies of justice and balancing are taken into an enjoyment of the use of power rather than the stillness and detachment that arises out of embracing the virtue of courage. Here the seraphim are invoked for their ability to burn and destroy rather than for purification and Khamael strengthens our wilfulness rather than our dedication to the light, the deep strength of Geburah supporting our sense of a separated self instead of strengthening our connection to all life. The magical image of this sphere is the goddess Minerva, a woman bearing a sword in red armour and wearing a helmet with a red plume. The qliphothic image, Golachab גולחב, is a wildfire or a nuclear reactor in meltdown.

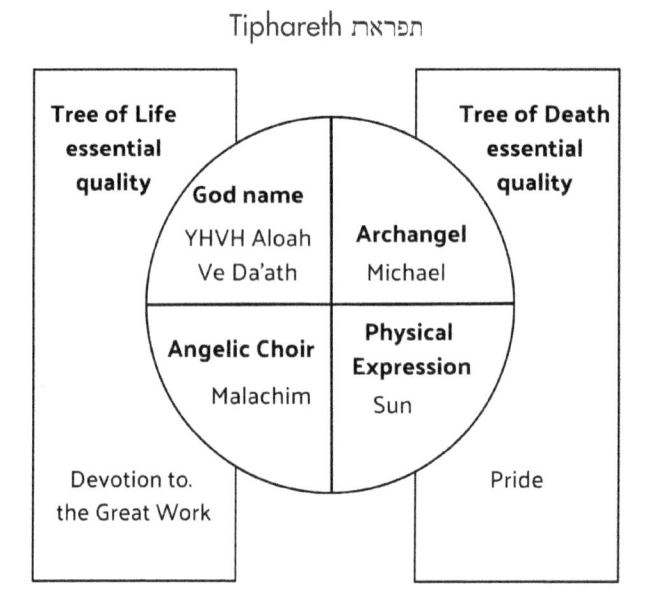

Tiphareth תפראת

Tree of Life essential quality			**Tree of Death essential quality**
	God name YHVH Aloah Ve Da'ath	**Archangel** Michael	
	Angelic Choir Malachim	**Physical Expression** Sun	
Devotion to the Great Work			Pride

Tiphareth translates as "Beauty" and "Balance", and its physical expression is the Sun. It is the central sephirah of the Tree of Life, mediating between the deeper spheres of the tree and the outer ones. It can be visualized as a field of golden light. Here we meet the sovereignty we engaged with in Malkuth, but at a deeper level, for here is the archetype of sacred kingship and queenship. The Hebrew name for the sun, *shemesh* שמש, is worth contemplating here. The letter *shin* ש is associated with the fiery breath of the divine, whereas the letter *mem* מ is water, giving us a conjunction of opposites and a sense of the *shin* being reflected in the waters of *mem* which gives us the mediation of Tiphareth. The sense of sacred kingship is reinforced by the choir of angels, the *malachim* מאלחים—"the kings". These may be envisaged as multi-winged beings of golden fire with shining faces like the sun. Michael מיחאל is the archangel of this sphere; his name means "one who is like God" and he can be visualized in robes of gold and red holding a sword of light in one hand and a pair of scales in the other. Michael is both guardian and protector, and a guide and teacher. As the quintessential angel of light and balance he has much to teach us about working with the qliphoth. He is emanated from the God Name YHVH Eloah Va Da' at יהוה אלוה ו דעת, "God made manifest in consciousness".

The Tree of Life Quality assigned to Tiphareth is devotion to the Great Work, and it is this intention that enables us to remain centred here in the place of mediation, balance, and sovereignty. The Tree of Death quality is pride, the sense of inflation that comes when the qualities and energies of this sephirah are owned or acquired by the sense of self. Devotion to the great work of transformation takes away this sense of personal aggrandizement and enables us to work with this enlightening and balancing presence in peace and safety. Pride, however, takes this sense of light and radiance and attaches it to our personal sense of presence, hence we mistake ourselves for the radiant source of life, a kingly one. We assume the role of the one who is like God and the arbiter of what is balanced and unbalanced, and instead of allowing the sense of the divine to overshadow our consciousness we make our consciousness divine. The magical image is that of the priestly king or queen who is also the sacrificed god and the child. The qliphothic image, Thagriron תגרירון, is a tyrant who radiates coldness and despair.

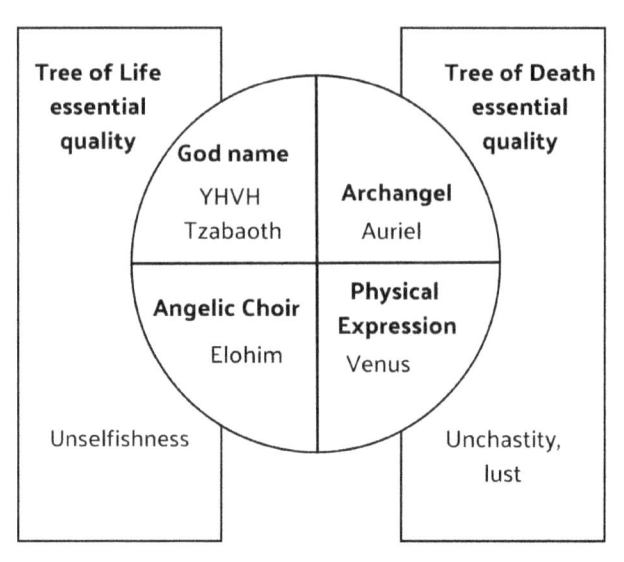

Netzach נצח

	Tree of Life essential quality		Tree of Death essential quality
	God name YHVH Tzabaoth	**Archangel** Auriel	
	Angelic Choir Elohim	**Physical Expression** Venus	
	Unselfishness		Unchastity, lust

The complementary sephirah to Hod is Netzach, נצח or "Eternity", which represents the nature of desire—the will to manifest and live. It can be visualised as a field of bright green light. The planetary archetype here is Venus, the sphere of love and desire, and as we contemplate it we come into relationship with our own desiring nature, but also that of the divine desire to create and bring forth. This is called in Hebrew *nogah* נגה, the shining star of the morning that opens the way for the sun. This is the path of nature mysticism accessed by feeling. Dion Fortune called this the path of the green ray, which touches and inspires our hearts through the art of feeling in sympathy with and loving the specific nature of all we come across. The angelic choir is the *elohim* אלהים, "the divine hosts" (the reflection of the manifesting power of Binah in the field of multiplicity). These are the many wills that desire to be, the desires that—by being housed in shape and form—come into life and expression. We directly encounter the power of desire that is as specific and direct as the will of a god or goddess, and we may contemplate the god images of human history to get a sense of the work of this angelic choir. They might also be seen as multi-winged beings in green and gold with a rose at their centre. Above and beyond the elohim we find the archangel Auriel אוראל, "the Light of God", sometimes also called Peniel פניאל, "the face of God". It is the task of this archangel to enable the prismatic action of the divine will to bring many out of oneness, to enable the arising of the hosts of the divine wills, which will later take form in Hod, acquire charge and density in Yesod, before achieving expression in Malkuth. Auriel can be envisaged as a hooded figure in deep green robes holding a prism at the heart of which is a white flame and from which many rainbows emerge. At the heart of Auriel is the God Name YHVH Tzabaoth יהוה צבות, the masculine creative power that generates the many wills out of the one. The Tree of Life quality of this sphere is unselfishness, the capacity to work with will and desire without seeking to own or appropriate it.

The Tree of Death quality, unchastity, does not simply apply to sexuality, though of course that is a key part of the nature of desire and feeling. It is the inability to manage boundaries, to blur edges and to allow desire to overflow; it is an absence of the purity and precision needed for the desire to clearly express its nature. Lust, similarly, comes out of the absence of unselfishness as it is the desire to possess, use, and satisfy one's own needs—it binds the divine will into personal need. In this case the Venusian energy, instead of loving and delighting in the emergence of all life, becomes manipulative and self-centred, choosing that which pleases and rejecting that which does not, as the sense of self becomes central. Equally, the elohim, instead of suggesting the divinity of all life, take that divinity into the self, creating inflation and arrogance. Our relationship to Auriel is also altered as the light of God is replaced by the sense of the light of self. In turn, this replaces YHVH Tzabaoth as the divine quality that creates multiplicity, with the consequent sense of our self becoming the god of our own universe. The magical image of this sephirah is that of the goddess Aphrodite, the mistress of desire. The qliphothic image, Oreb Zereq ערב זרק, is the parasite that steals life.

Hod הוד

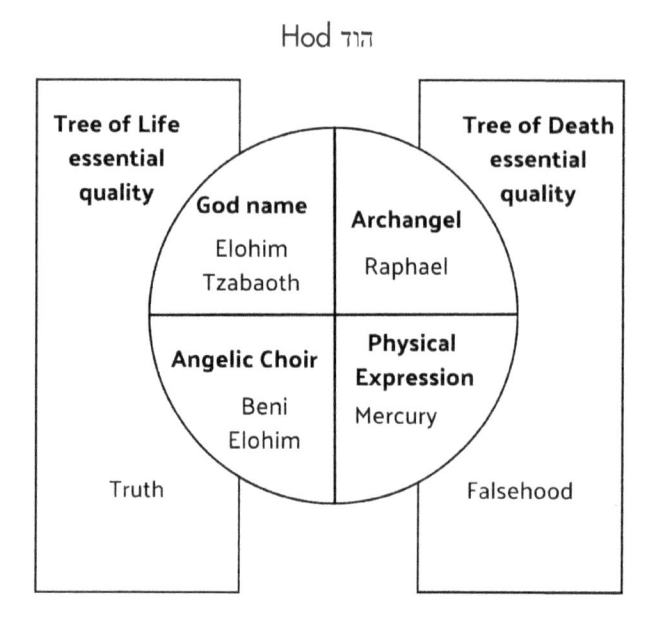

Tree of Life essential quality			Tree of Death essential quality
	God name Elohim Tzabaoth	**Archangel** Raphael	
	Angelic Choir Beni Elohim	**Physical Expression** Mercury	
Truth			Falsehood

The next sephirah is Hod, הוד or "Glory", which represents the capacity of the mind to create form and the capacity of the divine mind to generate specific forms. It can be visualised as a reflective field of mercury. Our first access to this sephirah is through contemplating the nature of our mind and the archetype of the planet Mercury whose name in Hebrew is *Kokab* כוכב, the shining swift-moving star. In this sphere we encounter the image of Hermes and the hermetic way; here we find the mind in its creative, shapeshifting form, creating thoughts, ideas, arguments, stories, histories. These are the shapes that will emerge in Yesod as the charged and potent images of the inner sea of the subconscious.

As we come to more deeply understand this creative fluidity, we encounter the angelic choir, the *bene elohim* בני אלהים, "the sons of God", the creative host responsible for generating the host of forms that that the divine wills articulated in Netzach require in order to incarnate. They might be visualized as a great host of caducei, staffs entwined by living serpents, continually generating new forms and transmitting them into Yesod.

The archangel of this sephirah is Raphael רפאל, the great teacher of the hermetic way and the mastery of the mind and its artisanal functions. He is often envisaged as a traveller bearing the serpent staff and carrying a jar of ointment with which to heal injuries. He is the teacher of truth and Socratic dialogue. He leads us to the God Name *Elohim Tzabaoth* אלהים צבות, the feminine creative power that generates forms and shapes, the blueprints of each entity that the universe gives rise to.

Fundamental to all of this is the Tree of Life quality of the sephirah—truth. It is vital that these blueprints, the transcendental DNA, be an accurate reflection of the divine will or all can go astray. In the hands of the Tree of Death quality, falsehood, the creativity of the mind and the universe shifts to manipulation and the distortion of what should be. Thus, both the human will and the divine become trapped in forms that twist and turn aside the energy of that will, so that it is expressed partially, not at all, or even opposite from its true intention. In this place, the messenger Hermes is a false messenger; the bene elohim instead of being sons and transmitters of the creative power become lords in their own right, using their capacity to shape for self-referential and manipulative ends while presenting themselves as faithful servants; and Raphael, instead of teaching true dialogue and proving truth, teaches the art of lying and manipulation. Elohim Tzabaoth instead of manifesting the forms of beauty and truth gives birth to monsters who deceive and entrap. The magical image of the sephirah is the god Hermes. The qliphothic image is Samael סמאל, the seductive serpent, who speaks with a forked tongue.

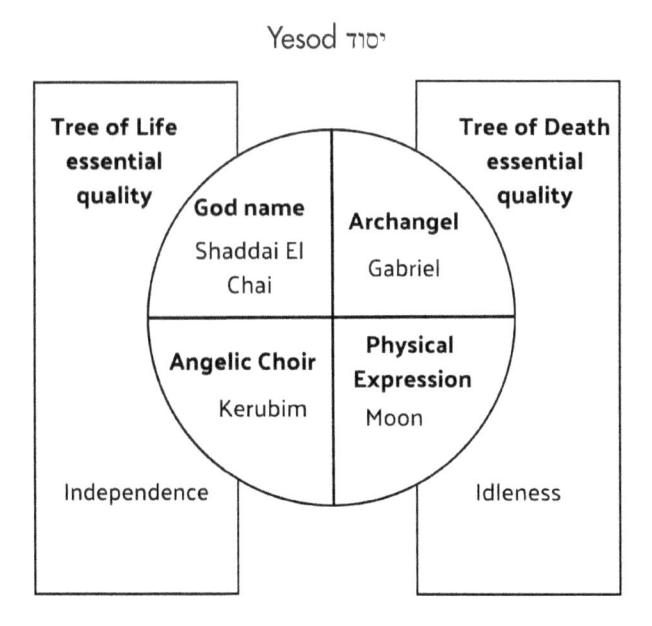

Yesod יסוד

	Tree of Life essential quality			Tree of Death essential quality
	God name Shaddai El Chai		Archangel Gabriel	
	Angelic Choir Kerubim		Physical Expression Moon	
	Independence			Idleness

The sephirah Yesod יסוד, "the Foundation", is deeply linked to the conditioned and shaped imagination. It is also called "the inner sea" and "the treasure house of images", and "the place of sweet and bitter waters". It can be visualised as a field of swirling silver, green, and blue light. It is just below the threshold of consciousness, an edge-place just before things are perceptible by the senses. Here, we enter into relationship with *levanah* לבנה, the Moon, and find the foundations of our psyche and the formative foundations of the universe. We are confronted with the ways in which we have created ourselves; by the bright and dark images we have built into both our sense of self and sense of universe. We discover the field of subliminal images; the luminous icons that point us into depth and new possibilities; the opaque idols, which point back into the surface and into the repetition of history. The key function of a foundation is to create stability and the challenge here is to find stability in movement by being able to work fluidly with opposites or, if not, we sink within the sea of history and memory. The moon cycles are deeply linked to the appearance of life and growth on earth, and the capacity to work creatively with the moon cycles both in ourselves and in the world can make all the difference between successful birth and stillbirth.

The challenge of this sephirah is indicated in its Tree of Life quality: independence. This means being able to confront and meet these great energies and to remain present and aware of our capacity to choose, to assent and dissent. If we consider the Moon and her cycles it is the ability to work with them, not to be bound by them or to be simply reactive to them. We next encounter the angelic choir of the *kerubim* כרובים, "the strong ones", the formative energies that make the latent image into the subliminal strange attractor and we are strengthened by our understanding of the power of the living image. They might be experienced as multi-winged beings with the faces of bulls. In encountering Gabriel גבראל, the strong one, the giver of vision and revelation, we are able to meet the vision cleanly and are present in the act of choice whether to fulfil the vision or to pass by it. We may contemplate Gabriel as a pillar of silver, green, and blue, a living mirror. Gabriel is the active embodiment of *Shaddai El Chai* שדי אל חי, "the almighty power of life", and we are asked here to discover the source of that life and power within us and honour and sanctify it.

The Tree of Death quality that is given here is idleness, which may not seem very significant but the demarcation between the qualities of life and death here is very sharp, for if we are not present and capable of independent choice in working with this sphere we become either dreamy and removed from life or at the mercy of whatever images are presented from within or without. We allow the Moon to make us "moony" and become a worshipper of idols. This is the place of dreams that will never be realized, or being the unquestioning member of a cult. The strength of the kerubim will be applied to fending off the world or used in the service of a qliphothic image of separation. Similarly, the visionary gifts of Gabriel will either be wasted and ignored or distorted to serve the will of one of the idols that squat at the heart of the psyche. The Almighty Power of Life will be dissipated or, instead of being at the service of all life, diverted to serve the needs of a particular image that has replaced the deeper will of our heart. The magical image is of a beautiful, naked, vigorous man. The qliphothic image, Gamaliel גמליאל, is a drunken satyr with an erect penis.

Malkuth מלכות

Tree of Life essential quality	Tree of Death essential quality
God name: Adonai ha aretz	Archangel: Sandalphon
Angelic Choir: Aishim	Physical Expression: The Elements
Discrimination	Avarice, Inertia

We conclude with the sefirah Malkuth מלכות, "the Kingdom"—of the elements and the Earth and our own physical body, called *olam yesodoth* עלם יסודות, or the world of the elements of earth, air, fire, and water. It can be visualised as a field of shining black light shot through with green, red, blue, and yellow light. We enter this sphere by becoming present to our bodies and the world around us, and in that process entering into our own sovereignty, treating seriously our own sense of body and world as we do so, becoming aware of the qualities of warmth, flow, space and solidity, which are the direct experience of the four elements. Deepening into this we come to a sense of the living, fiery nature of body and world, stepping into the place of "the souls of fire", the *aishim* אישים. They might be experienced as sparks of living, rainbow-coloured light at the heart of matter. As we establish ourselves here we enter into the place of Sandalphon סנדלפון, the creative intelligence behind matter and body, and start to understand something about the deeper aspects of prayer. We might experience Sandalphon as a shrouded, hooded figure in autumnal colours making the gesture of prayer. Then we take our seat as *Adonai ha Aretz* אדני ה ארץ, "Sovereignty of Earth", embodying this principle of sovereignty, understanding, and honouring the essential divinity underneath earth and body.

The Tree of Life quality of the sephirah is discrimination: being grounded and able to create useful and effective boundaries. The Tree of Death quality of the sephirah is avarice and inertia—in place of the sense of centre and balance we have either the desire to annexe what is not ours, to accumulate for the sake of accumulation or, instead of ground and rootedness as a basis for movement and life, the sense of inertia in which that quality of ground has so deepened that there is no life or activity. If we consider how the Tree of Death quality affects the sephirah we may see how the sphere of the elements, instead of simply moving from phase to phase, becomes deadened and inert or becomes unbalanced in that there is receiving without releasing and giving out.

Similarly, in relation to the souls of fire, that fire dims in the face of inertia and through avarice becomes the fire that instead of warming the world wishes to consume it. Equally, the impact of the Tree of Death on the form of Sandalphon brings us either into the sense of the futility of prayer, or the sense of prayer as being purely for self alone. Coming to the God Name *Adonai ha Aretz*, the Tree of Death quality points at a sense of sovereignty being built around the separated sense of self, using the density of inertia and the acquisitive energy of avarice to build a bulwark against connection or communion with those around us and with the wider world. The magical image of this sephirah is Demeter, the earth mother, who brings the grain out of the ground. The qliphothic image is Lilith לילית, the night hag, part woman, part raptor, who devours life.

CHAPTER 5

The paths of light and shadow

The paths are not so much archetypal structures, in the way the sephiroth are, but are rather created as we link the sephiroth together. They are dynamic territories formed from the interaction of the archetypes of the sephiroth they link, and their field nature is influenced by the experience of those who have trodden the path in the past. They have both a collective and an individual nature, hence your own encounter with them will be both uniquely your own and influenced by those who have walked the paths before you. The paths are the linkages of the Tree of Life and show the active mirroring of the sephiroth as one unfolds into another, as one balances another, so that the entire mandala of the tree comes into being. As we pay attention to the paths, therefore, we are putting ourselves into the mirroring process and, depending upon our capacity to function as icon or idol, we enable or obstruct the transmission between the sephiroth. We might consider the paths as mandorlas formed by the overlapping fields of the sephiroth.

Sephirah 1 — Path — Sephirah 2

Earlier in this work we considered some aspects of the paths in describing the ascent of the tree, noting how the triangles of the tree interlock. In particular, we looked at the paths of the middle pillar. In this chapter we are going to consider all twenty-two paths; classically the paths are numbered from eleven to thirty-two, the numbers one to ten being the sephiroth.

The primary experience of the path is discovered by placing oneself in the overlapping fields of the sephiroth, but the quality of each path is further indicated in the hermetic Qabalah by assigning a Hebrew letter to each of the paths.

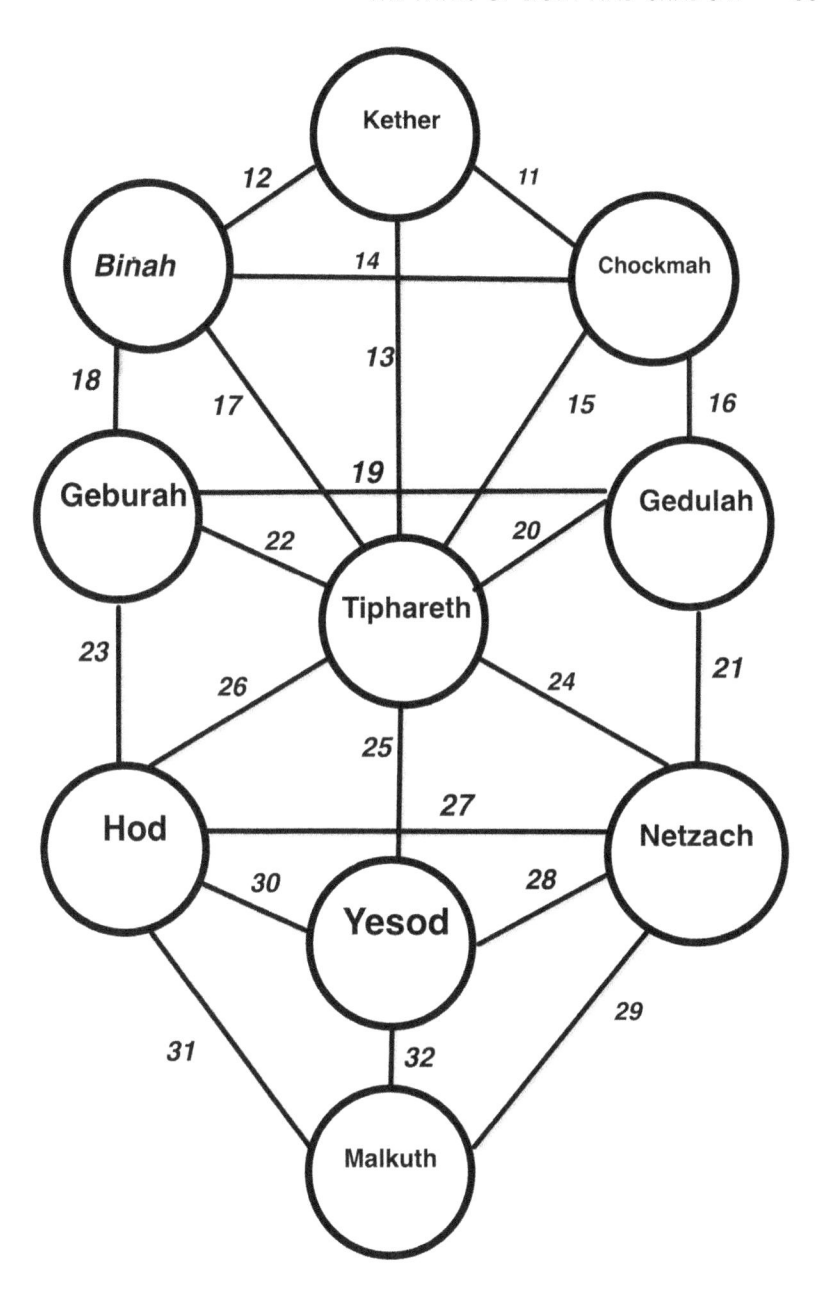

THE PATHS OF LIGHT AND SHADOW   63

```
                    Kether
                 12       11
          Binah    14    Chockmah
         18    13         16
              17   15
          Geburah   19   Gedulah
               22     20
                Tiphareth
           23  26    24   21
              Hod    25   Netzach
                 30  27  28
                   Yesod
              31         29
                    32
                  Malkuth
```

Path 32 Malkuth—Yesod

We will begin our exploration of them from Malkuth, beginning with the thirty-second path from Malkuth to Yesod.

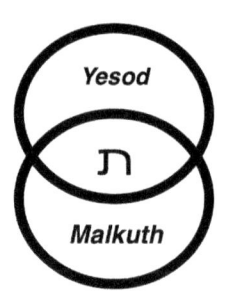

This we have encountered earlier in the book as "the underworld path". This is the path that leads from outer to inner experience. Here we stand between Malkuth, the sphere of the elements, and Yesod, the Moon sphere, the treasure house of images; and also between Sandalphon and Gabriel. We experience the solidity of the body and the fluidity and cyclicity of the Moon sphere, touching also upon the transition between inner and outer. Here we see the way in which the charged images of Yesod come into expression and the way in which outer experiences impact our subjective universe. The Hebrew letter *tav* ת, "the mark", is given to this path, the letter of completion and emergence; it is the last letter of the word *emet* אמת, "truth", called "the seal of God", which completes creation. It is also the first letter of the word *tikkun* תיקון, which means "mending" or "repair", and of *teshuva* תשובה, which means "repentance" or "turning back to the divine". The shadow path is the embodiment of the images of sterility, death, and entropy, that energy the ancient Egyptians named "Apep". This path of embodiment therefore is where we literally make our mark, inscribing our name in the service of life or the service of entropy.

Path 31 Malkuth—Hod

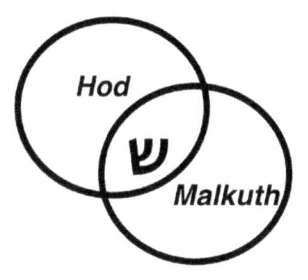

Here we encounter the overlapping fields of mind and body so that mind and body are as one. This is the mind-body integration of the martial artist and the patterns of the divine mind emerging in activity and behaviour that is the expression of deep thought whether human or divine, the fusion of the principles of Mercury and Earth. The Hebrew letter that applies to this path is the letter *shin* ש, "the tooth", which represents the divine breath that vivifies, that renews life, and that breaks apart to enable the expression of that new life. Here we stand between the archangels Raphael and Sandalphon and hold the coming into being of the new thought or idea. The shadow path here is the embodiment of the lie, of deception and seduction. This path brings into concrete being the truth or the lie.

Path 30 Hod—Yesod

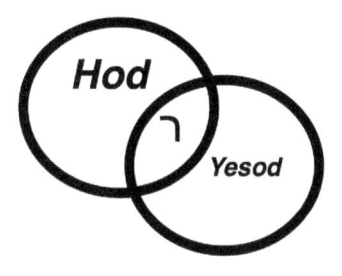

Here we stand between Mercury and the Moon, between Raphael and Gabriel. In this path we encounter the creative mind of Hod clothing itself in living images, acquiring life, texture, and generative potential. The Hebrew letter that applies here is *resh* ר, "the head", or origin, the initiation of the new. Here we draw upon the healing power of Raphael and the strength and purifying power of Gabriel as we enable the mirroring to be true. The shadow path is the generation of idols that serve corrupt ideas that seek to increase separation and entropy—the conjunction of Samael and Gamelial.

Path 29 Malkuth—Netzach

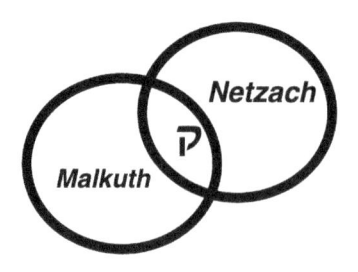

This is the uniting of Earth and Venus, Sandalphon and Auriel, the meeting of the instincts with the mechanism of the body. The Hebrew letter applied to this path is the letter *qoph* ק, "the back of the head", which indicates all the automatic systems that are necessary for life to function. On this path we bring together the quality of Auriel or divine light with that of Sandalphon, the prince of prayer. The combination of the light of awareness with the active practice of prayer brings that light into the automatic instinctual patterns, into the systems of the body, and ultimately into the chemical and physical patterns of the universe. The shadow path linking the life denial of Lilith with the parasitic energies of *oreb zereq* combines our negative instincts with our desire nature, so that we live a vampiric existence drawing life and energy from all around us instinctively and unconsciously.

Path 28 Yesod—Netzach

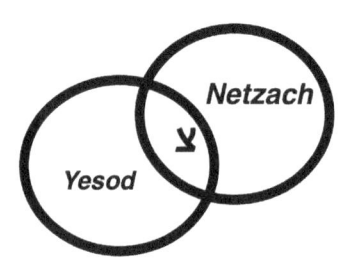

This path is concerned with the interplay of the desires and wills of Netzach with the creation of the living images of Yesod. Here we stand between Auriel, the divine light and fire, and Gabriel, the messenger and purifying intelligence. This conjunction looks at the expression of the prismatic will—or rather, wills—and desires arising from Netzach and generating the eidola of living images that take form within the psyche and the universe. It is also the place of the laws of nature coming into being in Netzach and acquiring life energy in Yesod. The Hebrew letter *tzaddi* צ, "the fishhook", the first letter of the word *tsaddik* צדיק, "the righteous one", the adept who generates Maat, is applied here. The extent to which we can be the *tsaddik*, the one who bows before the divine will, or else becoming the one who asserts our own separate will, determines how much this path is oriented to the Tree of Life or the Tree of Death. The shadow path gives us the conjunction of the Oreb, the parasitic ravens, who feed upon dead flesh, with Gamali'el, who joins together that which should not be joined. Here we are shown the generation of forms of parasitism at all levels from spiritual to physical.

Path 27 Hod—Netzach

This is the first of the paths that join the pillars of the tree, bringing together Mercury and Venus, mind and desire, and the archangels Raphael and Auriel. This shows us the conjunction of the alchemical light of Auriel joining with the swift, mercurial expressiveness of Raphael; a mirroring of life and new possibilities and a matching of will and pattern so that the generated thoughts and patterns are active and alive. The Hebrew letter assigned here is the letter *peh* פ, "the mouth", which further amplifies the sense of the creative expression of self and universe. The shadow tree here conjoins Samael, the deceiver, with the ravens, joining deception to parasitism.

Path 26 Tiphareth—Hod

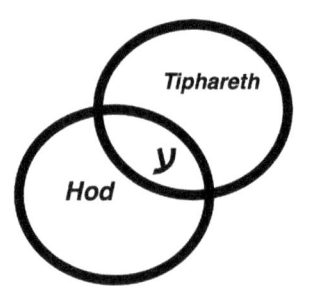

This path joins together Mercury and the Sun, the mind with the radiant presence of the heart. This is one of the paths that pierces the veil of the temple and connects the outer sephiroth with the deeper spheres of the tree. It is given the Hebrew letter *ayin* ע, "the eye", the experience of sight and insight. It is related also to the idea of an arising spring of water. Here we find the conjunction of Raphael, the messenger angel, with Michael, the priestly angel who transmits the divine presence. We contemplate the nature of vision, illumination, and the empowerment of the divine and human mind. The Tree of Death path comes from the conjunction of Samael, the liar and deceiver, with the Thagriron, the disputers, who work with the averse name. Here the deception and lying quality of Samael is augmented by the energy of the dispute and the disruption of harmony caused by the averse name. Here too is the sense of the evil eye—that is, projection of malignancy, the generation of a vision that is concerned with the disruption of the divine plan.

Path 25 Tiphareth—Yesod

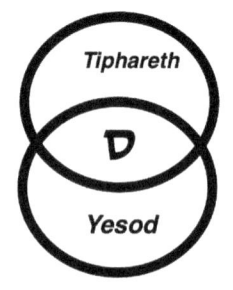

The path between Tiphareth and Yesod we have met earlier as the alchemical path of the conjunction of opposites. It unites the Sun and the Moon and Gabriel and Michael. This is one of the major paths of transition that pierce the veil of the temple and enable a shifting of the locus of consciousness from the thoughts, feelings, and known sense of self and universe into a direct, intuitive perception of the soul and the inner universe. One of its key images is the light of the angel of Tiphareth illuminating the pool of Yesod so that the images that give rise to the expression of both our sense of self and universe become as icons transmitting the deeper light of the divine. The Hebrew letter applied to this path is *samekh* ס, "the support" or "prop", and refers to the support of the divine and that aspect of the divine, the holy guardian angel, who is our particular guide and companion in the inner journey. The contrary path of the Tree of Death is formed from a conjunction of the Thagriron, the builder of ugliness, and Gamali'el, the impure, and here we see the capacity of Gamali'el to join together that which should not be joined empowered by the Thagriron, so that in place of the clear icons of new life arising out of the pool of Yesod we have distortions and dark and powerful-seeming idols dedicated to separation and struggle.

Path 24 Tiphareth—Netzach

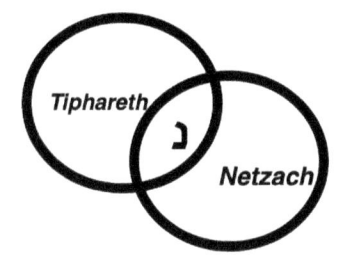

The twenty-fourth path similarly bridges the veil of the temple and unites the Sun and Venus and Michael with Auriel, uniting the harmonising and centralising light of the Sun and the mediatorship of Michael with the revealing capacity of Auriel. The divine faces manifest as inner and outer laws come into being. The Hebrew letter applied to this path is *nun* נ, "the fish", which represents the fertility of the deep and the process of death and resurrection because the arising of multiplicity from unity or, indeed, the arising of unity from multiplicity, involves

70   THE TREE OF LIFE AND DEATH

the death of the prior condition. In the shadow path we find the parasitic energies of the Oreb empowered by the building and empowering energies of Thagriron so that in place of the fertility of the deep we find endless struggle to feed and consume the other.

Path 23 Geburah—Hod

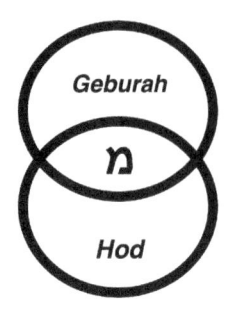

The twenty-third path marks the transition between Hod, the sephirah of the creative mind, and Geburah, the sephirah of will and clarity. The Hebrew letter applied to this path is *mem* מ, "water", which appears in the open form just given or at the end of a word in a closed form ם. It holds the possibilities of reflection and flow or stagnation. We stand here between the warrior archangel, Khamael, and the hermetic archangel, Raphael, in a powerful conjunction in which the mind focuses and is illuminated by the will and direction of the deeper soul. The shadow path places us between the Golachab, the burning ones, and Samael, the liar, so that in place of the clarity and purpose of the straight path we are given a path of deceit that destroys all who walk it.

Path 22 Geburah—Tiphareth

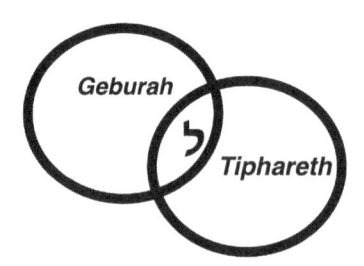

This is one of the paths of the middle triad of the tree, joining together the principles of will and presence and mediatorship. It is assigned the Hebrew letter *lamed* ל, "the oxgoad", which represents the principle of teaching and transmission of will applied to a good purpose. Here we stand between Khamael, the warrior, and Michael, the priest, feeling the conjunction of will, discipline and direction and blessing and mediatorship. It is above all a path of balance and beauty. The shadow path places us between the burners and the transmitter of despair so that the sense of coldness and pain is amplified by fiery will.

Path 21 Gedulah—Netzach

The twenty-first path connects the sephirah of love and compassion with the expressiveness of desire as the will of love to grow and expand expresses itself through the prismatic multiplication of Netzach. The Hebrew letter applied here is the letter *kaph* כ, "the palm of the hand", which contains the proto chalice, for this path is about receiving and containing so that the water of life can be passed on. Here we stand between Tzadkiel, the archangel of growth, expansion, and blessing, and Auriel, the archangel who, as the vessel of the divine light, reveals the faces of the divine. The shadow path places us between Gamchicoth, the love that devours, and the Oreb, the parasitic ravens.

Path 20 Gedulah—Tiphareth

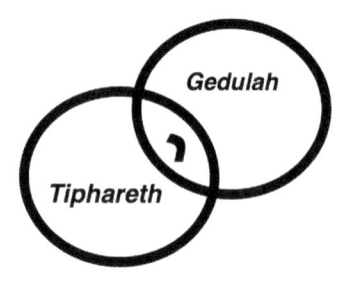

The twentieth path brings together the expansive love of Gedulah with the presence, beauty, and balance of Tiphareth. The Hebrew letter of this path is *yod* י, "the hand", the first letter of the divine name *YHVH* יהוה, and here we see deep will arising from love and finding balance and rest in Tiphareth, preparatory to its expression in multiplicity. Here we stand between Tzadkiel and Michael, between love and blessing. The shadow path is between the devourers and the builder of ugliness, and between the love that consumes and the transmission of pain and coldness.

Path 19 Geburah—Gedulah

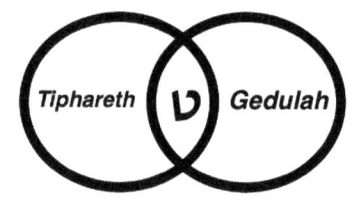

The nineteenth path places us between the principles of love and will and between Tzadkiel, the bright archangel of mercy, and Khamael, the dark archangel of severity. The Hebrew letter of this path is *teth* ט, "the serpent"; this is the first letter of the word *tov* טוב, or "good", and takes us into the mystery of the serpent who is the saviour, and the capacity of the serpent to shed its skin and to free itself from the husks and shells that conceal the light. The bringing together of love and will unities our forces and the forces of the universe so that all becomes aligned.

The shadow path places us between the burners and the devourers, between the will to destroy and the will to consume.

Path 18 Binah—Geburah

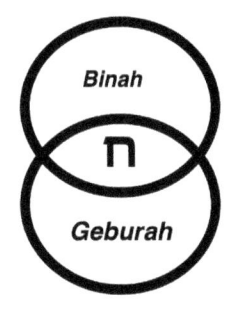

The eighteenth path crosses the abyss into the non-dual world of the supernal spheres, uniting the non-dual sephirah of love with the sephirah of will. The Hebrew letter for this path is *cheth* ח, "the fence" or "container", the first letter of *chai* חי, or "life". It enables us to contain and house the will that arises out of the field of non-dual love and understanding of Binah, the divine mother. As a movement between the dual and non-dual it helps us also contain and work with that tension. We stand here between Tzaphkiel, the archangel of the love of the deep mother, and Khamael, the warrior of deep heaven, the sword of will. The shadow path places us in the place of hidden or concealed hatred, the wish to destroy, and poison expressed in dark contemplation.

Path 17 Binah—Tiphareth

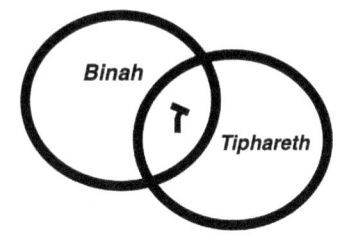

The seventeenth path also bridges the supernal sephiroth and the middle triad of the tree and brings us into communion with the sphere of non-dual love and the sephirah of balance, blessing, and mediatorship. Here the priestly capacities of Tiphareth are enhanced and empowered by the sense of non-dual love and understanding arising out of Binah, enabling the capacity to join opposites and to enable separation without loss of connection. The Hebrew letter of this path is *zain* ז, "the sword", which represents cutting and division and that shows us the principle of this path: the mystery of separation and union. Here we stand between Tzaphkiel, the contemplative archangel, and Michael, the priest, who blesses the multitude. We encounter the mystery of the one and the many. The shadow path puts us in a hidden place where Thagriron mediates the God Name that brings pain and separation.

Path 16 Chockmah—Gedulah

The sixteenth path similarly connects the supernals to the middle triad, here uniting the non-dual sephirah of will to the sephirah of love. The expansive compassion and growth of Gedulah is augmented by the deep, generative will of Chockmah. The Hebrew letter of this path is *vav* ו, "the nail". This is the letter of joining together and indicates the union of the dual and non-dual, and the union of all beings within the Tree of Life. Here we stand between Raziel, the archangel of the generative will, the power that moves the stars, and Tzadkiel, the archangel of love and compassion resting in that will and the communion of all beings. The shadow path is the conjunction of cancerous generation and the will to devour.

Path 15 Chockmah—Tiphareth

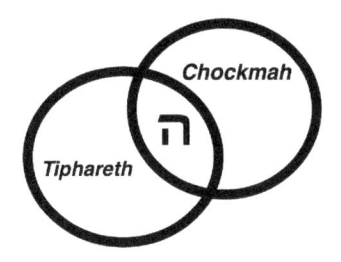

The fifteenth path unites the non-dual will of Chockmah with the mediatorship and balance of Tiphareth so that the balance and presence of Tiphareth is backed by that sense of deep will. The Hebrew letter that applies to this path is the letter *heh* ה, "the window", the second letter of the divine name *YHVH* יהוה. The art of this path is the surrender to that will, allowing its light to enter into the house of the soul. It is the letter of breath and represents the breath of the non-dual soul, creating new life in the centre of the tree so that the priestly blessing that manifests here is fresh and generative. Here, we stand between Raziel, the archangel of the generative will, and Michael, the priest. The shadow path places us between chaotic and cancerous generation and the priesthood of the averse name, which mediate darkness, coldness, and separation.

Path 14 Binah—Chockmah

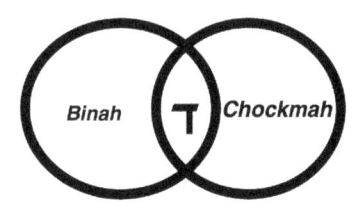

This is the first of the paths above the abyss and combines non-dual love and will, the supernal mother and the supernal father. It is the great conjunction on which all lesser conjunctions are founded. The Hebrew letter of the path is *daleth* ד, "the door", and represents the fact that this path opens and closes the doors of life. It is deeply connected with the mysterious sephirah, Da'ath, as the letter that begins it, for it is from the conjunction of Binah and Chockmah that Da'ath arises and the roots of the appearance of the dual from the non-dual are found. Here we stand between Tzaphkiel, the contemplator, and Raziel, the doer. There is no shadow in the supernal paths, but the reflection of this path in the abyss is the hidden cancer that gives birth to all the forms of the qliphoth.

Path 13 Kether—Tiphareth

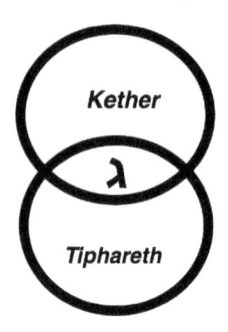

This path brings the root and crown of the tree into relationship with Tiphareth, the central sephirah of mediation. The letter of this path is *gimel* ג, "the camel", and it holds the image of the desert way, the journey from presence and connection to the divine root. The desert way is given as an image for this path as it involves the letting go of all knowing and provisions into the starkness and simplicity of the emptiness of the divine, symbolised by the desert. The camel is one who has the necessary capacity to make this journey and return. Here we stand between Metatron, the archangel of the divine presence, and Michael, the priest, who is like the divine and makes the divine presence manifest. Here is the mystery of the icon. The shadow path here places us between the eternally opposed heads and the priesthood of the name of despair.

Path 12 Kether—Binah

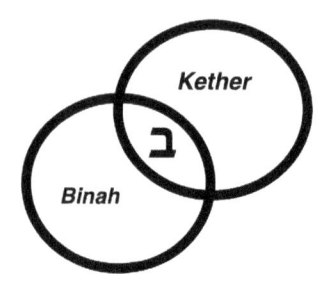

The twelfth path brings us to the conjunction of the divine root with the sphere of non-dual love, asking us to reflect on the roots of love. The Hebrew letter of this path is *beth* ב, "the house", the letter that begins the words for "blessing" and "creation". Here we are in the very beginnings, the foreshadowing of the appearance of duality as love arises within the simplicity of the divine essence. We stand here between Tzaphkiel, the contemplative, and Metatron, the angel of the presence. The shadow reflection of this path in the abyss is eternal concealment and refusal to appear.

Path 11 Kether—Chockmah

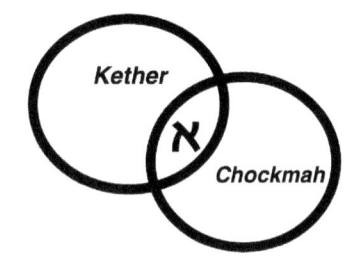

This path deals with the arising of will from within the body of the divine and the very beginnings of the principle of reflection, of twoness. It is the root of the 0 = 2 equation. The Hebrew letter of this path is *aleph* א, "the ox", the letter of unity that is in itself a paradox, for in asserting absolute unity it also asserts a degree of separation, just as the point of absolute presence also creates the point and ground. It is the first letter of *achad* אחד, or "unity"; the first letter of *Adam* אדם, the archetypal human being; the first letter of *adonai* אדני or "lord". Here we stand between Raziel, the archangel of generative will, and Metatron, the archangel of the presence between absolute being and non-dual willing. The shadow reflection of this path in the abyss is the will that eternally opposes unity.

The contemplation of the paths brings us into relationship with the dynamics of the tree and the principle of reflection that operates between all of the sephiroth. Working with them enables this principle of reflection to clarify as we emerge from the coils of the shadow paths of the Tree of Death. We may also notice the way in which the core principles of being, love, and will, found in the supernals, are transmitted down the tree. The paths take us into the heart of the 0 = 2 equation, for in each path we are working with the principle of conjunction of two sephiroth, +1 and –1, so to speak, which takes us into the generative ground of the path 0.

CHAPTER 6

The dynamics of creation and the nature of evil

We will now look more deeply into the nature of the Qliphoth and the dynamics that create and sustain them. In these contemplations on the Tree of Life there is an intention to move from the surface into depth and from an experience of exile and separation to the experience of being in communion with the universe and with divinity. Our deepening experience of the 0 = 2 equation and the processes of reflection that sustain the universe brings us into an embodied relationship with the Tree of Life. The virtues that are cultivated in the contemplation of the sephiroth, from the discrimination of Malkuth to the independence of Yesod, the truthfulness and unselfishness of Hod and Netzach, the devotion to the great work of Tiphareth, and the courage and obedience of Geburah and Gedulah, create in us a sense of balance and deepening communion and trust in the nature of things that enables us to be open to the capacities of the deep will and to contemplation of Chockmah, Binah, and the oneness and absence of separation of Kether.

By contrast, if we have cultivated the vices of the sephiroth: the inertia of Malkuth followed by the idleness of Yesod, the duplicity and unchastity of Hod and Netzach, the pride of Tiphareth, the cruelty and hypocrisy of Geburah and Gedulah, then we more than likely will be led into the shadow realm of the abyss where we work with the energies of hiding, hindering, and eternal opposition. Here the process of reflection becomes a hall of distorting mirrors that disrupt the reflective process of the tree.

The combination of clear mirroring and distortion creates our own unique constellation of relationship to the Trees of Life and Death and, in deepening into this work, it is increasingly important to understand the ways in which we shut ourselves and others out of the light.

The root word for "sin" or "badness" in the Bible is *ra* רא. It is derived from the word *bra* ברא, which means "creation" but, lacking the letter *beit* ב, which represents both the house of God and blessing, it suggests a creation that is outside the divine life and is not blessed. We will find that the Hebrew Bible has three words to describe degrees or levels of sin:

- *Chatah* חטא means "missing the mark" and suggests error or absence—the movement away from presence and relationship. It has connotations of becoming unconscious, unfocused, and reactive. This is the word most commonly translated as "sin".
- A more serious example is given by the word *pesha* פשע, which suggests an engagement of the will and an act of choosing separation. This word is normally translated as "transgression" and has qualities of becoming opaque and self-centred.
- Another word, *avon* עוון, represents another, deeper step into separation; one in which there is delight in the places of separation and a willed corruption of the spiritual, a twisting of the energies of the deep spirit in the service of the separated self.

These describe three steps in the creation of qliphothic forms and rely on our capacity to work creatively with will and imagination to fashion both a sense of self and sense of universe. *Chatah* is the aspect of the Qliphoth most commonly encountered; it is a turning away from awareness into unconscious reactivity. It is the inertia and idleness of the distorted Malkuth and Yesod in which our inner fire is dimmed and our capacity to act independently is subsumed. Yet even this is an aspect of our capacity to create, for our ability to create the shells that obstruct light relies upon the power of our imagination. Considering this territory therefore takes us intimately into the nature of creation itself and into our identity as human beings.

The Book of Genesis tells us that we are the living image of the divine and, in its beginning, and at the beginning of John's Gospel, we are given the images of darkness, emptiness and chaos, which is supplanted by the speaking of a word that evokes the appearance of light. This light creates boundary, shape, and order, and multitudes of beings, and concludes in the creation of the image of the human being who is deeply rooted in the light and whose role it is to bear witness to it.

It is this creative light that both Dion Fortune and Ernest Butler refer to in their work. Dion Fortune called her school "The Fraternity of the Inner Light", and Ernest Butler called his "The Servants of the Light". They are drawing on the qabalistic tradition of the work of creation that can be found in both the Judaic and the Hermetic Qabalah. Both the Gospel of John and Genesis ask us to return to the experience of the beginning so that we can seek to discover our origins and the process by which we have come to be. Our contemplation of the Tree of Life has given us much understanding of our current shape, but now we must look at the dynamics that cause the tree to grow in the way it does.

The cosmology of the Qabalah begins with a sense of negative existence, of a no-thingness out of which all existence arises. This is a concept we find in the ancient Egyptian tradition of the cosmos arising out of the waters of chaos as the primal mound of earth rises out of the sea. The tree grows upon the mound and all beings take shelter in the tree. This sense of the first garden is central to qabalistic tradition, so we begin our contemplation of this verse from Genesis:

> Now the earth was formless and empty, darkness was over the surface of the deep, and the spirit of God was hovering over the waters. (Genesis 1: 2)

If we take this verse step by step using the *PRDS* process we will see that we are asked to contemplate the nature of Earth as being formless, *tohu* תהו, and empty, *bohu* בהו. Like the primordial waters of Egyptian tradition this is a state without differentiation—a pregnant darkness with the *ruach elohim* רוח אלהים, "the breath of God", hovering over it. This is the beginning place of contemplation. There is no order, form, shape, or meaning, so we hover over the waters of chaos and emptiness as we contemplate. We enter the verse, the verse enters us, and we await the rising of revelation and insight.

Genesis 1: 3 shows us the next stage:

> Then God said, "Let there be light", and there was light.

The key phrase here is "Let there be Light", *yehi or* יהי אור, where *yehi* is the arising of will and *or* is the luminous image that houses and transmits the will.

This takes us to Genesis 1: 4 in which:

> God saw the light, that it was good and God divided the light from the Darkness.

The key word here is "good", *tov* טוב, in which the luminous creative image is seen and is declared fruitful and balanced, and so it separates from the inchoate darkness and through it a world comes into being.

This contemplation of formlessness and emptiness, *tohu ve bohu* תהו ו בוה, followed by "Let there be Light", *yehi or* יהי אור, the separation from darkness, *hosech* החשך, and then the sense of goodness, *tov* טוב, creates a ground of contemplative awareness in which we move from the sense of emptiness and confusion into the activity of deep will and deep love. This involves a new sense of self as creator and a new sense of the universe as containing the fruitful and creative light. This may only be a faint sense but most of us can identify with the sense of goodness and expansion that appears when we have done something creative. This is literally the creative light manifesting through the human form. It is in this act that we are the living image the *tselem* of the creator. This light and the image which it forms can also be a false light, and the image, instead of being *tov* can be *ra*—that is, instead of an icon that widens and deepens our connection to the universe there can be an idol which encloses us within our own separate world, which we will in turn label as *tov* or "good" as it gives a sense of safety. The key is in the beginning *intention*: whether we act in the service of the divine will or from self-will. To free ourselves from the convolutions of the false light and its creations we must return to the beginning.

This returning to the beginning is what Jesus speaks of when he tells Nicodemus that he must be born again by water and by spirit and is the inner meaning behind the baptism rite. It is the descent into the inner sea of Yesod, the foundation of psyche and world, and continuing that descent under the guidance of Tiphareth that takes us through Da'ath into the deep waters of Binah, where the deepest image of ourselves is found in the keeping of that part of our soul that remains in the non-dual world of the supernal sephiroth.

It is this act of return and the manifestation of the deep will and luminous image of the divine that the Gospel of John is principally concerned with, and we may find much in it that can help us navigate these difficult waters. Ernest Butler drew a great deal from this gospel, seeing the apostle John as the archetypal priest working with the name *Eheieh* אהיה, "I am", and having at the heart of his gospel the image of Jesus walking on the sea of Galilee. This is an act that parallels the account in Genesis of the spirit of God hovering over the waters of chaos and bringing forth light and creation. The sense of working with the waters of the inner sea is the heart of this work, for it is by engaging with the mixed waters of Yesod and working with what is found there that we reach through them to the presence of Tiphareth, which can descend into the pool of Yesod to purify it and bring healing.

Both Yesod and Da'ath are profound transition points that can either be negotiated successfully or can lead us astray. Yesod is the foundation of our inner world and, as we have seen, is linked to the Moon, the angelic choir of the *kerubim*, "the strong ones", the archangel Gabriel, the giver of visions, and the God Name *Shaddai El Chai*, "the Almighty Power of Life". It is a central part of the inner dialogue that creates the veil of the temple which, in turn, either opens to reveal our deeper nature or is opaque and hides it. The power of the inner dialogue to overwhelm thought, feeling, and even sensation, so as to maintain its stability, should not be underestimated. This is the reason why qabalistic meditation begins by paying attention to the body through relaxation exercises and breathing before using the ritual of the qabalistic cross and the exercises of the interwoven light (described in Part Two) to create a field of presence within which the waters of Yesod can be worked with. These practices engage with Malkuth, Yesod, Hod, and Netzach to bring a sense of presence and new life into places that may have become dead and lifeless. They are followed by the practice of descending into the inner sea and working with images so as to interrupt the unconscious idol worship we are engaged with. Initially this typically involves introducing an image or series of images that come from deeper aspects of the collective human psyche which, as they unfold within us, become active in our personal sense of inner sea, introducing new elements and opening us to the presence of Tiphareth.

Ernest Butler used a trigger phrase that begins, "Now do I descend into the inner sea, whose waters rise and fall within my soul. Let the inner elements be subdued and still as I immerse myself within the living waters and emerging therefrom unfold from latent stress to potent image ..." as a way of accessing the energies of Yesod. The use of this phrase and the image contained in it holds the immediate descent into Yesod, but also the descent into the deep waters of Binah, accessed through Da'ath. The phrase was followed by the description of an image which was unfolded in consciousness in order to be worked with before being returned into the inner sea. For example, the phrase might end: "unfold from latent stress to potent image the sanctuary of Sandalphon, prince of prayer" at which point the sense of the temple of Sandalphon would unfold within our inner senses; we would work with it and then, when the work was complete, let the forms dissolve and repeat the following phrase: "Now do I descend into the inner sea whose waters rise and fall within my soul. Let the inner elements be subdued and still as I immerse myself within the living waters and emerging therefrom unfold from latent stress to potent living image the symbol of my own true self."

The images of the inner sea are subliminal and are the foundation stones of our sense of self and world, constituting our own particular treasure house of images. The images that we hold close to us in this way are those that we have found relevant to our life and experience and are not normally experienced as images with their own life energy and will, existing within us and influencing our understanding, but rather are experienced as the way things are. By having been gathered into our sense of identity our "I am"-ness they gain a solidity and sense of truth and are why it is difficult to change at a deep level. As they function in this autonomous way they are aspects of the qliphoth—self-referential shells that promote separation at all costs. They prevent us from exploring unknown aspects of our nature, taking risks and behaving spontaneously. Their presence within us binds our senses, mind, and feelings into a stereotypical form that feels like "us". If we consider for a moment the way in which a child's sense of self fluctuates, shifts and flows, as they move through the events of the day, playing games, being pirates and heroes and heroines, being sad and happy, filled with a great sense of life and energy, by contrast most adults have a much more limited range of expression are much less rooted in present experience and are less connected to the raw energy of life. The constellation of Yesodic images which have become bound to our sense of identity are responsible for this, through having been enshrined as idols in our house of life. These are the aspects of the Qliphoth that are nearest to us and where we must begin our work.

This beginning level of the work is sometimes called the "house of the soul" as we are using the mandala of the Tree of Life to plant seeds of new life within us that start to reorganize the constellation of images that live in our inner sea. Ernest Butler often would use a phrase from alchemy to illustrate this work, "the flyer must descend into the sea", by which he meant that the constructed ego that is generated by the inner dialogue must let go its grip and descend into the mystery of the inner sea of dissolution and reformation. This is the alchemical formula *solve et coagula* or "dissolving and reforming" in which, each time we perform the process, a little more of the density of the inner images is dissolved and we are coagulated into a shape that is more transparent and capable of expressing the presence of Tiphareth. As we continue to work with this, we will start to relate to the roots of the Qliphoth within us; to our *chatah* or reactive ignorance, our *pesha* or wilful antagonism, and even the roots of *avon*, the desire for complete and utter separation. It is these powerful embedded tendencies that create and maintain the idols of our nature and that are challenged by the careful, patient work of hovering over the chaos, darkness, and emptiness of whatever presents itself and then, in an act of will and surrender, manifesting the luminous image in the midst of the chaos so that the light and the chaos mix together and a new world arises from it. This practice of will and imagination, of surrender and mixing together of light and darkness in hope and trust, is the heart of this work and takes us right back to the verse in Genesis of the spirit of God hovering over the waters and, in the gospels, of Jesus walking on the sea and stilling the storm.

CHAPTER 7

The linen-clad priest

The Book of Ezekiel is the third of the latter prophets in the Tanakh and one of the major prophetic books of the Old Testament. It is also one of the originating documents of the Qabalah and speaks powerfully of the nature of our capacity to create icons and idols and the consequences of so doing.

It shows us the work of transforming the Qliphoth, which requires us to go into the waste places of both the personal soul and the collective human soul in order to bring the divine breath and light to them, to free the lost sparks of light and bring them home. Ezekiel is a priest writing at a time when the people of Israel are in exile in Babylon and the book begins with him looking into the waters of the River Chebar, a similar act to both Ernest Butler's descent into the inner sea and the contemplation of the waters of Genesis.

Ezekiel passes through three barriers that relate to the three levels of the Qliphoth: first, a stormy wind in constant chaotic motion that is the reactive quality of *chatah*, next a dense opaque cloud that has the wilful ignorance and determination of *pesha*, and then a consuming fire that has the quality of *avon*. As he passes these barriers, he perceives both a sense of dawning light within the darkness and a quality called *chasmalim* חשמלים, "the speaking silence". This is the presence of the angel of Tiphareth presenting itself to guide and teach.

This begins with Ezekiel experiencing the potent icon of the divine as the likeness of a man enthroned in the midst of the holy living creatures: these are figures of fire and light having the face of a man, an ox, a lion, and an eagle. They have six wings extending above, around, and below, and interlocking wheels filled with eyes that are constantly in motion. Above them is a dome like shining ice, and in the midst of it is a throne like a stone of sapphire, and upon it is the likeness of a human being. All around there is movement and rainbow-coloured light. In the description, two terms are continually made reference to: likeness and appearance. Thus, he says there is the likeness of the man upon the throne, or there is the appearance of wheels, because what is being shown here is a functioning icon that takes us beyond the image into a powerful experience of the divine as light and movement, perception and will. It is also an image of the four worlds of the Qabalah: the turning wheels are the world of Assiah, the holy living creatures show us the world of Yetzirah, the angelic world of formation; the throne is the world of Beriah, the world of creation, and the appearance of a man the world of Atziluth, so that as we pass into and through this icon we are involved with the dynamics of the four worlds.

What follows is worth a good deal of pondering over. Ezekiel is addressed as "Son of Man", a term that asks him to stand in the place of the archetypal human being. He is able to do this because he has passed through the veils of the Qliphoth and is under the tutelage of the speaking silence of Tiphareth. He is now taught about working with the Qliphoth in the collective human soul. He is told that he must bear a message to Israel and to those who have transgressed against the divine. A scroll is placed in his hand and he is asked to take a tile and draw upon it an image of Jerusalem and to contemplatively lay siege to it because of its iniquity.

As we have seen, the word "iniquity", or *avon* עוון, is highly specific and refers to the deepest kind of evil, the delight in evil for its own sake and in particular the corruption of holiness. Ezekiel is told to lie upon his left side and contemplate the iniquity of Jerusalem; this is the beginning of contemplation of the nature of the Qliphoth and of the nature of the idol as compared with the life, lucidity, and movement of the icon that brings us to the divine presence.

He is told that Israel has become corrupted and is worshipping idols, so that the divine presence is no longer to be found in the temple. He is then taken in vision into the temple so that he may see the "abominations" with his own eyes and, as he enters into the court of the temple, he sees what he describes as many detestable and creeping forms, all the idols of Israel. He then sees the seventy elders of Israel with censers of incense creating a great cloud of darkness and the divine presence says to him, "Son of man, hast thou seen what the elders of the house of Israel do in the dark, every man in his chambers of imagery?" (Ezekiel 8: 12). In contrast to the movement, life, and lucidity of the icon, which opens us to the wider life of the universe, here we are in a chamber of darkness and hiddenness where each is within their own separated chamber even when standing together in the holy place.

He is next referred to as "the man in linen" and asked to go into Jerusalem and mark all those who are distressed by the work of iniquity and then to destroy all who do not bear the mark by prophesising against them. This apparently casual reference to linen brings us to a very important principle in performing this work. Linen, as far back as ancient Egypt, is an image of the illuminated body: the semi-transparent nature of fine linen allows light to pass through it. What is being shown here is Ezekiel the priest descending into the places of darkness and finding within it the sparks of light and marking them, so that they will be preserved when the qliphothic energies and beings are destroyed.

The Divine Presence goes on to comment, "Son of man, these men have set up their idols in their heart, and put the stumbling block of their iniquity before their face" (Ezekiel 14: 3). This graphically shows that what is being described here is the power of the internal image. The Hebrew word for "heart" is *lev* לב and means heart or mind, just as does the Egyptian term *ab* we have already considered. The connotation is of centrality of personhood and we see that this power of this qliphothic form within us places a barrier before us that means we can neither reach past it to have a direct experience of the universe, nor can the universe without help reach past the form to free us. The Hebrew word for "stumbling block" or "obstacle" is *mikshul* מכשול, but its root meaning is "idol".

The presence goes on to show Ezekiel, the linen-clad priest, that his task is to cleanse Jerusalem of the iniquity of idols and that he must enter into the darkness as a way of connecting with the deeper archetype of Jerusalem:

> For in My holy mountain, in the mountain of the height of Israel, saith the Lord GOD, there shall all the house of Israel, all of them, serve Me in the land; there will I accept them, and there will I require your heave-offerings, and the first of your gifts, with all your holy things. (Ezekiel 20: 40)

The quaternity of the Holy Mountain, Holy City, Holy Temple, and Holy of Holies is right at the centre of this work and here we see an indication that Ezekiel is aligning with the true archetype behind all the disturbance he has been contemplating.

Next, he is given a sword with which he will cleanse the city and destroy the qliphothic energies; the sword is the symbol of Geburah on the Tree of Life. It is that energy of clarity, will, and awareness that frees, that cuts through the bondage. It is also the quality of discrimination that can distinguish between the false and the true and between the icon and the idol. This quality is then contrasted with the image of Israel as a harlot. We are given the image of two sisters who take many lovers and are not faithful to YHVH יהוה. This is not a conventional teaching about sexual morality, rather it describes a state of heart without the capacity of the sword that becomes attached to many images who become dominating idols. He is also asked to gather all the sparks of holiness, described as "the good bones", place them in a pot and boil the pot until the bones are purged. This is the work of the cup, the alchemical container within which all impurities are dissolved and through which the seeds of light are reconstituted. Having broken through the binding energy of the Qliphoth and dispelled the cloud of obscuration by the art of the sword, the broken and lost forms and souls are brought into the cup of the heart and there undergo the alchemical transformation. It is this process that Dion Fortune describes when she absorbs the wolf form, and which we see Simon Iff carrying out in *Moonchild*.

Having looked at the Qliphoth within Jerusalem, the text then moves on to looking at these energies at work within the wider collective. Having identified Jerusalem as the place of the Holy Mountain, Holy City, Holy Temple, and Holy of Holies, it shows us the countries of the plains that threaten her existence: Egypt, Assyria, Tyre, among many others. This is of course drawn from Israel's history, but Ezekiel here is using them as illustrative of qliphothic archetypes that constitute a threat to holiness and balance. Among them is Edom which, in later tradition, comes to be representative of the qliphothic energies as a whole. The word "Edom" means red, and the Edomites are said to be the descendants of Esau, the red man who sold his inheritance to Jacob (Genesis 26). Esau is seen, therefore, as not having received the patriarchal blessing. He also marries outside the clan, thus representing a wild and chaotic energy that is alien and unpredictable. Later, in the book of Genesis, we find his descendants named as the Edomite kings who ruled before there was a king in Israel (Genesis 36: 31-43). The Kings of Edom are seen as primeval beings who, like Esau, are chaotic and alien and antagonistic to the balance and ordered growth that comes from the place of holiness. In later thinking they are linked to the kings whom Abraham has to overcome in the rescue of his nephew, Lot, and where he meets the priest-king of Jerusalem, Melchizedek. Here again we see the centrality of the idea of balance and order, the Egyptian principle of Maat, and its absence is the very hallmark of the Qliphoth. The Edomite kings are said to be dead and their crowns are lost, so we are asked to consider beings of death, kings without crowns, who embody darkness and chaos. Ezekiel is here being shown the vast scope of the enterprise of balancing the unbalanced energies, that it is more than addressing these energies within him and within his culture, it is woven into human collective history and into the fabric of the universe itself.

He is next shown the vision of the valley of dry bones. He must go into a wasteland, a lifeless place, and find a hidden valley filled with bones—an off-putting and eerie place—and bring the divine breath to them, bring them to life, in that process listening to the wounds that brought about their sense of death and disintegration, and then restore them, putting them back in their own true place, a process that involves the opening of graves. This he can only do because he is a servant of the temple and the holy living one, and the creative process that he sets into being comes out of his alignment with the divine breath.

The book concludes with the vision of the Holy Mountain, the Holy City, the re-establishment of the temple, and the return of the presence of the divine into the Holy of Holies. As this happens, a river arises in the east of the temple, flowing through it and out into the world. Wherever the waters touch there is renewal and healing; putrid waters are made clean, sick fish are made whole. Trees come into fruit and we are told that their leaves will not wither and they will produce fruit every month; the leaves of the trees will heal us and the fruit will feed us.

Having worked with the forms of iniquity by entering into the places of corrupted holiness, Ezekiel is then present with the restoration of the energies of the garden. He is in the midst of the flowing river of life as both agent and witness of the salvific energy.

CHAPTER 8

Holy Mountain, Holy City, Holy Temple, and Holy of Holies

This formulation, which completes the Book of Ezekiel, is central to a particular qabalistic tradition that has its origins in the Book of Psalms and to which both Ernest Butler and Tom Oloman were party. Oddly, my first experience of this tradition was long before I met either of them when, at the age of fifteen, I read Dennis Wheatley's *The Devil Rides Out*. Fifty years ago, I was living in a small village in South Wales and looking for something more than the local church and chapel could offer me. As a child I had devoured the *Mabinogion*, a collection of Welsh myths and legends, and the Arthurian stories, but I also loved the Bible with its many myths, poems, stories, and acts of magic and miracles. As a young child I had attended a private school run by nuns and, though not a catholic, was able to attend the Latin mass, which was sonorous and full of mystery. I felt therefore that underneath the formal teachings of the church was something else, something magical. *The Devil Rides Out* was the first external indication that there might really be something else. I knew, of course, that it could not be as described in the novel, but something about the references that were being made rang true. The principal character, the wonderfully named Duc de Richleau, the adept figure in the book, was regularly exorcising the dark forces whenever they turned up, which they did frequently. One of his standby methods for these situations was to chant: *Fundamenta ejus in Montibus, sanctis!* This is the beginning of the eighty-seventh psalm, one of the psalms of the sons of Korah, who are thought to have been a distinct group of priests in early Israel, specialists in the art of exorcism and in working with the unquiet dead. The Korahite psalms (42–49, 84–85, and 87–88) are concerned with the sense of Zion as the archetypal fountain of holiness and the place where YHVH יהוה dwells, and also are concerned with the descent into dark places and the establishment of balance and peace. Dennis Wheatley's use of the eighty-seventh psalm was more than just a dramatic effect; he was drawing on a genuine tradition of exorcism.

The psalm is very condensed and gives us a framework for this work of transforming the Qliphoth:

> "By the sons of Korah, a psalm, a song,
> His foundation is in the Holy Mountain,
> YHVH loves the gates of Zion,
> More than all the dwelling places of Jacob.
> Glorious things are said of you,
> City of God. Selah.
> I mention Rehab and Babylon to those who know me,
> Behold, Philistilia. Tyre with Cush,
> This one was born there.
> But of Zion it was said: A man and a man was born in her,
> And he, Elyon, established her."
> YHVH takes account when he writes down peoples:
> "This one was born there." Selah.
> "And singers as well as dancers-
> All my springs are in you." (Rautenbach, 2010, p. 22)

The first question when contemplating this psalm is who is meant by the term "His"? The divine is the conventional way of understanding it, but a more inner meaning is that it applies to the contemplator. Our foundation then is within the Holy Mountain, which means that we align the foundations of our being with the sense of the Holy Mountain of the divine. This is an act of commitment and inclusion; it says that we who do this are dwellers in the Holy Mountain. "The dweller on the mountain" was one of the phrases that Ernest Butler used to denote the deeper reaches of the human soul—the presence of Tiphareth—and aligning your foundation with the Holy Mountain is an invitation to the angel of Tiphareth to descend into and dwell within the pool of Yesod.

This beginning statement of not just taking refuge in the mountain but making it our foundation, and the implicit invitation of the angel to descend into the sweet and bitter waters of our foundations of life, begins a process of deepening contemplation. The next step we are invited to take is to contemplate the Gates of Zion in the phrase, "YHVH loves the gates of Zion". This is, in effect, the entrance into the divine city whom YHVH loves more than the other dwelling places of Jacob. This is a coded reference to entering into the middle triangle of the tree, into Tiphareth, the archetypal place of balance, harmony and presence.

We are also given the name *YHVH*—the divine name that both outlines the universal creative process and is an image of both the divine and the human being. While the Tree of Life gives a structural mandala for self and universe, the path of the name יהוה shows how to work with flow, and the transmission of energy and consciousness from level to level. It contains the dynamic of the four worlds and the structure of the tree. Aligning with this name enables us to be a vehicle for the deep will of the universe. The name *YHVH* יהוה in Judaism has a very particular status; it is the name spoken by the high priest in the Holy of Holies at Yom Kippur and that in being spoken brings the direct presence of the divine into operation as an act of redemption. It is also said of it that it is the name that must not be spoken, and its pronunciation remains unknown. Those who were able to work with the energies of the name were given the title of *Baal Shem*, a name that means "master" or "Lord of the Name" but which, more deeply, means one who has surrendered deeply to the name and is a transmitter of its sovereignty. The contemplation of the name begins with the point above the *yod*, which equates with Kether, the place of pure being. This simple point gives rise to the *yod* י Chochmah, deep will; the letter *heh* ה Binah, deep love, deep imagination; the letter *vav* ו the sephiroth of formation (Geburah, Gedulah, Tiphareth, Hod, Netzach, and Yesod), the principle of transmission, and the final letter *heh* ה, the sephirah Malkuth, embodiment and action. The point above the *yod* is sometimes attributed to the letter *shin* ש in the Christian Qabalah as representing the divine breath, and then the contemplated name is *YHShVH* יהשוה where the *shin* is seen as operating secretly within the creative flow of the name, uniting the name of creation *YHVH* יהוה with the name of deepest being *AHIH* אהיה. We will look in more detail at the practical applications of this in sections two and three, but what we are asked to do in this part of the psalm is to begin the contemplation of the mystery of the name. This has the effect of bringing our previous work together and preparing us for a new phase, for in addition to making our foundation the Holy Mountain we now dedicate ourselves to the service of the Name יהוה, aligning our being, our will, our imagination, our capacity to transmit and enliven, and our embodiment with that of the divine.

There is a whole series of meditations, which arise from this contemplation—from the initial encounter with the gates to the exploration of the Holy City and the temple that is at its heart. The gates of Zion are the inner dialogue created by the interplay of Hod, Netzach, and Yesod, and these gates open or not depending on our capacity to interrupt the dialogue. While the dialogue persists the gates of Zion remain closed. As we come into stillness the gates open, revealing to us the triad of Tiphareth, Geburah, and Gedulah, finding ourselves therefore within the Holy City in which our mind acquires the clarity of Geburah, our feelings the loving-kindness of Gedulah, and we commune directly with the angel of presence found in Tiphareth.

Having become a dweller on the mountain we then contemplate the enemies of the Holy City: Rahab, Babylon, Philistia, Tyre and Cush. They are the historic enemies of Israel, but this is not literal for they are aspects of the qliphothic energies that arise to challenge the emergence of light, truth, and beauty. They are seen as being far from the place of holiness and therefore inhabiting the wasteland of chaos and meaninglessness, the time of the Edomite kings before the mountain, city, and temple were established.

The worker with this psalm becomes one who can identify the beings that arise from those cities, who knows those who are born from there. We know this because as workers with the name *YHVH* we are born out of Zion; one who is seen by YHVH and who is recorded by the divine presence, who drinks from the springs of YHVH, who participates in the sacred songs and dances of divine service.

A particular phrase is used in relation to Zion: "A man and a man is born there". The Hebrew phrase is איש ו איש and, poetically, the repetition of the word for "man" focuses our attention on what is meant by a man being born from Zion. The psalm goes on to explain that Zion is

HOLY MOUNTAIN, HOLY CITY, HOLY TEMPLE, AND HOLY OF HOLIES 97

established by Elyon, the most high divinity, as opposed to the cities that are established in chaos and emptiness. Those who are born out of Zion are in direct relationship with the divine; they are taken account of and written down. The act of scribing in this way is to make permanent the status of those who are inscribed, much as in the Egyptian Ished Tree the Pharaoh's name is inscribed on the leaves. As part of Zion we are connected to the divine springs of life, the paradisal river that we find in Ezekiel, and take part in the divine service of singing and dancing before YHVH.

Becoming born of Zion, being *aish ve aish*, involves communing with our deeper soul and discovering ourselves to be a resident in the divine city who contemplates the places of unbalanced life. We are connected both to the springs of divine life that irrigate the city and the world, and we carry out the divine service of the temple with the singers and dancers of YHVH.

The principal practice of the temple priesthood is to bless with the divine name so that the angels who transmit the divine presence are sent out to touch all of the Earth with the sense of blessing, including those places who are opposed to the city of Zion. The blessing formula of the priesthood is this:

May the LORD bless you and guard you—יְבָרֶכְךָ יהוה, וְיִשְׁמְרֶךָ
(*Yevhārēkh-khā Adhōnāy veyishmerēkhā*—)

May the LORD make His face to shed light upon you and be gracious unto you—יָאֵר יהוה פָּנָיו אֵלֶיךָ, וִיחֻנֶּךָּ
(*Yā'ēr Adhōnāy pānāw ēlekhā vihunnékkā*—)

May the LORD lift up His face unto you and give you peace—
שלום לך וישם אליך פיגו יהוה ישא
(*Yissā Adhōnā y pānāw ēlekhā viyāsēm lekhā shālām.*)

The blessing begins traditionally by the priest placing his prayer shawl over his head and thus symbolically embraced by the divine presence in the tabernacle. His hands are raised, thumbs extended, with first and second and third and fourth fingers together, to form the shape of the Hebrew letter *shin* ש. The letter *shin* represents the divine breath, the *ruach ha qodesh*, which manifests as the blessing is spoken.

The first phrase engages us with the processes of blessing itself and the creation of protection. We are held safely in a place of inner protection, the temple, and start to understand the nature of the blessing of the Name *YHVH*. This is aligned with the sephirah Yesod, the place of the foundation, and addresses the qliphothic level of *chatah*, ignorant reactivity, placing bounds upon it as we draw all into the house of God.

The second phrase in which the name reveals its face and shines is the direct encounter with the living presence and the light that shines from it. This is aligned with the sephirah Tiphareth. This addresses *pesha*, the wilful choosing of evil, and shines light upon our choices.

The third phrase in which the face is uplifted and we experience peace is the experience of "face beholding face" and entering into the great stillness of *shalom*. This is aligned with the sephirah Da'ath. Here, the angels are sent forth to create peace and balance. This addresses the level of *avon*, iniquity, for here we meet the divine face-to-face and are given the choice to either renounce our dedication to evil or fall into the abyss.

The psalm gives us a way of aligning ourselves with the Holy Mountain, Holy City, Holy Temple, and Holy of Holies. The steps of making a foundation, contemplating the name, entering the city, and the critical step of becoming *aish ve aish* prepare us to be able to transmit the blessing by successively penetrating the veils of *chatah*, *pesha*, and *avon*, initially in ourselves and then more deeply in the world. It can be useful to envisage the city on the mountain, to contemplate its gates, and to wander the ways of the city before finding our place in the temple and within the Holy of Holies. The Temple is accessed through the sephirah Da'ath and is the supernal triangle of the Tree of Life. It is the work of one who has become *aish ve aish* to work with opposites to contemplate the Qliphoth and to bring the blessing into operation so that the *chatah*, *pesha*, and *avon* are lifted into the light.

CHAPTER 9

The living image and the body of glory

Here we look at the true image of the human being, the one who works within the Holy of Holies, who pronounces the blessing that binds and transforms the Qliphoth. In Hebrew the word for image is *tselem* צלם and is taken from Genesis 1:27: "And God created man in his image. In the image of God did He create him. Male and female created He them."

The root meaning of *tselem* is "shadow" or "representation" and takes us into the heart of the icon-idol dynamic, for an icon is an image or *tselem* that reveals the light, but an idol one that blocks the light and reflects the shadow of its own form. The human being as the *tselem* of the divine then either dissolves its form and bridges into the formless light, which it offers to all, or clings to its form, obstructs the light, and casts its shadow on the earth. This contemplation of form and formlessness and light and shadow is a pivotal aspect of our deeper work. If we look more deeply at the phrase we see some interesting ideas. The actual phrase in Genesis is בצלם, meaning "in the image", although the use of the of the prefix *beit* can also mean "with". The letter *beit*'s archetypal meaning is "house" and it is the prototype of the temple (as we shall consider more deeply in Chapter Fifteen). The function of the temple is to make manifest the divine life and enable interchange between human and the divine. So too, the *tselem*, the true image of the human, is the living temple that makes manifest the glory of the one who is both male and female, singular and plural.

If we consider this word in more detail בצלם as a formula for the expression of the true image or *tselem* it begins with the letter *beit*, "the house", which suggests that our first step in the work of becoming the true image is to create the house within which the image can live. This is simultaneously the house of our body and the house of our incarnation. We move on from this to the letter *tzaddi*, "the fishhook". This is the first letter of the word *tsaddik* צדיק, which means "holy or righteous one" and is the title of an adept worker with the name and the root of the true image of the human being. The *tzadddik* is said to be humble, hence the letter *tzaddi* צ bends, bowing to show the act of surrender to the divine; they are the door through which the divine and human meet, hence the next letter is the letter *daleth* ד "the door"; in their heart they hold the letter *yod* י the divine will, and this will penetrates into the deep repetitive patterns of the heart and body in the letter *qoph* ק which means "the back of the head".

Having prepared the place and aligned with the true image we step into the place of the *lamed* ל "the ox goad", the divine will in expression. It is this focus that moves both the wills of God and human—our true will. This will is applied to the final letter *mem* מ the mother letter that is the deep sea and stands for the deep imagination, the womb of creation.

The central practice of the *tsaddik* is the art of blessing, an art that has its origin in the priestly blessing discussed in the previous chapter. It is however more than a formal liturgical act, being a practice that both enhances the sense of light and peace and binds, illumines, and ultimately transforms the Qliphoth. This returns us to the dynamic of the icon and the idol and the fact that either we are transmitting the light or through opaqueness casting a shadow; we are either manifesting the blessing of the divine or, like the corrupted elders, generating clouds of darkness from our own chambers of imagery.

It is the function of the blessing practice first of all to gather the qliphothic energies and provide protection from being caught up in them, then to illuminate, and finally to bring what is blessed into union with the divine presence. All that is responsive to the divine is then magnified and made potent and all that opposes the divine will withers and ceases to exist.

This blessing is mediated through the human form which, as the living image of the divine, acts as a lens or focusing point for the divine presence. This sense of the illuminated body or "body of light" is given a great deal of attention in the Qabalah. Our capacity to activate it is directly linked to our ability to embrace our own true image. The whole thrust of Egyptian inner tradition was to bring about the arising of the immortal body that was simultaneously present on Earth and in the inner worlds. The mummification process in which the body is wrapped in layers of linen and beautified with gold and jewels is a symbolic enactment of the achievement of the body of light. It is significant in the Book of Ezekiel that we are told that the visionary is the man wrapped in linen; it is he who enters into the corrupted Jerusalem to find the sparks of goodness that remain.

The body of light is the reality behind ideas like astral projection. It is a created form that our awareness inhabits and which enables us to become active within the subtler aspects of the universe. At the heart of this form is the sense of being the fulcrum and confluence point through which the outer and inner universes combine and communicate. It is linked also with the mystery of light itself and the declaration *yehi or*—"let there be light". It is our own living luminous image that is the vehicle through which our own deeper will manifests. In the inner Christian tradition it is the "resurrection body"; in Tibetan Buddhism it is called "the rainbow body"; in the Qabalah it is the inner golem or the *Adam Kadmon*, the primal human image through which the practitioner of this art of the transformation of the Qliphoth reaches out into inner and outer worlds.

The root of this form in the Qabalah is the creation of the magical personality. This process makes use of the lower spheres of the Tree of Life (Malkuth, Yesod, Hod, and Netzach) to create a form that represents our deeper self. This form becomes stable within our inner dialogue and is indwelled by our deeper presence in Tiphareth which, as our experience of working with it increases, successively infolds the deeper spheres of the Tree of Life into the form. We begin by contemplating our sense of ourselves using the *PRDS* meditative process:

> *P* Direct awareness of our body and our senses. The entrance into Malkuth.
>
> *R* We experience our body as a living symbol, entering the sephirah of Yesod.

D We enter the search, seeking awareness of our living image. This brings us into direct awareness of the inner dialogue that supports this image. Yesod, Hod, and Netzach—the veil, Paroketh.

S Revelation. The presence of the stillness behind the motion of the inner dialogue. Tiphareth.

From that place of stillness and holding our sense of the different aspects of self—physical sensations, the yesodic image, and the dialogue of thought, feeling, and memory that sustains it—we descend into the inner sea of Yesod and emerge as a figure of light. This is the seed form for our magical image of ourselves, which, as we work on it step by step, becomes more and more embodied.

This is a practice deeply concerned with the question of identity, will, and creativity. Here we are aligning our personal sense of self, our persona or mask, with the image of the true human being whose function it is to bridge between opposites and bring life and light into dark places.

In taking on this image we re-enact the return to the garden, the return to Zepi Tepi, to the mound and the primal light. Through our will and imagination, through that mysterious fluid awareness, we enable the divine images to become flesh here and now for the redemption of all worlds.

In the inner Christian tradition, the figure of Christ is the prototype of the image of the true human being and the figure of the Apostle John is seen as the image of this image. There is a very early Christian tradition which says that the reason Judas had to identify Jesus with a kiss when the servants of the high priest came to arrest him was that Jesus was known to be a shapeshifter so that no one knew his true form. What is being hinted at here is that Jesus' true form was the body of light, the resurrection body, which is infinitely creative and capable of assuming many forms depending upon need. This idea is shown also in the traditions of the Apostle John who is seen as the "Christed" human being so that his form reflects the form of Christ. He becomes the icon of the one who is the living icon of the true human being and, in his form as John the Presbyter, he becomes the icon of priesthood. Jesus's declaration on the cross, in which he says to John, "Son behold your mother and to Mary Mother behold your son", is a declaration of this twinship or iconographic union. Interestingly, John is often depicted as holding a chalice with a green serpent arising out of it. This is based on a legend of John having been given poisoned wine which, as he blessed it, the poison emerged in the form of a green snake. This is a clear link to the work of blessing and purifying the Qliphoth, as well as indicating that this work is one of absorption and blessing, not banishing. There is another important legend about the Apostle John in that it is suggested that he did not die in the normal way but, like both Jesus and Mary, ascended into heaven through the body of light.

The practice of manifesting the magical personality that will in time arises as the body of light begins as we practice the training exercises described in Section Two. There is much to contemplate here as it is not simply a visualisation exercise but deeply related to our sense of identity and the vehicle that holds our awareness.

PART 2

THE TRAINING

The training in this art is based around the three images of Maat found in Egyptian tradition:

1. The Eloquent Peasant—this is the capacity to stand firmly on the earth, to irrigate and tend the land, and to speak with the voice of *maa kheru*, "the just voice". Here the focus is on developing an embodied sense of presence, of being able to work with inner energies and sense when they are in balance and out of balance.
2. The Good Shepherd—the capacity to remain centred in Tiphareth and to work with and help to transform the split-away aspects of our nature and the split-off aspects of the world. The focus is on the dialogue between the angel of Tiphareth and making the transition from the lower triangle of the tree so that our consciousness routinely dwells in the middle triangle. The other piece of training is in the development of the body of light as a vehicle for the salvific work of the Good Shepherd.
3. The Man or Woman of Silence—the *Geru Maa*. Here the focus is on Da'ath, the connection to the supernal triangle, and on the deepening capacity for silence. The *Geru Maa* is immersed in silence and by radiating it enables the growth and life of all that he and she encounters.

CHAPTER 10

Becoming the Eloquent Peasant

This first stage of training is organised around the figure of the Eloquent Peasant—the man or woman of earth who stands on stable ground and who clarifies the boundaries between the different elements of creation so that life can grow in an optimum way. The earliest image of Maat is the primal mound that arises out of the waters, creating the stability and boundary that is needed for the manifestation of life. The intention of this stage of training is to create an internal sense of ground and stability and balance, which involves addressing all the aspects of ourselves that are ungrounded and out of balance.

For this reason, the beginning exercises are designed to reconfigure our habitual sense of self and universe. They consist of body awareness and relaxation exercises, breathing exercises, the development of the imagination, the practice of the qabalistic cross and the middle pillar exercises, and working with the *PRDS* meditation so that the Tree of Life becomes deeply integrated into our nature.

The effects of these practices are:

- The body awareness and relaxation exercises bring us into relationship with the body and the load of tension and stress that the body

routinely holds, and begins the work of unlocking tension and held, old pain.
- The breathing exercises connect us to our vitality and open us to the rhythms of body and universe.
- The development of the capacity of the imagination brings our creative abilities into conscious awareness.
- The qabalistic cross is an act of alignment and holds the intention to serve the light and be a centre of blessing.
- The middle pillar exercises are an alchemical practice of circulating light through the subtle body, creating a fountain of vitality and clear edges to our energetic field.
- Contemplation of the Tree of Life incorporates the tree within us so that it mediates between the surface and the depth and between our soul and the soul of the universe. It opens us to a web of connections and relationships.

The continuing effect of these six forms is to create a physio-energetic matrix aligned to the embodiment of the light. Initially these exercises can feel mechanical and repetitive but, with practice, the relaxation exercises are experienced as an embrace of bone and body; the breathing exercise as the renewal of life; the magical imagination as the flowering of our creativity; the qabalistic cross as a prayer of light that promotes balance and blessing; the middle pillar exercises as a fountain of light or nourishment by a green and growing tree; and the *PRDS* process as the exploration of a responsive and living field.

Relaxation exercise

These are both the simplest and most fundamental exercises of occult training. They consist of systematically relaxing the body by consciously tensing and relaxing the muscles. We begin by tensing our toes, holding the tension for a moment, and then relaxing; next, tensing our calves, holding for a moment and then relaxing, followed by tensing our thighs, and then gradually working our way up the body including the face and the scalp muscles.

These exercises may seem too simple or peripheral given the deep matters we are considering, but the whole of magical training depends upon reorganising the reflexes of the body and, because the body itself is the fulcrum of the magical will and imagination, acquiring skill in this area is essential.

The intention of the relaxation exercises is first of all to help us become aware of our body and to engage with habitual tension and worry. The aim is to induce a state of alert peacefulness or dynamic stillness that is the substrate or ground for the inner work to follow. This is not as easy as we might think because whereas the systematic tensing and relaxation of the muscles has immediate effect (normally), we quickly find tension patterns reasserting themselves, and one effect of repeated practice is as superficial tensions dissipate deeper tensions become revealed. This is actually progress but may not feel like it.

As mentioned previously, Ernest Butler felt that the root of the inner work we were trained in derived from ancient Egyptian tradition. The body is central to that tradition and the emphasis on mummification and the elaborate funerary traditions have an inward correlate in that the body is the locus of operation and ground of the soul. The myth of Osiris, which involves his death and the scattering of his limbs, is—in a way—our situation when we come to inner work. We are inert and fragmented and, like Isis, must gather the pieces and create a centre of presence within us. This centre of presence the ancient Egyptians called the *ab* or the heart—it is that part of our nature that is weighed against the feather of Maat in the funerary traditions. The aim of cultivating the qualities of the heart is that it should be substantial and balanced.

This is a process with many levels, but it begins in this apparently simple process of working with tension in the body. The boring and repetitive process of scanning and rescanning the body involves qualities of both will and surrender. Will because, without will, we would not be able to keep doing it; surrender because the whole art of relaxation involves a softening into what is actually there and creating a dialogue between the body and the conscious mind. This involves connecting with a part of ourselves the Egyptians called the *khaibet* or "shadow". We might think of it as the unconscious self, the storage place of habit and reflex—in the Qabalah it is called the *nephesch* or "animal soul", centred in Yesod. Relating to the *khaibet* is a key part of this practice for once we get beyond the simple tension and release experience, we discover the deeper tensions held within its mysterious depths. To see the body as shadow, or as giving as access to shadow, is one of the deeper fruits of the exercise. In the Osirian myth the shadow can be seen as Set, the chaotic fiery energy that tears away at order. Engaging with those energies of rage, jealousy, fear, and even hatred is part of the work of surrendering into the body. These energies then rise to the surface in order to find their legitimate place. In Egyptian mythology, as well as being the murderer of Osiris, Set is the defender of the barque of the Sun in its journey through the mansions of the night; the myth indicates here the need for the inclusion of the shadow. Through this dialogue the deep tensions held in the *khaibet* come into relationship with the known aspects of body, and the dialogue between the two promotes a cycle of healing and release.

This repeated experience generates a field of presence in the midst of the body that extends to unify the separate parts of our being. This is the balancing of the heart and the coming to birth of the heart in the midst of the field of the body, so that the heart becomes as the ever-dawning Sun, continually renewing itself in the cycle of the day and night. These exercises, mechanical though they may seem, are the underpinning of this generative potential.

They can be extended beyond the tension and release practice so that we simply pay attention to ourselves not in the sense of thinking about ourselves either positively or negatively, but in the much simpler sense of bringing our attention towards our body. As we do this we start to discover the location and physical presence of the *ab*, our centre of metaphysical gravity, the sense of embodied self. Having found that fulcrum we will directly discover the body and the senses, beginning with the sense of touch, and successively adding hearing, seeing, smelling, and tasting. As we acquire the ability to hold all five senses together we may then engage with the proprioceptive sense of position in the world, the vestibular sense of balance, the sense of hot and cold, pain and pleasure, etc. This creates a sense of presence and a field of awareness that opens us into the present-moment experience of the body mediating between inner and outer worlds.

Breathing exercise

The rhythmic breathing exercise enhances and deepens this process. It is a particular way of breathing that involves breathing with belly and chest in a four-fold rhythm. Begin by pushing out the belly and then expanding into the chest for a count of eight, then hold for a count of four and breathe out for a count of eight. Pause for a count of four and repeat for at least five minutes.

This is a straightforward process of opening up the lungs, ensuring we make a whole breath, beginning with the belly, opening up the intercostal muscles, raising the shoulders then pausing and then completely emptying the lungs before again pausing.

Just as a physical exercise this has benefits: we are more oxygenated and feel more alive and the rhythm of the breathing helps the process of relaxation and touching stillness. From a deeper point of view, the breath is the life force, the energy of animation itself; it quickens, kindles, awakens. At first the rhythm of the breath feels clumsy and forced and it may take us some time to get used to it. Here, too, we must work with the principles of will and surrender for as the work deepens we may discover the breath moving effortlessly, at times conveying us into the sense of centre that is the *ab*. As this happens our life energy becomes more present, and we may feel a sense of deeper potency. For the ancient Egyptians this would indicate the enlivening of the heart and the activation of the *ka* soul normally indicated by the image of two hands and arms reaching out.

The *ka* is the vitality and life energy of Yesod, its great pool of life, energy, and imagination. This vital spark or energy has the capacity to reach out, and we could see it as the gravity well of the enlivened heart reaching out in response to the will and intention of the awakening process. We may reach out for many things as we become increasingly aware, but the intention of this exercise is to bring us to a dynamic stillness in which we reach out to the deeper soul, inviting it to take its place in the developing matrix of presence and energy.

There is much that can be learned from this stage of the process; the surrender to the rhythm of filling, emptying, and pausing brings us into alignment with the rhythms of the universe—daily, lunar, seasonal, etc. It can create a sensitivity to harmony and discord. The capacity to reach out, sustain the reaching, and the formation of what might be called a cup or chalice of active receptivity, all arise from this exercise.

The deeper soul, called by the Egyptians the *ba* soul, is described as a human-headed hawk.

Its connection with the matrix of incarnation is formed through the interplay of body, shadow, and heart. *Ka* is the deeper aspect of these apparently simple processes of relaxation and breathing. Its qabalistic parallel is in the entrance into Malkuth, the engagement with the internal dialogue and the invitation of the descent of the angel of Tiphareth. Its initial appearance may be in intuitions, feelings of peace or freedom, or a deepening sense of purpose as it increasingly takes the reins of the work. Working more and more deeply with the breath and body under the guidance of the deeper soul starts to bring what we might call "the imagination of the spirit" into incarnation. This is the capacity to embody spiritual realities through the active and empowered imagination that occurs when the field of the *ab* is stable and in alignment with the body and the shadow. In this way Tiphareth, Yesod, and Malkuth cooperate together and enable the activation of the magical imagination. This magical imagination is the subject of the next set of beginning exercises.

The magical imagination—the tree in the garden

The magical imagination mirrors the creative process in Genesis, which begins with the sense of the universe existing in a state of undifferentiation, having the qualities of *tohu* ("emptiness") and *bohu* ("chaos").

The divine spirit broods over them and then speaks the declaration *yehi or*, "let there be light!", which creates the separation of the dry land from the waters and the appearance of the living forms of creation, culminating in the appearance of the human being. Each time we exercise the imagination we recapitulate this process. We begin with the state of alert relaxation achieved in the breath and body exercise and, resting there, we imagine a great still sea of water—the inner sea. Then we imagine the rising of a mound or island in the midst of the waters. In the midst of the island is a tree from which four rivers flow, and then a garden filled with plant, animal, and bird life.

This is a multi-sensory experience connected to the felt sense of the body, so not a question of just seeing the image with the minds' eye but touching it, hearing it, smelling and tasting it, so that we are immersed in the image; feeling the sea and the growing of the tree; being a fish swimming in the rivers; identifying with plants and all the different beings that are found in the garden. One of the things that will be discovered is that the imagined image has a life of its own and the qualities of will and surrender developed in earlier exercises are central also here. Too much will and the image becomes static and dead; too little and it becomes chaotic and dispersed. This is the beginning of experientially learning about the qualities of *tohu* and *bohu*, or "emptiness" and "chaos", and the opposites that need to be worked with in any creative act. As *tohu* and *bohu* are balanced in the act of creation, the form that arises contains within it the dynamic stillness and potential of the beginning of *tohu*, and the generative potential of the fractal chaos that is *bohu*.

Of course, we do not know it at this point; we are just repetitively struggling with imagining the sea, island, tree, and garden. It is this struggle however that starts to develop what will become the magical imagination. There are many things that can be paid attention to imaginatively: the ecology of the garden, the balance of elements; we can be the whole garden or an element within it: a stone, a flower, the tree itself, water flowing around the garden, or a breeze blowing in the garden.

The key to this practice is that it is experienced as a felt, intimate sense; we are in the centre of the action and all our senses are involved. We are all stronger in some of our senses than others. If we are very tactile we will experience the garden through touch; if hearing is our strongest sense, we will hear the sounds of the garden; if scent, we will smell the flowers and the greenery. We will find as we continue that the other senses will add to the experience, creating an embodied, generative image.

This practice is a way of feeding the imagination by inviting it to be present and developing its potential to create the living embodied icon. This is the fundamental practice of deep magic for this energised, substantial yet flowing form that enfolds spaciousness and generative potential within itself, bridges the deeper soul and everyday physical reality.

The salutes of the Sun

One of the devotional practices that utilises this ability is the salutes of the Sun. This is a simple prayer-like statement to be used morning, noon, and evening, in which we pause, pay attention to the Sun, and align ourselves with its potency.

> Hail to thee the eternal spiritual sun whose visible symbol now rises/stands/sets in the heavens/rests at night. Hail to thee from the abodes of the morning/noon/evening/night.

A slightly more elaborate form, drawing on Egyptian tradition, can also be used:

> Hail to thee the eternal spiritual sun who rises as Ra Horakhty, the manifester of the morning. Hail to thee who makes us stand upright.
>
> Hail to thee the eternal spiritual sun who stands as Hathor at noon—the nurturing lady of fire and light who is Sekhmet radiant in power. Hail to thee who makes our limbs strong.
>
> Hail to thee the eternal spiritual sun who are Atum at sunset gathering all into the blessed west. Hail to thee who gives us rest.
>
> Hail unto thee the eternal spiritual sun who art Khephera, the sun at midnight. Hail to thee who renews our souls.

Whatever form is used the intention of this prayer form is to link us with the source of creative light, life, and power at regular intervals in the day. Here we employ the connecting ability of the magical imagination to connect to the cycle of the Sun and follow its sequence through the day so that the pattern of our day is linked to something bigger than our own daily life. The more vivid our imagining of these moments the greater the sense of presence and power we touch. We increasingly live against the felt experience of the eternal spiritual Sun. The use of the Egyptian god forms can help to deepen that experience, but we could use forms from any pantheon, or indeed forms that just appear in our personal work.

The night or evening salute is linked also to an exercise made just before sleep in which you contemplate the events of the day backwards, using imagination to reverse time and to digest the events of the day. This is linked with Khephera's process of self-renewal; again, this is a simple-seeming exercise but enables us to bring a deeper sense of awareness into our daily activities. This particular exercise is central to the work of *geru maa*, the man or woman of silence, and will be considered in some depth in that phase of the training. Here, we start to create the basis for that later work.

The qabalistic cross

The qabalistic cross brings together the skills developed in sensing the body with the magical imagination. We begin by standing, feeling the vertical dimension of the body, sensing our feet upon the earth, our head in space, our spine holding the weight of the body.

Imagine a sphere of diamond white light above our head. We touch our forehead with our dominant hand and say: "*Ateh*" (Ar-taay).

Aligning with the source of light and life, we bring our hand down the body to the solar plexus, imagining a river of diamond light flowing down the centre of the body into the ground.

Say: "*Malkuth*" (malkooth). Then we bring our hand to the right shoulder and imagine a sphere of intense red energy. Say: "*Ve Geburah*" (vay gebooraah).

Bringing our hand to the left shoulder we imagine a river of diamond white light flowing to it and forming a sphere of deep blue light. Say: "*Ve Gedulah*" (vay gedoolaah).

Bringing our hands together just above the solar plexus, we imagine a miniature sun shining there.

Say: "*Le Olam Amen*"—imagining the sun shining more and more intensely as we fully extend our arms to form a cross of light and fire.

This is the bare bones of the ritual which aligns us with the Tree of Life and holds the intention of generating light, power, and blessing. It is capable of great extension and is an unparalleled training tool.

Once we have memorised the basic practice we can add to it what is sometimes called "the magical voice". To find this, try chanting the phrases in a lower or higher note than your normal speaking voice. At a certain point we will discover a feeling of vibration spreading through the body in response to the note. This is sometimes called "vibrating" the names of power, and this vibrato effect brings in a deeper sense of connection with the phrase or intention.

The intention of the qabalistic cross is nothing more or less than the completion of the great work by incarnating the spheres of the Tree of Life within the field of human embodied consciousness.

Ateh is the sefirah Kether. It means "thou" or "thine", formed from the letters *aleph tav*, the first and last letters of the Hebrew alphabet. It is like the Greek Alpha and Omega and represents totality. *Malkuth* is "the kingdom", matter, solidity—the manifest world. When we perform this first part of the exercise, we are inviting the divine source to fully incarnate into matter through our living flesh.

The second part of the practice is to establish the horizontal balance of opposites through the invocation of Geburah and Gedulah. Geburah is the catabolic sphere of the tree, whereas Gedulah is anabolic. They are reflections of *tohu* and *bohu* in that Geburah breaks things down and creates space and simplicity whilst Gedulah generates forms and shapes and maximises the potentials of expression. Here the art of the practitioner is to create balance between these two possibilities. The spheres of Geburah and Gedulah can be seen also as fire and water, clarity and compassion, will and love, or any other dynamic pairs of opposites that need balancing. As the practice develops understanding, the many layers of opposites we work with become visible and reachable in the rite.

This is shown in the final part of the working, in which we bring our hands together at the centre of our body at the Tiphareth point. This is the balance point of the Tree of Life between the pillars of the opposites, and between Kether and Malkuth. Imagining this sphere shining out we say *"Le Olam"*—this means "the universe" or "the world" or "the all"—and then *"Amen"*, which can mean "so be it", as a word of sealing, but is also the name of the creator god, Amen Ra. At this point we open our arms embracing all and allow the blessing of the balanced and empowered form to radiate out through the heart.

This practice enfolds the energies of creation into the human form. It is an act of presence and incarnation. Repeated practise of the qabalistic cross brings us into the place of being the living bridge or incarnating the human archetype of linking, balancing, and generating new life.

The circulation of the light—the alchemical tree

Having acquired a beginning ground in the qabalistic cross the next practice is to build the middle pillar within the energetic field and begin the alchemical process of the interwoven light. In occult writing there are tomes written about the aura and the body of energy, astral body, etc. There is a particular concentration on the visual sense—for example, people claiming they can see the colour of your aura, or seeing forms or entities attached to your aura, etc.

Much more simply we can sense our energetic field through the felt sense of personal space and through our connection with vitality or *dynamis*, to use the Greek word. The practice of the interwoven light is designed to deepen our connection with *dynamis*; to empower our vital or energy body but also to balance it; to create an inner shape that is suited for the process of mediating between inner and outer. Plato considered that the true shape of a human being is a sphere, and there is a way in which this work balances the sphere of our being and aligns it with the actual shape of our physical body, which is a vertical shape divided into opposites of left and right, back and front. This balancing the qabalists achieve through the use of the image of the Tree of Life, establishing the middle pillar in the core of the body and working with flows of energy so as to align the opposites as they manifest in our physical form. The verticality of the pillar and the spherical and spiral nature of the flows of force unite the sphere and the cube as archetypal forms within us and sanctify the body as the living temple.

The practice begins by paying careful attention to the felt sense of the physical body, as we have learned in the relaxation and breathing exercise and in the practice of the qabalistic cross. We then let our attention surround our body, getting a felt sense of our personal space. This is not normally a visual impression, more a bodily sense of space. Spend time sensing this and getting a sense of where this field begins and ends, then expand the field and notice how objects and other people interact with it. We continue this process until we have a clear sense of the field that surrounds us, finding it responsive to our intention. It will wrap around us and penetrate objects so that they feel more connected to us. If we drive a car, we might notice how our energy field maps onto the car, so when the car passes near another car or object we feel close to it.

Having gained both a felt sense of the sphere of awareness and the physical body, we then commence the process of enlivening and alignment. Ernest Butler called the first step in this "the contact of power".

118   THE TREE OF LIFE AND DEATH

This begins by sensing a sphere of pure white radiance just above the crown of the head. This is our connection to the deepest part of our being, that which the Neoplatonists would have called the *nous* and the qabalists the *yechidah*. It is the sephirah Kether on the Tree of Life, the crown of being. Feel this radiant centre shining down upon the body, down into the ground. Chant the name *Eheieh* אהיה as a vibration of stillness at the heart of the light. Commune with this sphere, let it become a tangible part of our field, let it hold and communicate with us. Feel the presence of the deeper soul and contemplate the Orphic phrase, "My home is in the starry heavens".

When this feels sufficiently stable, bring attention to the area just below the soles of the feet. Sense here a sphere of luminous blackness, shot through with rainbow colours. Chant the name *Adonai Ha Aretz* אדני ה ארץ in the heart of the sphere, feeling it as a focus of the fire of the Earth. This is our connection to the energy and life of the Earth, the *anima mundi*, the soul of the world. Once again, spend time feeling this radiant sphere that roots us into the Earth and radiates energy upwards into us. Here, commune with the world soul; be held by her. Contemplate the Orphic phrase, "I am a child of Earth".

As this sphere stabilises, we will feel the interplay of the two spheres as they engage with each other through the form of our body. As we do so, we will be aware of another sphere forming in the centre of our being, a miniature sun that mediates between the deep soul and the earth soul. Chant the name *Yod Heh Vav Heh Aloah Ve Da'ath* יהוה אלוה ו דעת at the heart of the sun as the seed of its life. Feel the warmth and power of this sun and its centring and mediating capacity. Contemplate the Orphic phrase, "I am the kid fallen into milk".

Spend time with this growing tree, its two poles and its centre point. Feel the sense of the field of stars and the Earth and the radiant mediation of the new sun at the centre of our being. As our awareness deepens, we will become aware of two new points: the throat and the pelvis. These are the spheres of expression, movement, and sexuality at the pelvis, sound and vibration at the throat.

Sense a sphere of lavender, luminous grey at the throat. Feel the vibration of potential. Remember the *vox magica* of the qabalistic cross and chant the name *Yod Heh Vav Heh Elohim* יהוה אלהים feeling the vibration of quickening and awakening. Contemplate the Orphic phrase, "I am the voice of memory".

Sense a sphere of silver, blue, and purple energy at the pelvis. Feel the potency of sexuality and the power of movement. Chant the name

Shaddai El Chai שדי אל חי, feeling the flowing of the inner sea. Contemplate the phrase, "I am pure from the pure".

Then spend time sensing the whole tree, feeling the vibration of the names at the heart of each sphere. Be aware of the interplay of the whole of the middle pillar and chant the names from Kether to Malkuth and Malkuth to Kether.

Conclude with the orphic phrases as a prayer or declaration:

> My home is in the starry heavens.
> I am the voice of memory.
> I am a kid fallen into milk.
> I am pure from the pure.
> I am a child of Earth.
> Behold my serpent shape.

This is the establishment of the middle pillar and we should give considerable time to building it up and letting it build a new sense of self, based on both our sense of our physical body and our energy field.

When it is stable and secure enough, then we can proceed to the circulation of the light. This we begin by contemplating the ouroboros, the world serpent, which swallows its tail and is an image of the eternal circulation of life and energy.

Then we contemplate the phrase, "I am Ophion hatching the egg", using the *PRDS* process to deepen our understanding. In Orphic cosmology, Ophion is the world serpent who incubates the world egg until it hatches. Here it stands for the process of working with the flow of the pillar to awaken the inner energies. When we have found some sense of flow and incubation, we centre ourselves in the middle pillar. Breathing in, we become one with the crown centre. Breathing out, we sense a sheet of brilliant diamond light pouring down the front of the body, down into the earth centre. Breathing in, feel the light sweeping round the back of the body, up to the crown. Breathing out, circulate the light down again. The flow of light and breath is continuous, even as is the breath. Do this for six to eight cycles and then begin again, but this time sending the light down the left side of the body and up the right again for six to eight cycles.

In the third exercise, as we breath in and out we centre in the earth centre of Malkuth then, as we breathe in, we visualize the diamond light spinning upwards in an anti-clockwise direction to Kether, wrapping the body like a mummy. On the outbreath, the light is sent down the middle pillar to Malkuth. On the next in-breath the light spins upwards again, and so on for six to eight cycles.

The final exercise is the fountain exercise and begins by centring in the earth centre as we breath in and out. Then, on an in-breath, feel the light being drawn up the centre of the middle pillar, penetrating each of the spheres and fusing with Kether. Then, on an out-breath, let the light cascade through our whole field like a fountain. Then, on an in-breath and out-breath, gather the light in the earth centre and repeat the fountain for six to eight cycles.

We conclude with the Orphic prayer:

> My home is in the starry heaven. (Kether)
> I am the voice of memory. (Da'ath)
> I am the kid fallen into milk. (Tiphareth)
> I am pure from the pure. (Yesod)
> I am a child of Earth. (Malkuth)
> I am Ophion hatching the egg.
> Behold my serpent shape.

Initially these exercises can feel clumsy but, with patience, they unify organically so that breath and light and felt sense come together with increasing potency and presence. The circulation of the light from top to bottom, front and back, left and right, the spiral and the fountain, combine together to create the hatching of Ophion's egg.

As we become more experienced, the stages of sensing the sphere of vitality, establishing the middle pillar, and working with the circulation of energy will flow effortlessly together and form a foundation for much of the later magical work. The prayer that accompanies it is both prayer and mnemonic. It is drawn from the Orphic mystery tradition and is worthy of contemplation in its own right, as it is concerned with the establishment of opposites, balance, and the mystery of the egg, the serpent, and creation.

The *PRDS* meditations

The next major training is the integration of the Tree of life so that it becomes a living form within us that mediates both the sense of our own soul and the sense of the universe within which we find ourselves. This we do through the practice of the *PRDS* meditation that was described in Part One. Day by day, we contemplate the sephiroth beginning with Malkuth and ending with Kether, so that they are not just words on the page but come to life within us.

The practice begins with the use of the phrase:

> Now do I descend into the inner sea whose waters rise and fall within my soul. Let the inner elements be subdued and still as I immerse myself within the living waters and emerging therefrom unfold from latent stress to potent image the sephirah of [the name of the sphere you are contemplating]

For example, beginning with Malkuth we would name it and then contemplate Malkuth in Assiah, the sphere of the elements of earth, air, fire, and water, bringing our attention to them. We start with the level of *peshat*, contemplating the qualities of these elements, the solidity of earth, the expansiveness and lightness of air, the fluidity of water, and the warmth of fire. As we deepen into our contemplation, we experience the symbolic nature of the elements and open into the formative world of Yetzirah, meeting the experience at the level of *remez*. Here we encounter the *aishim*, the angelic choir of Malkuth, the souls of fire, which may be visualised as sparks of fire within matter. As we deepen into this contemplation we are drawn into the experience of *derash*, the contemplative inquiry that brings us into the creative world of Beriah and the presence of Sandalphon, the prince of prayer, who may be visualised as a hooded form in autumnal colours making a gesture of prayer. As we commune with Sandalphon and enter into the presence of the archangel, we become still and receptive, awaiting the touch of *Adonai Ha Aretz*, the direct sense of the sovereignty of the living earth and the living body. Conclude by contemplating the virtue and the vice, seeing how attuning to one or the other alters the whole nature of the sephirah.

Use this method to explore the whole tree using this framework:

>Day 1 Malkuth
>Day 2 Yesod
>Day 3 Hod
>Day 4 Netzach
>Day 5 Tiphareth
>Day 6 Geburah
>Day 7 Gedulah
>Day 8 Da'at and the Abyss
>Day 9 Binah
>Day 10 Chockmah
>Day 11 Kether

The process of these meditations is like a spiral, so that each time we contemplate the sephirah we gain a little understanding and experience. The next time we meet it, we will discover greater depth and our associations with the tree will widen so that, for example, when we are aware of touching something solid it will remind us of earth, of Malkuth, or when we connect to a dream-like, imaginative experience, it will remind us of Yesod. These meditations should be pursued until we feel the tree is both an intrinsic part of us and of the universe.

Contemplation of the paths of the tree of life and death

When we have gained a sense of the sephiroth as living forms we turn next to the paths using the *PRDS* process to bring the sense of the paths to life. We begin with the phrase:

> Now do I descend into the inner sea whose waters rise and fall within my soul. Let the inner elements be subdued and still as I immerse myself within the living waters and emerging therefrom unfold from latent stress to potent image the thirty-second path between Malkuth and Yesod [varying this according to the path being worked on].

Then bring to mind the mandorla of the two spheres, envisaging them as two overlapping fields of intention or energy. Bring intention into the overlap; we may sense them as overlapping fields of colour so that, in the Malkuth-Yesod path, we would experience a field of shining rainbow-coloured blackness encountering a silver-blue greenness. Within that field we contemplate the Hebrew letter that denotes the principle of the path so that we start to embody the fusion. Next, using the magical imagination and contemplative faculties, we bring to mind the archangels of the sephiroth, in this case Sandalphon and Gabriel, and the contrast between the straight path and the shadow path—the emergence of life versus the path of entropy. We may make this experience more concrete by visualising a bridge of light in front of us with the two spheres and the archangels on either side of us, letting the sense of the fusion bring us across the bridge into the consciousness of the living path. Be aware that it is the act of fusion that enables us to cross the bridge so that we can now work with the mirror between Malkuth and Yesod; it is not that we cross from Malkuth to Yesod. Pathworking is an act of inclusion and participation in the mirroring dynamics of the tree. As our skill in this increases and as we clear the qliphothic forms that obstruct the paths, we will perceive the oneness of the tree and the simplicity of its reflective process.

Take each path in turn, from thirty-two to eleven, deepening into the act of the bridge crossing.

The effect of these meditations, prayers, and practices is to create a sense of ground and location within us, and to root us within the universe so that we can feel the connection between inner and outer worlds. We have embodied also the principle of balance and can feel when an aspect of the universe, whether within or without, is in balance or out of balance, and when the pattern of the Tree of life has been internalised. We have created a ground of stillness on which we stand, and the next step is to actively involve ourselves with the ongoing creative movement of the universe.

CHAPTER 11

The work of the Good Shepherd

The next stage of the training involves engaging with the image of the Shepherd King or Queen, or Good Shepherd. Here the focus is not so much on clarifying structure but on the active energy of compassion and dynamic prayer that goes out into the places of imbalance and brings them into balance. In Middle Kingdom and later Egyptian tombs a common scene is the image of the tomb owner hunting in the marshes.

The owner of the tomb is shown as larger than human, surrounded by the abundant life of the marsh, wielding a throwing stick, and accompanied by his hunting cat who is also catching birds. This is an image of subduing the chaotic energy of the marsh, and of the tomb owner acting as the sovereign who brings order and balance. The image of the hunting cat amplifies this theme as the cat is seen as a representative of Ra, who opposes the chaos serpent, Apep.

The gesture of practice in this phase of the work is to step forward and, through the use of the principles of will and love, to restore order and balance. A subtle feature of the image is the focus on the human form writ large, which points us to the centrality of the human form in this work.

One way of understanding this is that we stand in our living, human, imperfect form for the perfected human archetype, manifesting the potency of Amoun Ra, the hidden generative life, and thus being *asar un nefer* or "myself made beautiful". The work of this level is concerned with the communion between our ordinary sense of self and "myself made beautiful".

One of the earliest written versions of this communion is found in the Middle Kingdom Egyptian text, *The Dialogue of the Man and his Ba Soul*, in which a man who is struggling with difficulties in his life debates the nature of life and death with his *ba* soul. This very early dialogue shows us a depressed man longing for death while his soul speaks for the beauty and joy of life. The poem ends with the soul and the man making peace with each other by uniting the opposites of life and death thus:

> my soul said to me;
> Throw lamentations over the fence,
> My partner, my brother!
> May you make offerings upon the brazier
> and fight for life as you have said.
> Love me here and set aside the West,
> but still desire to reach the West
> When your body is laid in earth
> I will alight when you are weary,
> And we will reach harbour together. (Wilkinson, 2016, p. 122)

We find this sense of the human personality and the divine double echoing down through history and different religious systems. Charles M. Stang in his book, *The Divine Double*, charts the development of the human and divine twinning, finding it in Socrates' relationship with his daimon, in Plotinus' Neoplatonism, but also in the Gospel of Thomas where the main character is called Didymus or "Twin" and seen as the twin brother of Jesus. Particularly significant for our subject is the way in which the evangelist John the Beloved is seen also as a twin of Christ.

In this practice we step into the centre of space and time, becoming the axis of the universe, in effect entering into the Holy Mountain of the eighty-seventh psalm and aligning ourselves with that mountain. In this stage of the work this psalm becomes a principal source of contemplation, and each verse should be carefully considered using the *PRDS* process to unlock its secrets.

In the first verse of the psalm we are told, "He has set his foundation on the Holy Mountain". This asks us to make our foundation, our Yesod, the foundations of our psyche within the Holy Mountain. Holy mountains represent the vertical dimension of the spirit, and as we place our own foundation within it we align with that sense of verticality. We are next asked to contemplate the name *YHVH* and to become איש ו איש, one who is born out of *YHVH* within Zion, connected to the springs of deep life that arise here and to participate in the services of the Holy Temple.

In Hebrew the word for "fire" is אש. and there is a certain way in which the word for man, איש, denotes a fiery being who bears the creative letter *yod* within them; it is not gendered and simply means "a human being". In Hasidic tradition there is a quality called *hitlavahut*, which literally means "the fire of ecstasy" that arises from the conjunction of love and will, in which we catch fire and become a radiant sun of life. The phrase "a man from a man", איש ו איש, is hinting at this quality of radiant presence. This is reinforced by the conjunctive letter *vav* ו, the nail that joins things together, and, as the third letter of the divine name *YHVH*, represents the active energy of love and compassion.

The phrase איש ו איש, "a man and a man", points us to the communion with the angel of Tiphareth and the mirroring that happens between this deeper aspect of ourselves and the known self that emerges as we pierce the veil of the temple. This act of mirroring aligns Yesod and Tiphareth, Hod and Netzach, and Geburah and Gedulah, so that the image of ourselves and universe becomes illuminated, our mind aligns with will, and our feelings open into the deeper sense of love and compassion.

This process is linked to the capacity to work with the pool of images of Yesod, so that presence of the angel can be deeply felt within it, and the modification of the *tselem*, to reflect the image of the angel and the source of the angel in the supernals. The angel is, in a sense, a beam of light that shines through the prism of Da'ath, appearing in Tiphareth and reflecting into the waters of Yesod. In order to create and maintain this dialogue and communion we have to continually deepen our capacity for inner silence, but also allow ourselves to be increasingly directed by the presence of the angel.

The process of recognising being "a man and a man", and of being recognised by the divine presence as one who is born of Zion, takes us into the practice of prayer and communion with the presence of the deeper soul presenting itself as the Good Shepherd.

The extent to which we can align ourselves with the Good Shepherd of Tiphareth, Geburah and Gedulah, and the deeper sephiroth of the supernals, is the extent to which this communion becomes effective. This means that we must consider our *tselem*, our image of ourselves, and the extent to which this image is an icon—thus allowing through the light of the deeper self—or else an idol blocking or obstructing this light in a self-referential way. Psalm 87 is pointing us in the direction of working with the image so that it becomes lucid, so that we enter into the experience of איש ו איש. If we remain satisfied with the sense of just being a human, just as we are, then we encapsulate ourselves. The quality of reaching beyond ourselves towards the unknown other, in hope and openness, is what is needed here—this is *hitlavahut*, the fire of the inflamed heart.

Martin Buber describes this quality as:

> the inflaming, the ardor of ecstasy. It is the goblet of grace and the eternal key. A fiery sword guards the way to the Tree of Life. It scatters into sparks before the touch of hitlahavut whose light finger is more powerful than it. (Buber, 2015, p. 31)

This process of making our foundation in the Holy Mountain, contemplating *aish ve aish* and the inflaming the heart, brings about an awakening in which we become recognised as being born out of Zion. We are known by YHVH as the living image of the divine, able to draw on the springs of life and to participate in the work of the temple that involves contemplating the cities of the plain that represent the qliphothic energies.

The practice begins by the contemplation of ourselves firstly as *aish*, as a human being paying attention to our body, our mind, our feelings, and our known sense of self. Then sinking into the heart we direct our attention to the deeper sense of soul—the presence of stillness and guidance, which we touch on as the interior dialogue is interrupted. Holding our attention there, through concentration we touch on *vav*, the nail, that keeps us focused on the deeper sense of *aish*, the divine double or angel. Then we speak, inviting the angel to commune with us and to become one with us so that we are truly *aish ve aish*. We speak our thoughts, hopes, wishes, fears to this presence just as the ancient Egyptian did, communing with his *ba* soul as if speaking to an intimate friend. Our words may be extensive or simple—even a single word like "help" or "teach"—and, as with any conversation, we then pause and listen for the response, which may come from any direction. We may hear an inner voice speaking to us, or an image might arise in our mind, or we might feel touched in some way. We might also be aware of an outer event that feels like a response. This is the process that is described in the medieval work *The Sacred Magic of Abra-Melin the Mage* as "the knowledge and conversation of the Holy Guardian Angel", in which a very intense form of this process is carried out for eighteen months. We are not seeking that level of intensity, more a day-to-day communion that brings the everyday sense of self together with the presence of the angel of Tiphareth. This is a process that feels clumsy at first, and mechanical, but as our sense of the deeper self comes to life it is as if our heart catches fire and we gain the sense of *hitlavahut*, the burning heart, and the feeling of the angel descending into the pool of our psyche. It is this fire that clarifies and alchemises the pool of Yesod so that it becomes clearer and clearer, and as this happens our sense of stillness and communion with the angel increases. In this way we become the living image of YHVH and able to contemplate the Qliphoth and bless them.

This is the primary practice of this level of training, which is supported by the following secondary practices.

Morning meditation—the contemplation of the name

Following the salute to the sun in the morning, enter into stillness and spend some time establishing our sense of *aish ve aish*, as described above, reaching out to the angel, feeling the sense of longing and inviting the fire of *hitlavahut*. Pursue this for most of the morning session.

Then feel the form of your body and its central axis, and within you sense the name.

- the sphere of the י in the head,
- the sphere of ה in your upper chest
- the sphere of the ו in your lower torso
- the sphere of ה in your hips and legs
- the sphere of the ש in the centre of your body

Be aware that you are the living image of the divine. Feel the interplay of the spheres and chant the name *Yod Heh Shin Vav Heh*, יהשוה, letting the name radiate to all beings. Repeat this at noon and at intervals through the day.

Evening exercise

Pay attention to your body, feeling the impact of the day upon it, and then contemplate the phrase *aish ve aish*, turning your attention to the silent witnessing presence and offering the fruits of the day to it.

The body of light

As we develop our capacity to commune with the angel, we move on to the next stage of the work, which focuses on the tselem, our inner image, as we work on the development of the body of light.

Step 1 — manifesting the body

This begins with the relaxation exercise, which at its simplest is the tensing and relaxing of our muscles, beginning at our feet and working up to our head. However, at this level we take the exercise deeper, working with the opposites of tension and relaxation, of focus and stillness, of form and formlessness. As we enter more deeply into the experience of the body we begin the work of *hitlavahut*, of moving beyond the form and structure of the body into the silence and stillness of the unmanifest and longing for that deeper sense to manifest. In a sense, we sink into the bones of the body and the deeper self. The body is manifested in four stages, beginning with the body of power, then the body of love and the body of wisdom, and in the fourth and final stage of the body of light and prayer, the three forms are integrated together. In the first stage we use the mantric form,

> Now do I descend into the inner sea whose waters rise and fall within my soul. Let the inner elements be subdued and still as I immerse myself within the living waters and emerging therefrom unfold from latent stress to potent living image the body of light and power.

Then we sense or imagine a robed, hooded form arising around our physical body. The robe is green and contains the fire of spring and the sense of potency and power; we feel the fire of the Earth and the fire of the stars; a deep sense of creative will and life; a balanced, generative capacity that affects inner and outer worlds. We align with the image of the Eloquent Peasant, the man or woman of earth, and feel this energy and quality come to rest and balance in us. Practice this until each time we evoke the body there is this natural sense of power and life. At the end of the meditation, draw the form into latency and, on emerging from meditation, notice the effect on the sense of self and sense of world. Do this day by day until the sense of the body of power and life feels stable and strong. Then change the mantram's ending: "… to potent living image the body of light and love". A second form, clothed in deep purple or red and carrying the qualities of love and devotion, rises and clothes us. Reach out to the image of the Shepherd Sovereign and let that fiery sense of love and compassion become manifest. Let this form come together with the quality of power, and then rest in this imaginal body.

When that form is stable next align the body with the quality of wisdom, changing the end of the mantra to say: "… to potent living image the body of light and wisdom", and from within us a hooded form, robed in blue and bearing the qualities of wisdom and discernment, embraces us. The creative aspect of mind arises. We touch the longing for wisdom and immerse ourselves in this sense of contemplative clarity and feel its effect on the inner and outer environment. We reach to the image of the Silent Sage, the *Geru Maa*, to support the rising clarity. We feel this form connecting with the bodies of power and love, bringing with it a sense of clarity and deeper understanding. As before, we draw the form within us and emerge from meditation.

When that is stable we come to the last part of the creation of the body of light, using the mantram thus:

> Now do I descend into the inner sea whose waters rise and fall within my soul. Let the inner elements be subdued and still as I immerse myself within the living waters and emerging therefrom unfold from latent stress to potent image the body of light and prayer.

The form that arises now has the qualities of love, power, and wisdom, and holds the implicit shapes of the peasant, shepherd, and sage. Let it take whatever shape or colour feels natural.

Step 2—splitting the moon and stepping forward

The next step in the training of the body of light involves it coinciding with our physical body so that as we perform any inner act we let the body arise and clothe us. Once we are used to this practice, we learn to project the body of light much as Ezekiel does when he projects his awareness into Jerusalem. This exercise begins with us summoning the body of light and sitting in it, letting its qualities of power, love, and wisdom expand our sense of self. Then visualise the hooded form stepping forward to stand in front of us. Practise moving awareness between the seated and standing forms, tipping awareness forward so that the body of light becomes more present and our sense of sitting down is lessened. It can sometimes help to visualise the body of light becoming more substantial and our physical body more ethereal. Increasingly, bring attention into the senses of the body of light; see through its eyes, hear with its ears, smell and taste with it. Walk around the room and touch objects with it. When we feel stable in the body, we perform the practice of the qabalistic cross in it, noticing the difference between performing it physically.

Step 3—expanding the body of light

Spend some time contemplating this verse from the *Corpus Hermeticum*:

> Become higher than all heights and lower than all depths. Sense as one within yourself the entire creation: fire, water, the dry and the moist. Conceive yourself to be in all places at the same time: in earth, in the sea, in heaven; that you are not yet born, that you

are within the womb, that you are young, old, dead; that you are beyond death. Conceive all things at once: times, places, actions, qualities and quantities; then you can understand God. (Salaman, 2004, p. 57)

Let the body of light take shape around us, feeling its qualities of power, love, and wisdom upholding us, making us a true image and vehicle of the presence of the angel. Contemplate our nature as *aish ve aish* איש ו איש and invite the presence of the angel to descend into us. Trust the promptings of the angel and experiment—expand the body so that we are as large as the universe, become smaller than an atom, project the body through space and time. Let the body flow into different forms, entering into communion with other beings organic and inorganic.

This whole process is pendant to the key work of communion with the angel as the body of light is used at the direction of the angel. At the end of the process, we draw the body of light back into the physical form. It is a specialised application of the deep imagination and is a vehicle through which our consciousness can reach places, situations, and people who have become enmeshed in qliphothic energies. It is the practice that is sometimes called astral projection, though it is often described in overly dramatic ways. It is rare to completely lose a sense of the physical body in this practice—it remains as a background sensation while our main attention is operating in the body of light and its environment. The sense is of being extended and able to reach and relate to situations that would otherwise be unreachable.

This sense of extended self, both larger and more fluid than our normal sense, is at the service of the deeper presence of the angel of Tiphareth. It is a bridging form that enables the communion with the angel to be intensified. Its manifestation represents love in action, for the key motivation of the angel is a formulation that Aleister Crowley described as "love under will". The capacity of love gives us the motivation to respond to disturbance and pain, but will determines if it is our work to engage with it.

The eight-seventh psalm is our touchstone in this phase of the work and should be continually reflected on, so that we discern what it is to be born out of Zion, the nature of those who oppose her, to be a worker with the name *YHVH*, to be within the temple and connected to the spring of deep life that constantly refreshes the universe.

CHAPTER 12

The *Geru Maa*—the silent one

The third aspect of training is based upon the image of Maat that the Egyptians called the *Geru Maa*—the person who is infused with silence and is described as a tree who gives fruit and shade. This stage is connected to the supernal triad, Da'ath, and the abyss. Aleister Crowley called it the grade of the Hermit or the Master of the Temple and spoke of the trial of the abyss, which involves a deep act of surrender in which the aspirant surrenders all volition to the presence of the deeper soul, envisaged as Babalon the goddess, who sits in Binah receiving all and manifesting all. This moment of giving all, and surrendering all previous mastery, is the equivalent to what John of the Cross called "the dark night of the spirit"—it is the veil of the temple on a higher arc. It is a process of stripping away all that is known, including the presence of the angel, and often experienced as abandonment and a sense of having failed in your quest.

The temptation that is offered at this point is the repudiation of the gesture of surrender and to lean back into what has been known and achieved. This apparently innocuous act is called falling into the abyss and, instead of proceeding into the deep and non-dual waters of the supernal triangle, the tree is crowned with shadow images that are self-referential in nature and cut off the person relating to them from the ongoing life of the universe. Thus Kether, the crown of creation, which represents the point at which all beings come together in the most profound gesture of love and will becomes Thaumiel, the quarrelling heads, the primal division of will and rejection of love. Chockmah, the place of the deep will that directs all becomes Augiel, primal confusion, and Binah, the place of non-dual love and the revealing of the living forms of the universe, becomes Sathariel, the concealed and hidden. These forms of splitting, confusion, and hiddenness become the foundations of the psyche of the one who has refused the path of surrender. Yet they are not experienced directly as this—they most often present themselves as aspects of knowing. The splitting of Thaumiel is experienced as the solidity of the self and a sense of separation and independence that feels strong and contained. The confusion of Augiel presents itself as the freedom to create, unhindered by external limits, and the hiding of Sathariel as being the possessor of hidden knowledge and of being a secret adept. All this is a defence against the experience of the nakedness of the act of surrender within which the deeper aspects of the soul reveal themselves in the unreserved love that arises out of Binah, which delights in each and every form that arises; in the unstoppable will of Chockmah, which delights in the act of creation; and the completeness of the being of Kether.

Piercing the veil of the temple that prevents us from entering into communion with the angel of Tiphareth requires us to still the internal dialogue and to be able to receive a deeper aspect of ourselves. The same situation applies here, though at a much deeper level. The ancient Egyptian phrase *Geru Maa* holds the quality that is needed here—to be infused with silence so that the act of possession and accumulation is repudiated, and so all aspects of our nature become translucent. Here our will is subsumed in Will, our love in Love, and our being in Being.

The process of becoming *Geru Maa* begins as our work on the middle triangle of the Tree of Life becomes established enough for that aspect of our soul to start to relate to the supernal triangle. One of the ways in which this perception arises is the sense of non-dual mirroring in which there is no division between the source and the reflection—there is instantaneous union, no matter the distance between them. Here the clarity and focus of Geburah starts to be subordinated to the profound understanding of Binah; the expansive kindness of Gedulah is taken up into the generative will of Chockmah; and the active balancing energy of Tiphareth finds rest within the dynamic stillness of Kether. This transition is a genuine leap of faith, however it presents itself for the world of the supernals is, in a way, beyond the looking glass and everything is reversed so that understanding can look like stupidity (knowing nothing), wisdom like folly (willing nothing), and being like non-being (being nothing).

In the novel *Moonchild*, the figure of Simon Iff represents the one who is *Geru Maa* whilst his apprentice, Cyril Grey, is operating at the level of the Shepherd King. Recalling his dealings with the thing in the garden, Iff says of himself that his secret is:

> "To have assimilated all things so perfectly that there is no longer any possibility of struggle. To have destroyed the idea of duality. To have achieved Love and Will so that there is no object to Love or any aim for Will. To have killed desire at the root; to be one with every thing and with Nothing.
>
> "Look!" he went on, with a change in tone, "why does a man die when he is struck by lightning? Because he has a gate open to lightning; he insists on being an electrical substance by possessing the quality of resistance to the passage of the electric current. If we could diminish that resistance to zero, lightning would no longer take notice of him.
>
> "There are two ways of preventing a rise of temperature from the sun's heat. One is to oppose a shield of non-conducting and opaque material: that is Cyril's way, and at the best it is imperfect; some heat always gets through. The other way is to remove every particle of matter from the space which you wish to be cold; then there is nothing there to become hot; and that is the Way of the Tao." (Crowley, 1971, p. 53)

It is this way of the Tao which is pursued at this level of work and, as we can see from Crowley's example, this is a way of apparent paradox when looked on externally, but from within has its own pure logic and pattern. The transition place is often called "being a Babe of the Abyss"—an accurate and precise image that evokes the ancient Egyptian image of the child Harpocrates sitting in the midst of the blue lotus, holding his finger to his lips and making the sign of silence. The experience of being silent and being a babe who has no agency is right at the heart of this transition as the infusion of silence penetrates us to the core and our capacities to will, love, and be, are freed from entanglement. Similarly, our sense of our body becomes a door into mystery as the absence of volition and relating opens us to the simple mystery of just being.

One of the hints that Crowley leaves for us in working with this transition is that we should take the oath of the abyss, as follows:

> I ...., a member of the Body of God, hereby bind myself on behalf of the whole Universe, even as we are now physically bound unto the cross of suffering,
> 2 that I will lead a pure life as a devoted servant of the order
> 3 that I will understand all things
> 4 that I will love all things
> 5 that I will perform all things and endure all things
> 6 that I will continue in the Knowledge and Conversation of my Holy Guardian Angel
> 7 that I will work without attachment
> 8 that I will work in Truth
> 9 that I will rely only upon myself
> 10 that I will regard every phenomenon as a particular dealing of God with my Soul. And if I fail therein my pyramid be profaned and the Eye closed to me. (Prescott-Steed, 2019, p. 176)

He, then, with his trademark sense of humour, goes on to suggest that anyone who takes this oath can then regard themselves as a Master of the Temple and one of the secret adepts that run the universe, a joke that has been responsible for many an alienated teenager taking refuge in an inflated sense of self.

However, properly contemplated, this oath can give us a sense of direction when we contemplate this profound transition. The oath has ten clauses, each of which applies to one of the sephiroth. What is common to them all is an intention to identify with the whole nature of the universe—thus, the first part, where we declare ourselves to be a member of the body of God working on behalf of the universe to solve the mystery of suffering. The second part proclaims our intention to align our will with that intention, so that nothing else signifies. The remaining clauses amplify our personal Tree of Life, so as to align it with the universal tree. The two final parts of the oath are worthy of particular notice—reliance only upon oneself, and regarding every phenomenon as a particular dealing of God with our soul. These are, of course, contradictions, and following both of them will lead us into the unknowing mystery of Da'ath. Similarly, the other aspects of the oath lead us into the mystery of identifying with all and identifying with nothing. For example, to understand all is to deconstruct all, including the one who is doing the understanding; to love all and to perform and endure all likewise takes us into the mystery of identification with the one and all. There is a sting in the tail of this oath in that, if we do not allow it to undermine our sense of known self, it can cause massive inflation in which the egoic sense of "I" tries to eat the universe.

Let's explore the implications of working with these two principles of relying only on oneself and on regarding every phenomenon as a particular dealing by God with your soul. If these are properly applied, then the rest of the clauses of the oath fall into line. One of the effects of contemplating them is that they bring out of hiding all the places of inflation where we take ourselves too seriously. Relying on ourselves takes away our props, and regarding every phenomenon as a particular act of God intensifies our relationship to the present moment and demands that we exclude nothing from our direct experience.

To regard every experience that presents itself as a particular dealing of God with my soul demands that we have both some sense of our soul and of divinity. Crowley wisely does not define this territory but, in indicating the categories of soul and God and the relationship between them, locates our attention firmly in this ground, challenging the inertia and unconsciousness of the shadow Malkuth. If we consider both the nature of our souls and the nature of our God and what happens between them, our sense both of our own subjective universe and of the objective universe starts to sharpen and awaken. One of the discoveries that is made in this process is how much of our experience is occluded by habit; much of this occlusion will have been diminished by the previous two levels of training, but the work of this level is to make visible and deal with the remnants of unconsciousness that remain as subtle veils. One of the genuine difficulties in carrying out this practice is in sustaining awareness. We will find that it is very tiring, and there are deep-rooted tendencies to succumb to the inertia of Malkuth. The counter to this is the intensity and fire of *hitlavahut*, from the previous training, and the development of an attitude of deepening curiosity about our waking and even our sleeping experience. A very common experience in this stage is the discovery of how much of it is manipulated through the subliminal images that arise automatically out of Yesod in response to inner and outer events. For example, let us say we buy something in a shop and are cheated in some way. The oath would ask us to contemplate the experience of being cheated as a particular dealing of God with our soul, potentially opening even the experience of being cheated into a profound experience—a sense of depth and unknown possibility accompanied by the particular silence of the energy of the beginning. Initially we enter that field of new possibility, but what may also arise, from the storehouse of images found in Yesod, are past images of having been cheated. If we can allow these arising experiences to be seen also as particular dealings of God with our soul, the sense of depth and new possibility deepens, but if we fail to hold it in this way and become lost in the images we find ourselves succumbing to the automatism of Yesod and may often just replay old grievances and interpret the current experience as a repetition of past unfairness. Here, the second aspect of relying on yourself, which feels like the opposite of the previous injunction, is intended to interrupt the automatism of the habits and reflexes we find in Yesod. In the "particular dealing" clause we are addressing the principle of love as we embrace all experience, whereas in the clause "relying on oneself" we are working with will. If we pursue the next clauses of the oath, we find three principles of working with truth; working without attachment and continuing in the knowledge and conversation of the Holy Guardian Angel. Working with truth and, therefore, working with falsehood within us and in the universe, is again a work of the will as we face up to the actual operation of our will and, in so doing, own up to both who we are and how the universe is. Similarly, working without attachment frees our capacity to work with love and shows us ways in which this capacity is bound or free within us. Continuing with the work of the knowledge and conversation of the Holy Guardian Angel, begun in the prior training, now has a very particular focus as the angel assists us to keep the will focused on the contemplation of silence and love, on the resolution of opposites that is the hallmark of this stage. As such, the sense of the angel as a dynamic presence will often be absent as the active sense of other would undermine both the deepening silence and the conjunction of opposites. This we can often experience as being abandoned by the angel, and our only refuge is the contemplation of this too as a particular dealing of God with our soul.

As the process deepens, we increasingly become identified with the process of the universe so that the next clauses of performing all and enduring all universalises the principle of will, and the clause of loving all universalises love. This principle of universalising continues in the clauses of understanding all, which deepens the principle of love into the non-dual and of being the pure servant so that our will serves the all. The final clause of being a member of the body of God, binding ourselves on behalf of the whole universe, affirms our identity with the divine and the universe. These clauses are contemplation points, which we return to again and again, deepening our sense of identity and our capacity to work with love and will. The work of becoming the silent one is a work of undoing, hence Crowley's definition of this stage of being a Babe of the Abyss. This has a precise meaning, it is not simply being mystically reborn (an experience that may happen at various places on the Tree of Life); this is specifically being the babe who floats on the water of the beginning making the sign of silence.

Pharaoh Iuput as Horus the Child, adapted from faience plaque—
Twenty-Third Dynasty

The image above of Pharaoh Iupet shows us the babe seated on the lotus, keeping silent and contemplating the mystery of the abysmal waters. This is the essential gesture of this stage of practice; we must be the silent child placed in the major point of discontinuity and transition, the unknown place. This keeps our will focused on mystery and working with love to resolve the whole series of opposites that we have made accommodation with to create a sense of sense of self and universe that we can bear to live with. The silence of the child and the child's capacity to rest within the lotus is the silence that the *Geru Maa* is suffused with; to be the child is to become new again to allow the transformative power of the lotus to dissolve and reform us.

Crowley juxtaposes the oath with an instruction on working with what he calls "the magical memory", in which we learn to turn our consciousness backwards. This parallels the journey of the sun found in the New Kingdom Netherworld books in which, at sunset, Ra is envisaged as an old man who, as he passes through the hours of the night, becomes younger and younger, finally being reborn at sunrise as the infant sun of the new day. This practice involves us following our memory backwards, initially for just a few moments but, with practice, travelling backwards through our life assimilating the causes and conditions that have brought us to this present moment. This apparently simple practice of moving backwards through our life enables the dissolving of the fixed forms of self and allows the free energy released by that to emerge in a new way. It is not an easy practice however, and we should begin by taking a small period of time (say, five minutes) and move backwards through it. Initially the mind will just jump to the beginning of the five minutes and so we must focus, step by step, on the events of those five minutes using our magical imagination and will to gain an embodied experience of reversing time. When that felt sense is definite and perceptible then we may work with longer and longer periods of time.

Another way of approaching this is to sit in silence and to be aware of all of the universal forces that are in action enabling us to sit here, from gravity, the motion of the Moon around the Earth, the Earth around the Sun, the movement of the Milky Way around the galactic core; then the internal forces, our skeleton, our bodily systems that enable us to sit here, our psychology and history that has interested us in this subject and which has led to us reading this book and trying out the practice. Having got a sense of the conjunction of inner and outer elements responsible for us just sitting here, we then isolate a key element and contemplate it. For example, we consider our will to sit here silently and motionless and investigate the immediate cause of this will. Having discovered this we may pursue the matter more deeply—what enables this cause to come into being?—until we enter into a contemplation of our whole relationship with will at all its levels. Similarly, we may consider our attraction to doing this practice and contemplate the quality of love that caused us to do this. Having discovered the immediate cause of our love for this, we then proceed to contemplate the root of the quality of love within us, contemplating it at all its levels from the non-dual love of Binah to, say, the love of chocolate. These contemplations, similar to the reversal method, undermine our fixed sense of self and universe and free our inner capacities.

This has parallels with the Buddhist formula from the Heart Sutra: "Emptiness is form, form is emptiness", in which we are invited to consider not just the emptiness of all existent forms but also to contemplate the nature of the form that arises from emptiness. It is this continual contemplation of opposites and the surrender to what happens in the act of juxtaposition that provides the thrust that enables us to cross the abyss and begin to operate in non-dual awareness. This then brings about the infusion of all our parts with silence and enables us to operate as the tree in the midst of the garden, producing fruit and offering shade as a direct consequence of our being.

The principal practice, however, is a way of being that Crowley, in *Moonchild*, has Simon Iff describe as "the way of the Tao"—this he derives from the *Tao Te Ching* by Lao Tze. This contemplative poem begins thus:

> Tao called Tao is not Tao.
> Names can name no lasting name.
> Nameless: the origin of heaven and earth.
> Naming: the mother of ten thousand things.
>
> Empty of desire, perceive mystery.
> Filled with desire, perceive manifestations.
> These have the same source, but different names.
> Call them both deep—
>   Deep and then again deep:
>
> The gateway to all mystery. (Addis & Lombardo, 1993, p. 2)

The dominance of the Good Shepherd archetype in Western thought, as a result of Jesus's embodiment of that form, has overshadowed this level of the Silent Sage and it was one of Crowley's particular gifts to the tradition that he included the Taoist teachings of the *Tao Te Ching* and the *I Ching* within the higher echelons of the practice of the Qabalah. Tao is a very similar idea to that of Maat as it represents the flow or movement of the universe and aligning with it involves entering into communion with a silence that has movement and direction but cannot be defined. The poem, however, points at the way in which the named arises from the unnameable; how light arises from darkness; how the particular arises from the universal. Working with the clauses of the oath of the abyss and the magical memory must be done from this intention as we return again and again into the living silence that underlies speech and action. The *Geru Maa* works with what could be described as the empty hand; that is to say, they work creatively with whatever comes to hand, seeing it as the manifestation of the Tao or Maat and as an aspect of the oath of the abyss.

There are 3 interlocking dimensions to this level of the training:

1. The way of the Tao.
2. The practice of reversal, contemplating the backwards movement of time.
3. Contemplating the oath of the abyss.

The effect of all three is to free the will from its entanglements and to increasingly align it with the flow of the Tao. Similarly, the quality of love becomes universal and free of attachments and our sense of identity also expands into identity with the soul of the universe. Put like this, it may sound like good news, but the actual experience is one of continual loss as the known sense of self and world dissolves and we move from a world of stable structures to one of continual interacting living processes. This sense of loss and stripping away continues so that even the sense of this living stillness itself and the presence of the angel who has been our guide passes away. In his poem *Liber Liberi vel Lapidus Lazuli* Crowley tells us:

> Not by memory, nor by imagination, nor by prayer, nor by fasting, nor by scourging, nor by drugs, nor by ritual nor by meditation; only by passive love shall he avail. (Crowley, 2015, p. 158)

This points us squarely into the ways in which will and love operate in this stage; the will is suspended and surrendered, pointing into the unknown, while love is awake and present in the process of dissolution. The verse shows the challenge of this stage and the experience of being a Babe of the Abyss; there is nothing to be done but offer love and will into the mystery.

This process is sometimes accompanied by key visions that govern the later work; these relate to the fundamental work of transformation. Crowley had a simple-sounding vision of the universe as being "nothingness with twinkles", which gave him a profound understanding of the body of Nuit and the experience of the $0 = 2$ equation so that all the rest of his work was spent articulating it. Ernest Butler's equivalent experience was an encounter with the risen Christ who showed him the omnipresence of love. For Tom Oloman, it was the experience of a depth of silence suffused with love. For me, it was the experience of the rising of an inner moon, very like Lucius Apuleius's experience of the rising of Isis over the gulf of Corinth, which revealed the conjunction of the universal goddess with a particular immediate form (Apuleius, 2011, p. 250). Typically, there is a memory of something; a phrase or image, but the true experience is the profound stillness, surrender, and sense of expansion into the universe. The concrete details that remain become the focus for work that follows; in Ernest Butler's case, the practice of a particular form of esoteric Christianity; for Tom Oloman, the practice of contemplative stillness; in mine, the exploration of the relationship between icons and idols and the ways in which the Yesodic foundations of life either free or bind. For Crowley, the exploration of what it means to be a star in a universe of stars, which he explored both in terms of the collective soul and human psychology.

In contemporary magical practice having this experience is sometimes believed to convey status; this could not be further from the truth of the experience. All experiences inform us and direct our later work and life, but we remain always a work in progress. There is a certain inevitable linearity in the three trainings; we have to acquire the solidity, ground, and commitment to truth of the Eloquent Peasant before we can practise the redemptive work of the Good Shepherd, and we must gain skill in embodying the shepherd before we can step into the non-dual waters of the Silent Sage. However, having gained experience of these three aspects of ourselves we will now find that our work will move through these three forms according to the flow of the Tao arising out of the supernal spheres. At times then, we may find ourselves concentrating on beginning aspects of the training of the stage of the eloquent peasant, such as the relaxation exercises, finding new depth and possibility in them. We are in the hands of the deeper presence that manifests through Da'ath into the spheres of dualistic life.

PART 3

THE PRACTICE OF TRANSFORMING THE QLIPHOTH

CHAPTER 13

The art of mirroring

The effect of the training is to prepare us to work with the practice of transformation of the distorted and lost forms and energies. It is necessary here to look at how distortion and separation happen. The impulse to split or move out of relationship is at the heart of the Qliphoth. The Qabalah gives us the image of the universe as being a Tree of Life in which each part connects to each other part and in which each mirrors each. Thus, the great world of the universe and the small world of the individual human soul mirror each other in that the pattern described by the Tree of Life is the foundation pattern of each. The teaching takes this further, however, in a simple-sounding statement: "There is a tree in every sephirah". Hence, we may contemplate Yesod of Geburah. This may give us a sense of the foundation or underpinning of the martial energy of will; and we may contrast this by contemplating Geburah of Yesod, which may illuminate how our will and clarity influences our use of our life energy, and may reveal the image of will that is held there. Using the *PRDS* contemplative method in this way enables us to penetrate the fractal and mirroring dynamic that is both our deeper nature and the deeper nature of the universe. But if we take the principle just one step further and, say, contemplate the sphere of Tiphareth of Yesod of Geburah, now we find ourselves touching the intention that causes balance within the foundations of will. Taking yet another step, we may contemplate Yesod of Tiphareth of Yesod of Geburah and find ourselves in relationship with the foundation of that balancing presence that works at the foundations of clarity and will. If we are too literal about this, we can end up with nightmarishly complex cognitive diagrams, but what is shown in this process is the way in which the pattern of the sephiroth replicates itself at all levels. Intrinsic to this process is the way in which the process of reflection creates true images or distorted images.

In the same way that cell division can produce cells that are exact copies or distortions and—for example—generate cancerous cells that act in a self-referential way and are not aligned with the health of the larger organism, so too can forms be generated within us and within the universe which do likewise. The profoundly interconnected nature of the universe shown to us via the fractal nature of the tree demonstrates the way in which a breakdown of mirroring in any part of the universe disturbs and affects the whole. Thus, when Simon Iff absorbs the thing in the garden there is the sense of the universe being restored to balance. Each part of the universe is a fractal of that universe. If it is not acting as a true copy of the living universe then it is mirroring or reflecting a distortion, which unbalances the whole. The "Thing in the Garden" is generated through the will to separate and is a denial, therefore, of the conjunction of the unity of love and will that binds the Tree of Life at all its levels together. At the heart of this process is the principle that we are the living images of the divine and thus possess the generative capacity to create life. It is therefore the function of any created being, built in the image of its creator, to also be generative and to reach homeostasis, finding a way of enabling its continued existence and growth. If the creation is based upon and connected to the Tree of Life in balanced form, then its life and growth is supported by the whole structure of the tree and, in particular, by the supernal triangle. This means that the form is connected to the non-dual presence of Kether; its seed of will is connected to the non-dual willing of Chockmah; and its archetypal form generated out of the non-dual love of Binah. In that case the movement into the activity of the worlds of duality is supported by this deep-rootedness, so that the growth and expansion of Gedulah, and the discipline and clarity of Geburah, find balance in Tiphareth, which then multiplies, generating energies and forms through Netzach and Hod that enable the possibility of multi-level expression before coming into full expression and activity in Malkuth.

If, however, this created form is not linked to the supernals in that it arises out of some version of the will to separation through, the operation of *chatah* (reactive ignorance), *pesha* (wilful narcissism), or *avon* (iniquity, conscious delight in evil), then it cannot root in the non-dual and will instead be arising out of the shadow tree in the abyss whose roots are separation, confusion of will, and hiding. The supernal triangle is the place where free energy arises from the unmanifest life of the universe which, as the word implies, we cannot directly know, but hints of its nature are given in the three veils of *ain soph aur* ("the endless light"), *ain soph* ("the endless"), and *ain* ("no thing"). It is our roots within this that continually refresh the life of the tree but, if we are not rooted here, then in order to sustain life then we must find other sources of life to feed on.

In essence, some form of parasitism is needed, the robbing of Peter to pay Paul. It has to be parasitism rather than symbiosis as, for the qliphothic form to subsist, it must maintain a sense of separation from the Tree of Life else it will be drawn into the dynamics of the tree, which will start to dissolve its separated status. It is this mechanism that is responsible for many physical disorders but can be most intimately seen in the split off portions of our psyche, which often maintain themselves by working against our greater sense of health and wellbeing. This is most visible in addictive behaviours and reaches its apogee in multiple personality disorder, in which there is no consistent centre in our psyche but rather a number of often quite different personalities struggling for dominance.

These internal qliphothic forms can be seen also in the external universe wherever there is an active will that is not aligned with the deep movement coming from the unmanifest and the supernals. The Qabalah maintains that the capacity to align with the Qliphoth is found at all levels of the tree up to Da'ath, which means that when we contemplate this problem we are not simply looking at our own behaviour and that of the world around us but the underpinnings of the psychic world of Yetzirah, and the creative world of Briah. This brings into view a landscape that involves working with both subtle energies and formed subtle beings as well as working with the creative energies that work within the manifest universe.

This opens up the whole territory of unquiet spirits, ancestral curses, as well as the worlds of archangels and archdemons that is normally the go-to place when we first start thinking about ideas like exorcism. In most popular accounts of this work, the image is of the exorcist banishing the disturbed being and sending it somewhere else—if a ghost, it is sent on to the afterlife; if a demon, to hell. This popular account is the opposite of the work, which is an act of inclusion and alchemical transformation rather than expulsion.

There are some aspects of the popular accounts that correspond to truth, principally the idea that things are in the wrong place and need to be sent to the place that is their true home, but this cannot be accomplished by an act of violence and exclusion. It is through creating connection with the split form, drawing it into relationship with our hearts and, through us, into relation with the multi-levelled web of relationship that is the Tree of Life that it finds its true home. In Christian tradition, the story of the prodigal son's return applies here.

In order to identify the way in which the mirroring process has become disturbed we need to consider the way in which the creative process operates in us as we exercise our will and imagination, creating either icons that transmit light, or idols that cast shadows and imprison.

One of the great teachers of this art of generating icons was the twentieth century qabalist Colette Aboulker Muscat who lived and worked in Jerusalem. To work with her one had to go to a suburb of west Jerusalem, pass through a blue gate and enter into a long narrow room on Saturday nights. She taught a form of Qabalah that worked with will, body, and imagination and relied upon simple-seeming, very swift meditations that implanted luminous images within us, combined with a particular way of sitting upright and breathing. They were intended to give a creative shock to our systems and implant seeds of new life within us. Her style of Qabalah came from an old Sephardic school of Qabalah, from Isaac the Blind and Jacob ben Shoshet from Provence. It worked with the divine injunction from Genesis:

Yehi or—Let there be light! יהי אור

This key phrase indicates the main feature of the path. *Yehi*, "Let there be!", is the deep will that initiates new life. *Or* is the luminous image or *tselem*, which focuses the will into substance.

THE ART OF MIRRORING   153

Just before her death at the age of ninety-four, in one of the Saturday night meetings, in addition to taking us through a series of meditations, she spoke a phrase in Hebrew:

The bone points to itself. העצם מצביע אל עצמן

She said that this phrase contained the heart of her teachings.

This poetic phrase is intended to focus our attention on the process of the manifestation of will; it looks at the interplay of the ideas of bone and flesh and the act of mirroring.

- The *bone otsem* עצם is the centre or organizing centre. Its deeper meaning in Hebrew is essence. It is related to the qabalistic world of Atziluth, the sphere of the divine. It is the root of whatever we are contemplating.
- *Points mTzbia* מצביע. This is the word of intention and direction—the will that arises out of the essence or deep organizing structure. It is related to the qabalistic world of Briah, the world of creation.
- *To al* אל. This is the word of conjunction, of coming together, and is related to the qabalistic world of Yetzirah or formation; the living image that arises in response to will.
- *Itself otsemen* עצמן. This represents appearance or flesh and is related to the qabalistic world of Assiah or the world of action; it is the process of embodiment and manifestation. It is the same word as "bone" with the addition of an extra letter.

If we take the contemplation a bit deeper and look at the Hebrew letters in the words we may discover further levels of meaning. The phrase begins with the letter *heh*, which simply means "the", but also one of its important correlations is with the idea of the divine breath, revelation, and light; it is the principal mother letter in the divine name *YHVH* יהוה; it is the marker of the work, the breath hovering over the waters.

The next letter, which begins the word *otsem* עצם is the *ayin* ע, "the eye", that perceives light, pointing us to the centrality of both perception and light. The next letter is *tzaddi*, "the fishhook", צ, the first letter of the word *tsaddik*, "the righteous one" who descends into the depths to transform the Qliphoth. As we have seen, this letter is said also to be bowing in prayer and humility. The final letter is *mem* final ם "water". It is in its closed form, which suggests a sealed and contained lake or sea.

If we put these ideas together, we have the sense of the contemplative responding to the divine breath by taking on the image of the righteous one, bowing in humility and prayer and contemplating the deep waters of Yesod and Binah.

The next word, "points" מצביע begins with the letter *mem* מ again but here the *mem* is opened and the waters are flowing; next, *tzaddi* צ the righteous fisher, and then *beit* ב, the archetypal house and temple; *yod* י, the archetype of will and direction, and concluding with *ayin* ע, "the eye". Here we are given the image of the righteous one in the temple, contemplating the flowing river and aligning with the divine will, which manifests in vision.

The third word "to" is the word of conjunction *al* אל. *Aleph* א, "the ox", represents the energy of creation. *Lamed* ל, "the oxgoad", represents the direction of that energy. Together they suggest the image of ploughing and of new life emerging as sprouting grain or, alternatively, the image of an ox turning a waterwheel and irrigating the land, which gives rise to new growth. Here we see in this work of formation the living image emerging in response to the will.

The fourth and final word, "itself" עצמן is the word of embodiment and becoming: the living image coagulated and expressing the will. In this we see the conjunction of the eye, *ayin* ע, the fisher *tzaddi* צ, and sea *mem* מ, which ends in the appearance of the fish *nun* ן, the fruit of the sea. This is a complete process beginning with the vision in the mind's eye being caught and landed as the fish is drawn from the sea.

This process of creation is something we are engaged with at all times, albeit mostly unconsciously, and the purpose of this phrase is to help us engage with the steps of the process so that we can work with it, so that the forms that we create are forms of light and holiness rather than forms of darkness and chaos. The interplay of essence and appearance, *otsem* and *otsemen*, suggests to us that within all forms there is an essence that is holy and true—a spark of light that has become exiled within the qliphothic shell that encloses it. As we have seen, when we apply the *PRDS* process to the Tree of Life, if the Tree of Death quality of the particular sephirah is active, then even archangels and god-names become founts of darkness rather than light. Nonetheless the true archetypes remain and, if we return to the essence, all can be remade.

We can discover more about this process if we return to the prophet Ezekiel's vision of the valley of dry bones (Ezekiel 37: 1-14). Ezekiel breathing over the bones is the letter *heh* ה; the contemplation of the bones is עצם; the bones coming together is מצביע; acquiring sinew and flesh is אל; and being placed in their own land is עצמן.

The priest and prophet Eziekiel has been through a process in which he been given a vision of the divine seated on the throne of the holy living creatures, the *chaiot ha qadesh*, the angels of Kether; and a vision of the destruction and restoration of the Temple. Here he is shown how to work with old, wounded situations, in order to restore them. He must go into a wasteland, a lifeless place, and find a hidden valley filled with bones—an off-putting and eerie place—and bring the divine breath to them, bring them to life, in that process listening to the wound that brought about their sense of death and disintegration. He must restore them, putting them back in their own true place, a process that involves the opening of graves. This he can only do because he is a servant of the temple and the holy living one, and the creative process that he sets into being comes out of his alignment with the divine breath.

However, this process, which is restorative and healing when aligned, is the same process that enables the inner dialogue to continue to manifest qliphothic forms. The key place is the starting point; if the starting point is the surrender to the divine breath then the ensuing process will reflect that. If, instead, the starting point is one of anger, or need for revenge, or any one of the qliphothic seeds, then what will emerge will be disturbed and poisonous.

This process of going into the valley of bones must begin with ourselves, so we must descend into the depths of our own soul, finding the places of unconscious resistance, willed separation, and the delight in iniquity in ourselves. The deep work here involves the realigning of the will, so as to enable the divine will to express itself through us in its fullness. That will in us is not whole, but splintered into many wills, each attached to an image or *tselem*, and each a copy of the divine *tselem* possessing the creative power of the whole. This is the field of idols, the lost and broken images that enthrone themselves continually. As we start to realign, these lost forms become available in a new way, but in order for that to happen they must be re-embraced and deeply known. There must be a descent as well as an ascent—the marriage in darkness as well as the sacred hierogamy in the light.

This is the descent into the depths to embrace the mystery of the soiled garments, descending through the murky ignorance of *chat'ah* or simple unconscious ignorance, through the chosen separation of *pesha*, in which there are deeper and deeper layers of conscious choice and active willing, to the depths of *avon*, in which the commitment to darkness is made and the will is sealed to iniquity.

At the heart of the work also is the experience of the body as the living image of the divine, the *tselem* of tselems. Engaging the will and imagination with our embodied presence in this way involves us in a process of dissolving the idols that hold both those images in place and generating fresh icons that seed ourselves and the world with new possibilities.

The body and the senses then are both a chalice and a doorway and act as a living vessel: Ezekiel's cup, in which the bones of holiness are gathered, and that generates icons in response to the movement of the will, and which continually manifests as a fountain of life, now bright, now dark, now like fire, now water. The contemplative discipline of meditation from the Eloquent Peasant training enables the act of attunement, but the prayer of the Good Shepherd is the active expression that brings the new *tselem*—the body of light—into operation. This, in turn, is held within the stillness of the *Geru Maa* as we make the act of descent, which begins with ourselves and then involves the descent into the collective field of human and planetary life. Our practice with the body of light will have helped us work with our will and imagination so as to connect us with these territories and begin the active work of rectification.

The process of creation of qliphotic forms in the collective can be seen in the antecedents of the Bosnian war. In 1992, the BBC broadcast a programme just before the war broke out that concerned Radovan Karadzic, then regarded as an example of the new Eastern European leaders who were bringing Eastern Europe into the light of democracy following the collapse of the Soviet Union. On the face of it, the programme was interesting and uncontroversial, but there was a moment in it that sends shivers up the spine. It showed Radovan and his friends up a mountain singing old Serbian folk songs that referred to the conquest of Serbia by the Ottoman Turks, and proclaiming that the white eagle of Serbia will rise again to drive out the Turk. It evoked a sense of the imminence of something terrible, in an inexplicable way, given that all that was been shown were some middle-aged folk singers. As history demonstrated, the Serbs did indeed try to drive out the Turks, ethnically cleansing Bosnian Muslims and committing many atrocities; literally the white eagle of Serbia was evoked into being and became an obsessing image for many thousands of people, influencing them to perform acts of horror and cruelty.

Incidents like this remind us that we all possess the creative will that can say *yehi or*, and as we project this will we gather around us a field of images that either act as icons and allow the deeper will of the divine to shine through the form, or, out of fear and the turning or bending of the will, become idols, qliphothic shells that turn on their own axis and obscure and lock up the originating spark. These shells are unstable fragments needing continual defence and assertion in order to maintain their integrity. They function as vortices, continually drawing more and more substance towards themselves. In this instance an ancient wound and resentment found in the collective history of the Serbs is revived by the will of politicians and military officers; speeches are made which revive these old images of resentment and rage in the population at large, and these qliphothic vortices infest a whole population that then enacts the will of the idolatrous images and carries out acts of horror. It is easy to demonise the people that carry out acts like this but, in this work, it is axiomatic that within even the most awful shapes of darkness there is a lost spark of light that has become trapped within the qliphothic shell.

The bone teachings and Ezekiel's vision give us a loose contemplative framework for determining the origin and the operation of the Qliphoth and the breakdown of the mirroring process of the tree. The bone, *otsem* עצם, gives us the root of the matter, *mtzbia* מצביע, "the pointing", "the vector", arising out of that root *al* אל, the conjunction of image and will that is behind the disturbance and the appearance *otsemen* עצמן, the embodied situation. Each of these points are potentially beginning points but, generally speaking, it is the conjunct image or idol that both distorts will and action which is the main focus of the work. For example, looking back to the world of Radovan Karodicz, the root energy we might see as the sense of belonging and pride at being Serbian, which is given in the image of the white eagle of Serbia. This is an image that is connected with what we might describe as "Christoslavism", the sense of the Slavic people as a holy Christian nation. This image could take anyone contemplating it into a communion with their ancestral roots and, through that, into a sense of the love of Christ for all beings. However, here it is linked to the defeat of the Serbs by the Ottoman Empire and to an idea that in order for the Serbs to fulfil their spiritual destiny they must drive out the Turk. Within the bones of this issue is a potentially powerful spiritual truth, which would bring about a sense of the holiness of all and a particular appreciation of the way that holiness has manifested in the Serbian people. This is, however, rejected in favour of organising around a sense of betrayal by the demonic other—the Muslim Bosnian. An impulse of ancient rage arises that translates itself into images of friends and neighbours transforming into alien and dangerous beings. This in turn justifies behaving towards them as if they were the enemy who must be suppressed and destroyed at all costs. These images then become the justification for the releasing of all manner of desires and rage and hence the horror of the Bosnian War. Despite this awful event, the possibility of rectification and the redemption of the image of the white eagle and the collective soul of the Serbian people remains a possibility, as it does for all peoples and their ancestral wounds if we work with them so as to connect them with essence of holiness. In the bones of the matter, we find the white eagle of Serbia linked with the white eagle of John the Evangelist, the living image of the Christ and whom, with Christ, believes in the holiness of all beings.

CHAPTER 14

The principal practice

In a certain sense, all of the book thus far has been context and preparation for this fundamental practice that now moves into centre stage and which is linked to the image of the true human being. It is a surprisingly simple practice of becoming present and available, opening our senses inwardly and outwardly, and embracing our body of light.

The key steps are these:

- We align our sense of self with the sacred and become a living icon of the divine light.
- We connect to the flow of the universe, both inner and outer.
- We notice disturbance and link to it.
- We draw the disturbance into our heart and into the living image of the divine within us.
- We hold it in relationship, digesting the disturbance and inviting in the principle of reconciliation until there is a sense of peace and both we and the universe return to a sense of balance.
- We offer that sense of peace and balance into the universe.

We will consider a number of ways in which this practice can be more concrete.

The practice of the healing name

The focus is on the practice of the name *YHShVH* יהשוה, seeing oneself as a servant and transmitter of the life and will of the healing name. In invoking the body of light, the letters of the name manifest in crystal white light vertically:

- The sphere of the *shin* ש is above the head.
- The sphere of the י in the head.
- The sphere of ה in the upper chest.
- The sphere of the ו in the lower torso.
- The sphere of ה in the hips and legs.

This central axis aligns us with the deep will of the universe and establishes us as the *tselem*, the living image of the name, by inviting the *shin* to descend into the heart. As *shin* descends, the letters of the name manifest horizontally. On our right side, the letter *yod* in brilliant red light; behind, the letter *heh* in brilliant blue light; in front, the letter *vav* in brilliant golden light; and on the left side, the *heh* final in deep green light. As the vertical and horizontal axes come together, we invite the four archangels of the quarters and the archangels Sandalphon and Metatron of the central axis to hold us and all that we contemplate.

> Michael, a presence in red and gold, holds the *yod*;
> Gabriel, in blue and silver, holds the *heh*;
> Raphael, in yellow and violet, the *vav*;
> Auriel, in deep green, the *heh* final.

Sandalphon and Metatron manifest as a single entity in white and black and rainbows holding the central axis and overshadow us, holding us in the balancing point and between the depth and the height. We become the archangel who is the archetypal initiate who once was Enoch, who "was not, for God took him"; our feet are in the hells and our head in the heavens and we stand between the four quarters of the universe.

Having established this form we commune with the angels, feeling the central axis and the balance point, and notice what arises in the field of awareness that is in need of blessing and healing. This could be a person, a situation, a principle, or trapped and distorted energy. We reach out to it, draw it into union with the sphere of our heart where the *shin* dwells, and speak the words of the priestly blessing:

> May YHVH *bless and keep us.*

The four archangels manifest their six wings, forming an interlocking sphere, which is the alchemical vessel. Then feel the containment and protection for both self and whatever is being worked on. Our hands are held at the level of our heart around the sphere of the *shin*, holding and containing the object of the working. This is the step into Yesod and the making of the foundation. Relaxing into the name say,

> May YHVH's *face shine on us.*

The vertical and horizontal axes ignite as the letters of יהשוה come together in radiant light. The task here is to allow the light to come together, to bring the blessing into the vessel and affect whatever is being worked on. The hands are held as before in the gesture of containment. The work is raised into Tiphareth and the healing energy of *YHShVH* shines into the heart of the disturbance. This is held until a sense of completion, at least for now, is reached.

Then say:

> May YHVH *lift up the face and grant us peace.*

There is a moment of uplifting and release, and a sense of perfect stillness and union as "face beholds face". The vessel dissolves, the angels turn outwards, and our hands open out in the gesture of blessing. As we do this, the sphere at the centre expands and is released into the world in the blessing of radiant peace. Then there is the surrender to the presence of blessing as the step into Da'ath and the supernals occurs.

We then spend some time in silent meditation, then thank and dismiss the archangels and allow the outer forms to fade away. We commune with the body of light and let its form sink back into the body.

As we become more experienced at working in this way, we will find that the simplest and in some ways most potent practice of this form is simply to align with and chant the name *YHShVH* יהשוה, inviting all that is lost and disturbed to come into resonance with it and to allow the name to hold us and direct our attention to wherever and whatever needs the blessing of the name. As we are held by and become the healing name then we naturally will bring the lost person or energies into our hearts and the process of transformation will naturally follow through. In the beginning, however, it is important to follow the outlined method so that the work is contained and safe.

Esoteric Christian—the way of John the Priest and the Christomorph

The New Testament figure of the Apostle John, who works with the transmutation of the Qliphoth, is one of the important figures within the Western mystery tradition. One of the key iconographic images of John has him holding a chalice with a snake arising out of it—this is linked with a legend of the apostle being given poisoned wine and, upon him drinking it, the poison became a serpent that came out of the cup. It is this principle of swallowing poison and transmuting it that is at the heart of this practice. John the apostle is sometimes depicted as a young man, an old man, an androgynous man, and as the living image of Christ. He was described as a "Christomorph"—one who embodies the transforming light of Christ by morphing into the form of Christ. In this way we might align our shape with that of John as a precursor to the act of absorption. This is the image of John as icon, who enables us to sense ourselves as living icons that offer no resistance to either the qliphothic form or the salvific light, but allows the meeting of both within us.

We might do this in a more focused way by aligning with the form of a servant of the light who is part of the lineage of John the Priest, as Ernest Butler did. This was linked both to his sense of the apostle John as the archetypal priest, his contemplations on the opening of the Gospel of John, and on the divine name *YHShVH* as the creative light that descends into darkness and that the darkness can neither catch hold of nor overcome. As we take on this identity of being a servant of the light, we step into a lineage of men and women who hold the cup, who transform poison and who draw from the androgynous, old and young figure of John the Priest.

Taking on the image of John is complex, for we take on the image of one who himself is taking on the image of the Christ, the living, incarnate image of the divine. The beginning of this practice is to evoke and sit in our body of light and to lean into the image of John the Priest.

We then contemplate these phrases:

- *In the beginning.*
  Here we enter into the stillness of the universe before form.
- *The name.*
  Here we contemplate the name YShVH יהשוה, as the root of our form and energy and that of the universe, drawing on our previous contemplations. This is the name that unites the manifest and the unmanifest *YHVH*, representing the four manifest worlds, and the *shin* representing the unmanifest under its three veils of limitless light, limitlessness, and no-thing.
- *The name is in the beginning with God.*
  Contemplate the sense of the name in the divine, unmanifest stillness at the root of all things.
- *All things came into being through the name, and apart from name nothing came into being that has come into being.*
  Contemplate the divine name at the root of all beings and the process of manifestation.
- *In it was life, and the life was the light of human beings.*
  Contemplate the unity of life and light working within all form.
- *The light shines in the darkness, and the darkness did not comprehend or take hold of it.*
  This is the light shining into the lifeless places of the Qliphoth and remaining free.
- *There came a man sent from God, whose name was John.*
  Here we contemplate the true human image, the *anthropos*, and take on the shape of John whose name is derived from the Hebrew *Yochanon*, which means the grace or blessing of *YHVH*. We allow ourselves to become the shape of the transmitter of light, the grace of the name, the *ruach ha qadesh* symbolised by the letter *shin*.

Having taken this form, we then let our awareness open outwards, allowing the *ruach ha qadesh* ("the divine breath") to present something to us that needs healing or rectification. This could be something within us or within the world. We will experience it as a sense of disturbance and lack of balance, like the thing in the garden. The first step in the work is to link to it, remembering the divine presence at the root of all forms, and then to step towards it. This may involve our awareness in the body of light experiencing a sense of travelling towards it, in the classic astral projection sense, or it may be that you feel that the person or situation is stepping towards you, or it may feel that both are happening. At a certain point you will feel that they are being absorbed into your heart. You might feel yourself to be a great flame of light, or a doorway, or as if you are feeding the other, or joining them to a great tree. In the Gospel of John seven images are used for what arises.

1. The light of the world.
2. The door.
3. The bread of life.
4. The way, the truth, and the life.
5. The resurrection and the life.
6. The true vine.
7. The Good Shepherd.

Many other forms may arise. We may find ourselves as the guide of souls, as a ferryman, as a mother gathering a child to her, etc.

The way of Simon Iff

Aleister Crowley, as Simon Iff, aligns with his version of the deified being through dissolving the forms of I, Me, and Mine, and arising as "Thou" that is all and nothing. Thus we see him beginning his work by aligning himself with the verse from the Thelemic holy book:

> I, and Me and Mine were sitting with lutes ... The music of the lutes was stilled. But Thou art Eternity and Space, Thou art Matter and Motion and Thou art the Negation of all these things for there is no symbol of Thee. (Crowley, 1971, p. 111)

He next proceeds to make a magical link with the thing in the garden, and proclaims the fundamental thesis of Thelema:

> Do what thou wilt shall be the whole of the Law. Be Strong! Enjoy all things of sense and rapture! There is no god that shall deny thee for this! (Crowley, 1971, p. 111)

He then walks into the thing, which envelops him and is drawn into him and into the burning ovoid of light at his core. The operation ends with him speaking the phrase: "Love is the Law, Love under Will."

Crowley's version of this practice is based on the cosmology he describes in his *Book of the Law*, which in turn draws upon the cosmology of Twenty-Fifth Dynasty Egypt.

We can see this cosmology depicted in the funeral stele of Ankh af na Khonsu, a priest of Montu.

The top and sides of the stele are formed by the body of the star goddess, Nuit, who represents both space, and the infinity of stars and of points of view, and the capacity to love and receive all. Just below her we find the winged sun-disk of Hadit, representing singularity, movement, and will. Beneath them, on the left-hand side, is the seated figure of Ra Harakhty, the new sun, creating the new day and thus an expression of will in action. On the right-hand side is the deceased priest, Ankh af na Khonsu, making an offering to the god as a gesture of devotion and thus representing the principle of love. It is through Crowley's work on this cosmology, his embodied relationship with these figures and his continual communion with his angel, that he came to his vision of the universe as "Nothingness, with twinkles", which underpins all his later work, and this practice in particular. By standing on the firm ground at the bottom of the stele, Crowley inhabits the form of the peasant. Being both the priest and that which is worshipped, he inhabits the world of the good shepherd. Through identifying with the goddess of the stars and the winged sun, he becomes the Silent Sage.

In order to follow this form we would do this:

1. We bring awareness to the sense of "I"-ness; then the sense of "Me" and "Mine", and dissolve it into the silence, entering the body of Nuit.
2. Then we arise as "Thou", the presence that is eternity, space, matter, motion, and the negation of all that aligning with the creative presence of the universe. We become the conjunction of the infinity of Nuit and the single point of Hadit.
3. Embodying that infinite presence, we link with the source of the disturbance and express the deep will of that creative presence that all should express their True Will. Here we embody Ra Harakhty, the creative reborn sun.
4. We step into the disturbed form, coming into a mysterious, inexpressible union as we speak the phrase: "Love is the Law, Love under Will". This is the offering of love to will that is the fundamental act of priesthood.
5. All returns to stillness and balance.

In this practice of absorption, we surrender to the light as it manifests through us, allowing ourselves to feel the disturbance, the pain, grief, rage, and hatred that is held within the qliphothic form, trusting the deep sense of the spirit that is working through us and cooperating with it, offering as little resistance as possible, as Simon Iff outlines in *Moonchild*. At a certain point there will be a shift of energy as the form dissolves and the universe returns to a sense of balance and peace. In early work, there can be strong senses of shifting and physical effects, even—though this is quite rare—poltergeist-type experiences. As we become more accomplished, however, then more and more it is a work of love and silence.

If we follow the path outlined by Simon Iff, we will deepen in our understanding of the formula "Do what thou wilt shall be the whole of the Law. Love is the Law. Love under Will", the sense of the cosmos as "Nothingness, with twinkles", and the $0 = 2$ equation. The study of Crowley's Holy Books will deepen our understanding of this form and give it depth, much as the study of the Gospel of John did for Ernest Butler. *Liber Lapidus vel Lazuli*, in particular, is filled with images such as, "Oh my beautiful God I swim in thy heart like a trout in the mountain torrent", which assist in entering the non-dual sense of "Thou" that Simon Iff invokes at the beginning of the work.

The Zen Qabalah of Tom Oloman

Tom Oloman used a more abstract, simple approach, in that he would enter into stillness, dissolving his sense of self into the silence, and would emerge from the silence in the form of a monk in a white, hooded robe with a mirror for a face. He would mirror the disturbed form, becoming one with it, and bringing it into the stillness until there was a sense of peace, which he would then radiate as a blessing to all. This is a form we will return to in the final chapter, as this simplicity is the fruit of a lifetime's practice of the path.

We may experiment with the forms of practice in this chapter until we find one that works for us, or we may find a different shape that is more suited to us.

CHAPTER 15

The sanctum sanctorum

In the Marvel comic book universe there is a series concerning Dr Strange, the sorcerer supreme, whose task it is to defend the Earth against attack by supernatural beings. He operates out of a building in New York in which he stores magical artefacts, has his magical library, and travels from there into different dimensions. It is the place from which he contemplates the universe, determines whether there are problems, acts from and returns to. The building is called the "sanctum sanctorum", which means "the Holy of Holies". It is a translation of the Hebrew terms *qadosh ha qadoshim* קדש ה קדשים which describe the holiest place of the Temple where the divine presence can be found. This primordial sanctum is the archetypal temple of Binah, which houses the universe. If we consider the account of creation in the *Zohar*, we see that out of the mystery of negative existence of ain sof, "the infinite", we see the appearance of what is described as a spark of impenetrable darkness, implying a light so bright that it is overwhelming, and describing the appearance of Chockmah out of the simple point of Kether. This paradoxical spark is then housed in the womb of Binah, which gives rise to the rest of the sephiroth. Binah is also described as "the palace of mirrors", giving us the image of a womb that is also a mirror. The sanctum sanctorum is a representation of these deep roots of the tree;

it is the first image of which all other images are fractals, constantly generating and receiving the outflow and inflow of the divine light and translating it into intelligible forms. It is an image which at one end opens into the mystery of negative existence and the mystery of the spark of impenetrable darkness, and on the other the thousand forms of existence. This archetypal temple is found in the deep places of the universe and the soul and, as we engage with it, we bring the soul and the universe into alignment.

Its earliest account in the Torah is the description of the tent of meeting in the wilderness; it is the inmost place in which nothing is found but the Ark of the Covenant, a wooden chest sheathed in gold that contains mythical objects, such as the tablets of the law, the bones of Jacob, and the rod of Moses. More important than the relics it contained was the space just above it, defined by the wings of two angels on either end of the Ark. The negative space defined by the curving wings was said to the be the dwelling place of the divine, the tangible and perceptible presence of the Shekinah. Only the high priest could enter this sanctum and only when protected by his robes, breastplate, and crown, which bear the divine name. It was the task of the high priest on entering the sanctum to speak the divine name that invoked the divine presence to bless the community of Israel. As the Israelites enter and take possession of the promised land, the Ark is taken to the sacred hill of Shechem, the first sanctuary, before being brought by King David to Jerusalem some generations later. We have no information on how the Ark was housed in Jerusalem before Solomon built the first temple. This has three divisions: the outer court for the people, the inner court for the priesthood, and the Holy of Holies where only the high priest could enter. This is identical to the pattern found in Egyptian temples where the outer court is open to the skies, the inner court is a roofed and colonnaded hall, and the Holy of Holies is a small, enclosed room containing an even smaller image.

Christianity drew strongly on the image of the Temple of Solomon but interpreted it in a new way. Drawing on the idea of the priesthood of all believers it did away with the outer court and the separation between the altar where the innermost mystery was celebrated, and the rest of the sanctuary was simply the symbolic barrier of the icon screen. Essentially, therefore, it brought the Holy of Holies into the midst of the world in keeping with its intention of the incarnation of the divine and the raising up of the human.

All churches to a greater or lesser degree reflect this pattern, but perhaps the finest remaining version is that of Hagia Sophia in Istanbul built by the Byzantium emperor Justinian in 537 CE. This church of Holy Wisdom shows in its proportions and design the pattern of the sanctum sanctorum archetype. Its very name indicates its root idea, for holy wisdom is the co-creator with the divine in bringing the universe into existence and often described as the mirror in which the divine sees itself. The building is a great dome set on four pillars surrounded by a cascade of half domes and buttresses, and thus brings together the sphere and the cube of sacred geometry. In the quarters, as if holding the whole building together, are images of four six-winged angels echoing the holy living creatures of Ezekiel's vision. The interior is sheathed in shining marble, gold mosaics, and images of Christ, the Virgin, the saints and angels. Just below the dome there is a circle of windows that allows shafts of light to penetrate the interior which, in early morning and in the evening, causes it to become incandescent, luminous, and alive. This building is based on the archetypal form of Holy Wisdom, which is the icon that contains all icons, the mirror that mediates between matter and spirit and the human and the divine. Its internal space is also deeply responsive to any sound made beneath the dome, and the divine office said within it was said to resonate throughout the world. Following the Ottoman conquest of Byzantium in 1453 it was converted into a mosque until 1931 when, following the establishment of the secular republic of Turkey, it was converted into a museum and the mosaics and images were once again revealed.

This ancient form is the basis of the inner sanctuary we will create. It is the place of contemplation in which the divine light becomes material, and the nature of humanity is lifted up. It arises out of the dynamics of the divine name *YHShVH* יהשוה and holds the intention of that name, namely the bringing together of the manifest and unmanifest worlds and the service of the *ruach ha qadesh*, "the divine breath". The sanctum sanctorum integrates the cube of *YHVH* with the sphere of the *shin* and directly echoes the purpose and practice of Justinian's Church of Holy Wisdom.

There are two ways of approaching the sanctum sanctorum: contemplative and ritual. The contemplative practice begins by turning our attention inwards, seeking stillness and then using this trigger phrase: "Now do I descend into the inner sea whose waters rise and fall within my soul. Let the inner elements be subdued and still as I immerse myself within the living waters and emerging therefrom unfold from latent stress to potent image the *qadosh ha qadoshim*."

We sink deeply into the inner waters until all around us is a deep black stillness and we find ourselves in the centre of a negative image of a combined cube and sphere, an unmanifest latent shape which yet conditions our awareness. As we continue in our contemplation it acquires shape and density becoming a square, domed room with the letter *shin* ש floating at the apex of the dome in brilliant white fire. We are standing in the centre of the room before an altar whose top is inscribed with the letters of the name *YHShVH* יהשוה. In each of the four walls is a stained-glass window with one of the four holy living creatures depicted. In the south there is a winged lion; in the west, a white eagle; in the east, a winged human being; and in the north, a winged bull. The floor is of shining marble and can seem like a sea of glass or shining water. There is a stairway in the northern quarter of the sanctum which leads into the crypt beneath it.

We contemplate the holy living creatures and have a sense that behind them is the presence of an archangel. Behind the lion is Michael, behind the eagle, Gabriel, behind the man, Raphael, and behind the bull, Auriel. The principal practice here is to simply rest within the form and to allow the sanctum sanctorum to transmit to us the divine pressure that fills it. As we become more confident in working with the sanctum we will notice particular features; we may be drawn to one or other of the holy creatures; we may explore aspects of the dome or the crypt; or we may have a direct experience of the archangels who stand behind it.

When we have completed our meditation we allow the form to return into latency, letting it revert to the negative image and finding ourselves in the deep, luminous blackness as we say, "Now do I descend into the inner sea, whose waters rise and fall within my soul. Let the inner elements be subdued and still as I immerse myself within the living waters and emerging therefrom unfold from latent stress to potent image my own true self."

When we have become confident of working with the sanctum in a meditative way, we may then evoke it into being in a ritual way, employing the body of light and the qabalistic cross.

We begin by entering the body of light and by becoming as large as the universe, letting our feet be at the centre of the Earth and our form encompassing the Moon, the Sun, the stars and the crown point aligning the spine with the central axis of the universe.

We reach up with our right hands into the unmanifest, into the limitless light, the limitless and the no-thing of the *ain*. Around us is what can be described as the negative image of a four-square domed building with four empty thrones in the four directions. These are not images but the echo of an image, like the sense of a black cat in a completely dark room. Feel the mystery of *ain* and the negative image above and the crown, stars, Sun, Moon and Earth below.

Say,

> *Ateh—Malkuth*

>> drawing the unmanifest light down through the central pillar into the earth appearing as white, yellow, red, blue, and green vortices. As the spiralling light descends to Earth it takes shape around you as the fusion of the cube and the sphere, which resolves into a four-square domed chamber of contemplation. The four archangels take their place in the four quarters of the room, appearing as vast six-winged figures that form the substance of the building as their wings embrace above, below, and around.

Contemplate the archangels and the letters of the name:

- Michael stands in the South, robed in red and gold, and holds a sphere of red-gold light that contains the letter *yod* י—the archetypal priest aligning with the divine will and fire.
- Gabriel stands in the West, robed in blues and greens and holding a sphere of blue light containing the letter *heh* ה—the giver of vision and clarity, the purification of the imagination.
- Raphael stands in the East, robed in yellow and violet, holding a sphere of yellow-violet light, containing the letter *vav* ו—the archangel of breath and life, the healer and balancer.
- Auriel stands in the North in robes of deep green and electric black and holds a sphere of green-black light containing the final *heh* ה—the archangel who holds the hidden light within matter, the alchemist of deep heaven.

Then in the presence of the archangels, balance the universe speaking

> *Ve Geburah, Ve Gedulah*

>> feeling the scales of the opposites aligning as the principles of will and love come into active expression.

Bringing your hands to the centre of your body, visualise the letter *shin* שׁ and say

Le Olam Amen

letting the radiance touch all quarters of the universe.

At the centre of the room is an altar with the letters of the name engraved upon it and in the apex of the dome is a radiant *shin* in fiery, white light. The floor is of shining marble, like a sea of glass and, at times, it is as if you are in the midst of the waters of the beginning. Stand in the midst of the room communing with the angels and the name, seeing the structure of the sanctum as the substance of the angels. In each quarter there is a door and a stained-glass window. In the East there is the image of a winged human being in the window; in the South, a winged lion; in the West, a white eagle; and in the North, a winged bull. You become aware also that there is a stairway leading to a crypt and that in the apex of the dome there is a circular opening. Spend time contemplating the sanctum and when you are ready simply seal the work by chanting the name *YHShVH* יהשוה, sensing the blessing of the sanctum radiating out to the world. Allow the forms to dissolve until you once again invite them.

Increasingly, as you spend time in your sanctum it will adapt to your shape, your imagery, and reflect the work that you are doing. We have described the basic form of the sanctum sanctorum but depending on the particular style of practice you have adopted it will acquire other attributes. For example, if, like Ernest Butler, you are working with the image of the Apostle John, the sanctum might appear like a Greek Orthodox church with frescoes and icons. If the way of Simon Iff has called to you, the ceiling of the sanctum may be the arched body of Nuit and, in place of the *shin* at the apex, there will be the winged sun disc. The floor of the sanctum might have a pool within which the blue lotus floats.

At other times it can appear as a primitive Celtic hermit's cell, the archangels appearing as living Celtic knotwork and interlace. In Tom Oloman's case, the sanctum was a place of light and abstract form—the angels were columns of light and the sense of the sphere and the cube and the dynamics of the name were primary. His altar was a round tree trunk filled with growth rings that he would use to contemplate the dimension of time just as he would use the organic image of the Tree of Life to attune himself to the living universe.

The principal function of the sanctum is as an inner place you go to in order to contemplate your life and work, but also the place from which you contemplate the next work that presents itself. You will find your attention being drawn to something, either from within your heart or something that presents itself to some part of the sanctuary. You may notice one of the doors or windows, or be drawn down into the crypt or up into the apex of the dome. There is a way in which the sanctum sanctorum is the universe so, as you are drawn to some detail of it, you are noticing something within the universe that needs attending to. You may move out through the doors of the sanctuary or invite some being or situation into it.

The main feature of the sanctum is the sense of the divine pressure which fills it and its most potent function for us is to simply rest within it and allow that pressure to work upon us and show us the way that opens before us. The practice of the extended qabalistic cross is an important beginning as it identifies the sanctum with the universe and should be used whenever you are doing active work. It is the place where you pray, bless, and send out light.

As you continue to work with the sanctum it will increasingly incorporate aspects of your life and work and will normally become more elaborate. While its basic form is the domed cube it may, like Hagia Sophia, acquire half domes, galleries, and a whole variety of other rooms and images. Some will be ephemeral while others will become essential and permanent features. As it is an image of the conjunction between your soul and the soul of the universe it will shift and change and evolve with you. It is above all a lens which focuses light and a mirror of contemplation.

CHAPTER 16

Contemplating the Qliphoth

Having established ourselves in our sanctum and become in effect one who dwells in Zion, we now turn attention to what Psalm 87 describes as "the cities of the plains", which are both far from and below the city of Zion and thus out of relationship with the divine presence. The images that are used in the psalm are Rahab (Egypt), Babylon, Philistia and Tyre with Cush, and represent the opponents of the divine. They are broadly drawn from Israelite history and then mythologised. Egypt and Babylon are places that held the Israelites in captivity, Philistia and Tyre are competitors to Israel and seen respectively as the sea people and as traders who will do anything for profit and will not keep the sabbath. Cush is seen as far away and alien and thus far from holiness and the springs of life that arise from YHVH in Zion. They represent therefore energies of opposition, imprisonment, and alienness—a breaking of the divine schema. In later Qabalah they are represented by the image of the abyss which separates the supernal spheres from the rest of the tree.

Remembering the mirrored nature of the universe we will see that the abyss is mirrored also in the continual experience of interruption—a break in the continuity of things. The abyss then is the home place of the qliphothic energies and is said to be the home of serpents who wrap themselves around the tree and distort the paths that connect the sephiroth. It is because of this image that working with the Qliphoth is often described as a descent, for we go into this place of interruption, twistedness, and distortion to find the lost sparks of holiness and bring them home. Aleister Crowley maintained (following the Enochian work of Elizabethans Dr Dee and Edward Kelly) that the abyss is the home of a devil called Choronzon.

> The name of the Dweller in the Abyss is Choronzon, but he is not really an individual. The Abyss is empty of being; it is filled with all possible forms, each equally inane, each therefore evil in the only true sense of the word—that is, meaningless but malignant, in so far as it craves to become real. These forms swirl senselessly into haphazard heaps like dust devils and each such chance aggregation asserts itself to be an individual and shrieks, "I am I!" though aware all the time that its elements have no true bond; so that the slightest disturbance dissipates the delusion just as a horseman, meeting a dust devil, brings it in showers of sand to the earth. (Crowley, 1983, p. 623)

Crowley with typical chutzpah undertook a magical working in the Tunisian desert with his disciple Victor Neuberg in which he sat in the triangle of evocation and Neuberg proceeded to evoke Choronzon into him, so that he experienced all the chaos and incoherence within his own frame. Now while I would not recommend this practice unless we are very experienced, we can see within it the heart of our method of working with unbalanced force in that Choronzon must be included and absorbed into us so that it loses its independent agency and returns into the flow of life. Perhaps one of the most direct ways for us to understand what Crowley was doing is to reflect upon our experience of the inner dialogue when we were negotiating the veil of the temple. One of our early experiences in touching this is the discovery that our mind and feelings and images have their own independent life because they have combined together to create a direction of will and a desire to survive and propagate. The abyss is an amplified version of that experience, being both subjective and objective. We will find that, as with Nietzsche, if we look into the abyss then the abyss will look also into us and will start to shape itself so that we can begin the work of bridging this primal interruption and align ourselves with the non-dual light of the supernals.

As we have seen, the Qabalah has used many different ways of personifying the dwellers of the abyss. We might, like Crowley, use the form of Choronzon, or the great, crooked serpent Leviathan, found in the *Zohar*, which was seen as the wicked serpent of Eden constantly trying to penetrate holiness to corrupt it. We might also contemplate them as the Edomite Kings. One of the most powerful formulations is given by Isaac Ha-Kohen in his Treatise on the Left Emanation (Dan, 1986, pp. 165–82) in which he tells us of Samael, the commander of jealousy, who desires to mingle his essence and unite with any emanation that does not have his nature, and his counterpart Lilith who is seen as the feminine principle that kills babies. They also take the form of two snakes that generate a multitude of snakes. They are the shadow equivalent of Adam and Eve and from them are created the demon Asmodeus and the younger Lilith who generate many distorted forms and, in turn, from them arises an anti-messiah who bears the sword of Asmodeus even as the messiah bears the sword of holiness. They are also thought of as the great Leviathan opposed by the heavenly serpent. Isaac Ha Kohen is here demonstrating a parallelism of opposites between holiness and impurity, showing us the generative capacity of the qliphothic energies which parallel the generative capacity of holiness. At the root of the qliphothic forms, however, is jealousy and the desire to possess and contaminate, and the wish to kill all new life. The offspring that arise from this are variously described as two-headed, leprous, having ulcerated faces, biting dogs, he- and she-goats, and taking the forms of men and women who lie and stir up quarrel and war. Right at the end of the text he gives us a hint that points us at the heart of our subject. He speaks of a figure alternatively called *tanin'iver* or *taninsam*, a blind, heavenly serpent. The serpent interrupts the bond of Samael and Lilith with the help of the archangels Gabriel (the angel of strength) and Michael (the angel of loving-kindness). The serpent eats poison, which becomes the elixir of life and transforms its poisoned flesh into the salted fish that will feed the righteous. The interruption of the qliphothic dynamic and the absorption and transformation of poison is, as we have seen, central to this work.

Rabbi Ha-Kohen's text is central to our subject and repays a great deal of contemplation for, at various points in the text, he shows us aspects of the work but not in a linear sequence. He tells us, for example, earlier in the work that jealousy and enmity can arise from the divine source but that is too great a mystery for created beings to grasp, and goes on to speak of the mystery of uniting and combination (*sod ha ibbur*), which is the way in which a soul may overshadow another soul as an act of love and blessing, enabling that soul to free itself from the qliphothic shell (Dan, 1986, p. 172). We are given here the possibility of the redemption of Samael and Lilith, and a similar teaching to that found within the bone teachings. A particular contemplation he points towards is the figure of the angel Masukhiel, who rules over the principle of duality, called "the dividing screen", and whose task it is to create separation. We are shown that initially three worlds are created and then destroyed because there was no balance and the principle of will overwhelmed the principle of love and kindness; the solely wilful beings in those worlds rejected connection to the divine source. These rejected and destroyed forms sink into latency and are held within the abyss until the current world is created, which is a mixture of will and love. Rabbi Ha Kohen also tells us that the secret knowledge of demons is part of the sacred work of being a prophet. There are many such gems in this short treatise which will become more evident as we gain experience. It was written in 1265 in Castille, making it one of the earliest qabalistic texts on this subject. The key thoughts that we may take away from this work concern working with opposites, working with boundaries, entering into the Qliphoth, being the intermediary, and consuming poison under the guidance of will and love so that it becomes nourishing food.

Another early form used in Jewish mysticism is the seven hells and seven heavens.

- The seven heavens begin with the heaven of the supernals, Araboth ערבות, which means "the desert" or "the empty places". It can also mean a mixture of fire and water, such as the sea of glass mixed with fire that we find in Revelation 15: 2. This is the non-dual world of the supernal triangle of opposites at peace.
- This is followed by the heaven of Chesed, Makon מכון, which has the meaning of a changeless, prosperous place; a thriving neighbourhood of goodness and good relationships.
- The heaven of Geburah is Ma'on מעון, which means "a strong refuge" and has the sense of a strong fortress.
- The heaven of Tifaret is Zebul זבול, a sure and centred habitation.
- The heaven of Netzach is Shechaqim שחקים, or "cloud of mystery", also the place of fountains and living gardens.
- The heaven of Hod is Reqia רקיע, the place that is like a golden canopy or expanse filled with beautiful dwellings.

- The heaven of Yesod and Malkuth is Veilon Shemain וילון שמים, "the veil of the heavens".

These suggestive images, we could say, are the icons of the deeper worlds, even as the hells are the idols.

- The hell of the supernals is called Sheol שאול, the deepest hell, sometimes called "the grave" and "the house of the devouring mother".
- The hell of Chesed is called Abaddon אבדון, or "place of destruction", "the bottomless pit".
- The hell of Geburah is called Bar Shachath באר שחת, "the pit of ruin and destruction".
- The hell of Tifaret is called Tit Ha Yeven טיט היון, or "the quagmire".
- The hell of Netzach is called Shaare Maveth שערי מות, or "gate of the grave".
- The hell of Hod is called Tzal Maveth צל מות, or "valley of the shadow of the grave".
- The hell of Yesod and Malkuth is called Gehenna or Gehinnom גיהנם, the ravine of the discarded the rubbish pit.

The heavens and hells can be used as contemplation objects using the poetic descriptions to attune us, first of all, to the environment of the heavens, next the hells, and then, using Rabbi Ha Kohen's principle of working with opposites, we can align them with each other. For example, as we bring together the sense of Gehenna, the discarded rubbish tip, with the veil of the heavens, we will start to see how that which appears useless or even toxic might be the doorway into beauty and light. If we bring together the valley of the shadow of the grave with the golden canopy, we may find the place where lost souls are protected. Similarly, bringing together the gate of the grave with the cloud of mystery and possibility may free those who are imprisoned in death. Uniting the quagmire with the sure and centred habitation will create life and movement in the midst of the mud, whereas the pit of destruction brought together with the strong refuge will create a sense of boundary and safety in the midst of war. Mediating between the bottomless pit and the changeless, prosperous neighbourhood will create a strong polarity of different possibilities that becomes even stronger and more potent as we align Sheol, the deepest hell, with Araboth, the heaven of the unity of all opposites. All the hells are reflections of the abyss whereas the heavens are reflections of the Tree of life and, as we place ourselves in the midst of these opposites, we will increasingly perceive the dynamics at play here both within ourselves and within the inner and outer worlds.

Another school of Qabalah, the thirteenth-century Iyyun circle of mystics, who produced the key texts *The Fountain of Wisdom* and *The Books of Contemplation*, took the notion of the Qliphoth as shells literally because their contemplations were based upon the image of the universe as arising out of the divine presence as a flowing fountain of wisdom that is continually arising and returning to the divine source. The practice of returning to the beginning and being recreated by the divine was central to their work. They describe the process of manifestation thus:

> Regarding this issue, wonders abound and are clarified. The wonders become more wonderful and from them come the flames and from the flame the thread extends outwards, and the threads thicken and in this thickened state they grow stronger until they become scepters. This then is the point: Everything is again and again dissolved and returns to the ether as it once was and the ether is the essential element. (Dan, 1986, p. 50)

This is contrasted with the process of congealing and fragmenting:

> … this flow extends and gushes forth by way of channels and the flow again becomes weak like a stream and the stream becomes minute turning into a thread. And in this exiguity it extends and is directed until it becomes tiny droplets. These droplets grow and become fragmented entities. (Dan, 1986, p. 51)

The fragmented entities continue to grow and intermingle and generate their own life but have become separated from the fountainhead of the divine presence. Here the contrast is, on the one hand, between flowing outwards and returning and, on the other hand, congealing and fragmenting and remaining separated.

As the Qabalah develops, its account of the Qliphoth becomes more detailed with a qliphothic image being attached to each one of the sephiroth. These are the forms we have already considered in our description of the Tree of Life and Death as they are the most accessible of the accounts of the Qliphoth. Like the figures of Samael and Lilith and the remnants of the destroyed world, these are what might be described as semi-autonomous complexes within the divine subconscious, if we can use such a term. These images are first described by MacGregor Mathers in his translation of Christian Knorr von Rosenroth's seventeenth-century book *Kabbala Denudata*, an encyclopaedic compilation of qabalistic teachings circulating at that time. Part of this work was translated into English by Samuel MacGregor Mathers in the late nineteenth century as "The Kabbalah Unveiled" and we find the qliphothic images described in the introduction to that book. These images were also used in the teaching papers of the Hermetic Order of the Golden Dawn and, since the Golden Dawn teachings were published by Aleister Crowley and Israel Regardie, have become ubiquitous whenever the subject of the Qliphoth is discussed. It is sometimes assumed that these ten images are the central teaching on the Qliphoth and that they arise out of the *Zohar*; this is not the case—the zoharic teachings use a similar formulation to Rabbi Isaac's *Treatise on the Left Emanation*. The confusion appears to have arisen because Mathers' introduction that mentions them is followed by a translation of three zoharic books. The ubiquity of these images is in part because they are direct and immediate and therefore are a good introduction to our subject. If studied in connection with the other teachings we have described, they can be very helpful.

They begin with the counterpart of Kether, Thaumiel תאמיאל, whose name means "twins of God" and that is given the image of two quarrelling, conjoined, bat-winged heads. In place of the unity of the crown of creation we are given the primal split, disunity, in which awareness is divided against itself.

Next we find Augiel, "the confusion of God", עוגאל, in place of Chockmah, wisdom and deep will being applied chaotically, a divine dementia containing a chaotic will to create but with no capacity to relate or reflect.

In place of the understanding and non-dual love of Binah, we find Satariel סאתאריאל, the wish to conceal and bind, to hide all in increasingly impenetrable webs of concealment.

These three form a shadow crown in the abyss and, like Kether, Binah, and Chockmah, form a dynamic from which all else arises.

The qliphoth of Chesed is Gamchicoth גמחיכת, "the devourers", those who consume the substance of the universe mercilessly—the ravenous open mouth that always requires more in place of the abundance of life and growth of Chesed. They may be visualised as vast beings with even larger mouths, or like black holes sucking in life.

The qliphoth of Geburah are the Golachab גולחב, "the burners", who destroy for the delight of destruction, sometimes called "the burning bodies" they are distorted reflections of the seraphim. They can be visualised as wildfire delighting in burning for its own sake, or like runaway nuclear reactors.

The qliphoth of Tifaret is Thagriron תגרירון, "the builders of ugliness"., the centralising point of the shadow tree that proliferates the sense of growing ugliness and despair. It is accompanied by a deep groaning and grief which is the expression of the averse name. They can be visualised as presences of pain, radiating a coldness that takes away all warmth.

The qliphoth of Netzach is "the ravens of dispersion", Oreb Zereq ערב זרק —the corrosive energies of death and disinterest eating away at the victorious life-giving energies of Netzach. They can be visualised as very large, red-eyed ravens tearing away at life and eroding it.

The qliphoth of Hod is Samael סמאל, the deceitful and poisonous. Here is the betraying and poisonous aspect of the lie and the generation of the lying universe in which no truth can be found, seen as deceptive serpents who seduce and corrupt the heart and mind.

The qliphoth of Yesod is Gamali'el גמליאל, "the impure", the corruption of the energies of generation itself and the creation of seduction and all forms of obscenity. They can be visualised as beings with exaggerated sexual organs who join together that which should not be joined.

The qliphoth of Malkuth is Lilith לילית, the night spectre, the mother of demons, who whispers by night a distortion of the shekinah and the generative earth mother—the mother that kills all life. She can be visualised as the night hag, part woman, part ravening bird.

Within all these different ways of expressing and describing the Qliphoth there is one important point we must remember: that this energy cannot penetrate to the supernal worlds and enter into non-dual experience. It arises out of splitting and distortion in the work of creation, just as in the bone teachings the level of the bone remains the intact archetype of holiness and the distortion enters in the act of the expression of will, which points in a particular direction, giving rise to image as idol and the expression of actions that assert separation and entropy.

Directly working with the qliphothic forms in this way takes the work into greater depth. We are not simply noticing disturbance and working with it, we are seeking it out. This is the act of descent, the gesture of the Good Shepherd who enters into the wild places to find the lost sheep. It is the journey of Ezekiel as he projects himself into the corrupted Jerusalem and the Holy of Holies and his journey to the Valley of Dry Bones.

CHAPTER 17

Baptising demons and freeing prisoners

This phase of the work should be begun by contemplating the forms of expression of the Qliphoth described above, until we feel ready to directly approach the split and disturbed energies. It is important that we are connected to our deeper soul and whatever represents the lineage of this work for us. Having done so as a servant of the Tree of Life we approach the qliphothic archetypes and begin the work of alchemising them and bringing them home into the heart of the Tree. The stability and truthfulness of the Eloquent Peasant, the fiery *hitlavahut* of the Good Shepherd, and the deep stillness of the Silent Sage will be both refuge and resource as we begin this work. Here we truly start to fulfil the principle of "the serpent is the saviour" for, as the qliphothic energy flows back into the source of life or is joined back into the tree, there is a great surge of free energy that manifests as new life and deep insight into the nature of things and creates new capacities within the Tree of Life.

This practice begins by establishing presence in the body of light and manifesting the sanctum sanctorum. We pay attention to the directions of space and feel ourselves to be the middle pillar, the balance-point uniting opposites, and then bring our attention to the direction below us, seeing there a stairway leading to a crypt sealed by an ancient oak door. Carved into this door is the image of two human-headed serpents coiling around each other in a great tangle. Around them and within them, many other distorted forms can be seen. This is the gateway of Samael and Lilith, the father and mother of the Qliphoth, who embody domination, possession, and the destruction of life. Within the coils, the form of the Tree of Life can be dimly seen, though overlaid by the tangle of serpents. As we place our hands upon the door it swings open and we cross the threshold. We enter into an underground room with a domed roof that is a distorted copy of the sanctum sanctorum—it is a room in ruins with many shadows. At its centre is a spiralling stairway descending into the abyss. This is the entrance into the shadow tree. It is labyrinthine and confusing, a genuine hall of mirrors, for the shadow tree has no constant structure because the shadow sephiroth are constantly in motion and the paths equally shift, twist, and turn. They are all reflections of the energies of Samael and Lilith who are the distorted reflections of the true human image. The work is begun by the speaking of the name YHShVH יהשוה, letting the energies of the name clothe us in the presence of the divine and in the intention of healing and release. As we walk the Tree of Death aligned with the name and overshadowed by the line of light we accept that all that we meet, however disturbing, will be drawn through us into relationship with the Tree of Life.

The foundation of this work is in the principle of mirroring and on a correct understanding of the bone teachings, which show us that at the root of all beings is the light and presence of the divine. Intention is the orienting principle here, so, as you stand in this entrance chamber of the shadow Malkuth and Yesod, the entrance Hell called Gehenna, "the pit of discarded forms", be aware also of the corresponding heaven realm, Veilon Shemain, "the veil of the heavens". Be aware of the sense of discarded and broken images and forms, feeling the destructive energies of Lilith and the dominating and oppressive energies of Samael, and be aware of the sovereignty and purifying power of Malkuth and Yesod. Notice here the conjunction of that which should not be joined, the absence of boundary and containment. Stand here as the living icon—the veil of Heaven. As you connect to both Hell and Heaven, to Lilith and the Shekinah (the divine presence), a process of catalysis begins in which beings will emerge from the shadows. These may be the spirits of the living and the dead, or non-human spirits of different kinds. You may even encounter the presence of Samael and Lilith in some form. Whatever emerges, the task remains the same: to offer light and blessing to whatever is met, to be the doorway through which any and all can pass to be reunited with the divine life and light so that Maat is re-established. This is the work of preaching to the spirits who are imprisoned in the case of those human and non-human spirits, who pass through us into the light, and the baptism of demons as we work with the aspects of Samael and Lilith that present themselves to us. They are Simon Iff's "thing in the garden" writ large, but the process of working with them is the same as working with any other form of disturbance. The conjunction of love and will and connecting with the line of light that supports us through the sense of presence in the heart enables us to act as the doorway to peace through which they re-join the flow of the universe.

This hell should be worked with regularly until you feel ready to make another step. You begin as before by passing through the gate of Samael and Lilith in the crypt of your sanctum, entering Gehenna by stepping forward on to the spiral stair which, Escher-like, seems to spiral in a number of different directions at once as if you are stepping on the coils of a serpent. Hold a clear intention to step into the hell of the Shadow of the Grave, Tzal Maveth—the hell that is the reflection of Hod. This is the valley of the shadow of death as described in the twenty-third psalm; here we find Samael at work as the poisoner, the liar who distorts truth and who taints and sickens all. As before, we align with the line of light, bring to mind the bone teachings, and speak the healing name *YHShVH* יהשוה. The hell takes shape before us as a place of whispers, promises, and seductions; one moment it might appear like a pharmacy, offering drugs that bring healing and relief, or a poisoner's den, or an ancient library filled with books of secrets, a demonologist's lair, or as a narrow enclosed valley with no exit. It is musty with a smell of old cemeteries and there is sense of a taint so that everything you touch is in some way unclean and compromised. It is a hell that makes promises that are never kept, and presents endless recursion that never concludes. Here we encounter Samael as the poisonous one and, as we stand in this place, we align with the heaven of Hod Reqia, "the place of the golden canopy", the place of protection, beauty, order, and clarity, the place of beautiful and ordered dwellings. We bring to mind the archangel Raphael, the healer. As we do so, just as in Gehenna, we start to become aware of human and non-human beings that are trapped in this place and also the aspects of Lilith and Samael that can be found here. Once again, being the living image of the divine, we preach to the spirits in prison, we offer baptism to the demons simply by opening to them and offering them the opportunity to pass through us into the light.

The next step is into the hell of Netzach, Shaare Mazvoth, "the gate of the grave". Again, enter through the crypt, step upon the spiral stair and hold the intention of stepping into the gate of the grave. Once again, there is the sense of coiling and spinning, but you hold your focus of intention and find yourself in a place that is like a charnel house or a battlefield. All around you are parts of bodies with strange, red-eyed ravens eating them. Here are Samael and Lilith spawning the life that feeds off other life; the mother and father of parasites, viruses, and cancers. There is a foul-smelling fog or mist drifting across the scene and a sense of decay; we speak the name *YHShVH* יהשוה, embodying the qualities of the name. We come into relationship with this vampiric field, bringing to mind as we do so the heaven of Netzach, Shechaqim, the fertilising cloud of sweet water, the place of gardens and fountains. We also bring to mind the presence of Auriel, the archangel who embodies divine light. Holding the qualities of Netzach in relationship with its shadow, we make the offering to whatever spirits emerge and to whatever aspect of Samael and Lilith presents itself to us.

The next step of the work involves holding the intention to descend into the hell of Tiphareth, Tit ha Yeven, "the quagmire". This presents itself as a marsh with no solid ground; this is the house of the builders of ugliness that work with the corrupted and averse name. This is the creative energy of the Name *YHVH* יהוה twisted from its origins to create distorted forms. There is a constant sound of groaning and grinding and dissonance that is the averse reflection of the music of the spheres, and a coldness that drains away all vigour. Here is found the demon king Asmodeus, the son of Samael and Lilith, a shadow reflection of kingship who combines the jealousy and possessiveness of Samael, and the denial of life of Lilith. We align ourselves with the heaven of Tiphareth, Zebul, the sure and centred habitation, the temple that is the house of holiness with the presence of Michael, high priest of Heaven. Bringing to mind the qualities of love and will we invite the spirits and presences of this hell to free themselves.

The deeper Hell of Geburah is Bar Shachath, "the pit of ruin and destruction", and as we hold our intention to arrive here we find ourselves in a torture chamber. This is the house of the accusers and the burning ones, the Golachab, who burn and destroy for the delight of it. Here we encounter the corrosive power of Samael in his shape as the accuser or inquisitor who breaks apart all that is holy so that he dominates all that he touches. As we stand here and speak the name, we link with the Heaven of Geburah Ma'aon, "the strong refuge" and protected fortress of God, and invite the seraphim and Khamael, the warrior of God, to link with us. We make the heart offering, inviting the imprisoned spirit and demonic forms to link with the Tree of Life.

The hell of Gedulah is called Abaddon, "the bottomless pit" and, as we step on the spiral stair and hold the intention to arrive here, we find ourselves in a place of quicksand or in the centre of a black hole that sucks everything towards its centre, and a sense of a ravening hunger that seeks to consume all yet remains empty of life and substance. Here we find the Gamchicoth, the devourers. As we speak the name, we link with the heaven of Machon, the changeless, prosperous place of goodness and generosity, the place of good neighbours who care for each other. We link with the archangel Tzadkiel, the angel of all *tsaddikim* and patron of those who forgive, and the angelic order of the *chasmalim*, the shining and brilliant ones. We make the offering to spirits and demons alike.

Finally, we come to the deepest of the hells, the abyss unveiled, the home of Samael and Lilith, Sheol, "the grave", the home of the wicked dead and the place of the shadow crown in which Samael and Lilith manifest as Satariel, the concealer, Augiel, the confused, and Thaumiel, the eternal divider and denier of unity. As we step onto the spiral stair and hold the intention to arrive here we find ourselves in the midst of the being that Crowley and Dee called Choronzon, incoherence caused by the constant dynamics of concealing, confusing, splitting—a place of cries and echoes, a sense of lives piled upon each other struggling and falling down for there is no co-operation, no unity, and all is chaotic, self-referencing struggle. Here as we speak the name we link to Araboth, the mysterious place of united fire and water, the sea of fire and glass, the desert in which God is found, and we link to the deep understanding of Binah and the contemplative archangel Tzaphkiel, the wisdom of Chockmah and the archangel Ratziel, and the profound unity of Kether and the archangel Metatron. This is the apogee of the art of the transformation of the Qliphoth and here we must truly surrender to the divine light that is infusing us and be as much as is possible the clear channel through which the lost spirits and demonic complexes can reach though to find peace, rest, and liberation. Here we stand as the true human being, Adam Kadmon, the *tselem* of the divine who knows that all is good.

The descent from level to level highlights different aspects of the Qliphoth and starts to create relationship between them and the sephiroth of the Tree of Life. There is a gradual movement from confusion and chaos into dynamic, ordered movement as the Tree of Death and Tree of Light start to align. As our understanding and awareness deepens, we will increasingly know the presence of the shadow tree in the midst of life and conversely be able to see the spark of holiness within the shadows. In this work we enter into partnership with the divine in acts of prayer and blessing and are directed by the voice of the stillness to go into the places of shadow in order to restore and bring healing. This, of course, begins with the house of our own soul but increasingly is concerned with the collective human experience and that of the planet.

Having worked with the Hells and the shadow sephiroth, there are a series of other forms we might use to deepen and expand the work. One is the shadow paths of the Tree of Death. We will recall that the paths represent the process of transmission and mirroring and are both archetypal patterns and are shaped and created by those who tread the paths. Earlier in our training we have worked with the paths of the Tree of Life, contemplating their mandorla-like form, and have made straight the ways between the sephiroth so that the tree within us reflects truly and accurately. Here we enter into a series of distorting mirrors, sometimes called "the Tunnels of Set", which produce distortion and entrapment and our work is to realign the path and bring it back into focus so that the mirroring process is true. The work begins in the sanctum sanctorum and, as we have done previously, we contemplate the mandorla that represents the path we are considering and recall the experience of crossing the bridge of light and making straight the path. We then go through the gate of Samael and Lilith while holding in our mind the image of the mandorla—so, if working with the thirty-second path, the overlapping fields of Malkuth and Yesod with the letter *tav* placed in the centre of the overlap.

Holding this image present as we step through the gate of the shadow tree will bring us into the shadow version of the direct path. As we step through into the shadow path we will find ourselves challenged by the disturbance it embodies. As with all qliphothic work, the main principle is to remain centred in and connected to the Tree of Life. In this case, remaining connected to the felt sense of the straight path represented by the mandorla with the Hebrew letter at its heart and your identity as a servant of the Tree of Life. As with the work on the hells, we begin on the outer levels of the paths of shadow and then descend to the deeper levels of the tree, beginning with path thirty-two and ending in path eleven.

As we become more skilled in this practice of the descent into hell, walking the paths of shadow and the baptism of demons, we will experiment with other ways of working with the Qliphoth. We may work with the serpent Leviathan, the Kings of Edom, investigate a specific qliphothic image, or contemplate the congealing and fragmenting process described by the Iyyun circle. If we feel very bold, we might even emulate Crowley and plunge nakedly into the abyss and embrace Choronzon.

PART 4

APPLYING THE PRACTICE

CHAPTER 18

The serpent is the saviour

As we deepen in our understanding of both the Tree of Life and its shadow, the Tree of Death, we develop a depth of presence which acts as an anchor or centre of gravity around which metaphysical space and time bends. In practice this means that we become increasingly aware of the polarity between the aspects of ourselves that align with the Tree of Life and those that align with the Tree of Death. The process of working with this was called by the Hasidic teachers "the elevation of strange thoughts", meaning by this not just intellectual thoughts but the constellation of thought, feeling, image, and sensation that is generated through the interrelationship of Hod, Netzach, Yesod, and Malkuth. The impulse of these strange thoughts is to draw us out of relationship with the Tree of Life and into the fragmented worlds of the hell realms of the Qliphoth. The art of elevation of these thoughts is the practice of noticing their appearance within us and, instead of allowing them to possess us, to hold them in awareness and to find the root of the particular thought within the Tree of Life. This means the discovery of the root of holiness within even the most disturbed and disturbing thoughts. For example, if we consider a thought of anger and humiliation that arises and follow this thought it generates density and attracts to itself memories, thoughts, and feelings that are similar, becoming stronger and more affecting. In response, our body may ready itself to attack or defend which, in turn, feeds back into the maelstrom of thought, feeling, and image. This creates a vortex that spins more and more strongly, filling our psyche and energetic environment, and it is from this state of heart, mind, and body that we may cause injury to others and ourselves. The hallmark of such thoughts is the sense of separation from the flow of life and the intensification of the sense of self. This produces a deepening experience of alienation from the interactive field of relationship that the Tree of Life describes.

The immediate locus of these strange thoughts is the conjunction of the sephiroth Malkuth and Yesod, so here we can apply the teachings of Rabbi Isaac ha Kohen, seeing it as the habitation of Samael and Lilith manifesting as intertwined generative serpents who appear here as Gamali'el, "the impure", and Nashashi'el, "the primal serpent", mingling their scents and creating a brood of serpents. These serpents entangle the rest of the Tree (bar the supernals) dragging the sephiroth out of balance and into the twisting coils of the averse energies of Samael and Lilith. This disrupts the balance and the mirroring of the sephiroth as the "strange thought" (i.e., the complex of thought, emotion, sensation, and image) establishes itself as central. This is the root of all the addictions that human life is prone to, and, like the addiction experience, is inherently unstable, needing more and more input in order to maintain its centrality. The image is of a mass of writhing serpents who continually join together that which should not be joined, becoming multiple and invading all of the sephiroth.

For example, let us say a thought of desire concerning a person emerges for you. If this is happening within a balanced Tree of Life, this thought will take its place among the organisation of thought, feeling, image, and sensation provided by Hod, Netzach, Yesod, and Malkuth, and is overseen by the intuitive balance of Tiphareth. In this case it will either be dwelled on and turn into some kind of action—which could be anything from writing a poem to making an approach to the person—or else it will be dismissed as not wanted, not needed, or too complicated, etc. In the case of a "strange thought" instead of it being processed through the reflective capacities of the sephiroth, they are pulled together in subordination to the qliphothic core of the thought so that in Hod, instead of being able to think about what has emerged and make a judgement about whether it is right or not, thinking about the desired one becomes primary. So too in Netzach, instead of clearly feeling the emotion it is pulled into the vortex of desire so that the person becomes increasingly exciting. The same happens with respect to the images of Yesod and the physical arousal of Malkuth. The internal dialogue becomes so focused around the strange thought that the balancing and intuitive presence of Tiphareth either cannot manifest or, in a worst-case scenario, becomes itself pulled into the vortex, in which case we may start intuiting signs that we are destined to possess this person. If this "strange thought" continues to advance then we may find the higher spheres of the tree becoming involved. In place of the clarity of Geburah we find the will to possess the other acquiring greater potency, and in place of the compassion of Gedulah an obsessive love of the desired one, leading to collapse into the abyss so that our whole existence depends upon possessing them as they become the source of all life. "Strange thoughts" can have any content so that the example we have just given about desire for another could equally be desire for a job, money, safety, even happiness. Their indicative feature is the way in which they dispossess the balance and mirroring of our Tree of Life.

The capacity for the "strange thought" to disrupt the tree in this way comes from this capacity to join together that which should not be joined. The word "to adhere" or "to glue" in Hebrew is *debek* דבק and is linked to the word *dybbuk* דיבוק which, in Jewish tradition, is a possessing spirit that seizes control of a person's psyche and body and dominates them unless exorcised. This possession can be literal if the will of another being is involved but it also applies to the unintegrated aspects of ourselves that can take possession of our seat of consciousness.

Rabbi Isaac goes on to describe this act of possession as the activity of the twisted Leviathan and asks us to pay great attention to the experience of adhering that enables Samael and Lilith in their forms of Gamali'el and Nahashi'el to entangle the tree. As we have seen, he asks us to consider the heavenly or pure Leviathan, which he describes as an eyeless serpent who slithers between Samael and Lilith, interrupting their bond and eating poison to transform it into the elixir of life.

The image of the blind, eyeless serpent recalls a seemingly insignificant but essential being: that of the humble earthworm who blindly moves through impacted and coagulated soil and, through digestion and literally passing it though its body, aerates it and makes it fertile again. This is the activity of the blind prince who swallows the poisonous reflux between Samael and Lilith. He is said to do this with the aid of Gabriel, the angel of strength, and to participate in the transformative act with the help of Michael, angel of lovingkindness. The clarity of Geburah thus breaks down the centripetal bonds that hold the components of the qliphothic form in existence, and the love and kindness of Gedulah frees and opens the way to the return into the bosom of the Tree of Life.

The art of transformation is precisely the interruption of the bonds that keep the qliphothic form of the "strange thought" in growth and motion, and then the drawing of that form into our hearts, experiencing the bitterness and disturbance and offering it all up to the source of love, light, and peace that we connect to. As we have seen in our discussion of the central practice, the connection to the line of light that upholds us is essential even for advanced practitioners of the art. We find Simon Iff quoting from the Thelemic holy books, Ernest Butler leaning back into the Christ, and I myself into the name *YHShVH* and the presence of Maat within my heart. Here we are inviting the divine presence into relationship with us and the disturbed energies we are in touch with. The act of absorption re-establishes the mirroring process of the tree as what is known as *devekut* דבקות comes into being. This is based on the same root as *dybbuk* but here what is adhered to is the divine presence as we offer both ourselves and the "strange thought" into the divine presence. Drawing upon the strength and clarity of Geburah, we hold the "strange thought" within our psychic and sensory field while, as an act of compassion, we lead that thought back into relationship with the Tree of Life. This is accomplished not as an act of will but through co-operating with the divine presence. Nor is it a mechanical process of cognitively matching a thought with a sephirah. The act of elevation is an intuitive one in which, as the form of the thought dissolves, the root energy returns to the life of the tree. For example, a thought of pride and inflation linked to the shadow side of Tiphareth will, as it dissolves, return energy and life to Tiphareth and thus increase our capacity to mediate and bring balance to the world. Similarly, a thought of desire will return to Gedulah and increase our capacity to love, and a thought based on fear and rage will return to Geburah and deepen our clarity. This is the practical application of the statement we discussed in the introduction to this book, "the serpent is the saviour" משיח הוא הנחש (above, p. 3). This phrase echoes back into the heart of Egyptian tradition and the twin principles of Maat and Isfet and the ancient Egyptian use of the serpent imagery to depict both creation and disorder. Apep, the principle of entropy, is envisaged as a great serpent but Re, the creative principle, is also protected by a serpent guardian known as Mehen, the spiral. Ra's journey through the underworld is overseen by Renenutet, a serpent with breasts who is seen as the mother of the harvest and as a wholly creative figure. The serpent energy is the conjunction of will, love, and imagination expressing itself in numerous forms and, depending on intention, can either be used to enable the movement and growth of life or can hinder and obstruct it. The Egyptian New Kingdom initiatory text, *The Book of Gates*, concludes with a series of women seated on serpents holding a star in their hand representing the image of the initiate who has passed through these mysteries, whatever their sex. They are depicted as women because they are perceived as generative sources who produce life. They are seated on the serpent because they have mastered the positive and negative aspects of creation and their deep imagination now upholds them. They hold the five-pointed star in their hand which is both an image of will and focus and the image of the true human being. This image represents one who has united the figures of the Eloquent Peasant, the Shepherd Sovereign, and the Silent One, and whose very presence catalyses the energies of life and diminishes entropy. Strangely, Aleister Crowley, who would not have seen in his lifetime *The Book of Gates* declared that the accomplished initiates of his occult order, the Astrum Argentum, were the servants of the star and the snake and, whatever their sex, were women.

Adept of *The Book of Gates*

This image of the woman seated upon the serpent, holding the star, is the ultimate conjunction of will and love, showing us how will emerges out of the sephirah Chockmah, the sphere of the stars, and the love that generates all forms arises out of Binah, the primal container and the mother of all. These principles are reflected down the tree, so we see will being reflected first into the clarity of Geburah and then into the fiery desire, Netzach, while love reflects into the compassion of Gedulah and then into many forms of beauty in Hod. They conjoin in Yesod, the foundation of world and psyche, and fountain of life, symbolically arising as the serpent that is both masculine and feminine, the straight line and the spiral. Yesod, as we know, is called "the treasure house of images" and "the inner sea", for it is here that conditioned aspects of will and imagination based upon the experience of life are collected and are a major source of the momentum and energy for the internal dialogue that keeps our sense of self and of the universe stable.

Qliphothic forms such as "strange thoughts" have the vigour and generative capacity of cancer cells. Having their own conjunction of love and will to sustain them, like cancers they erode and can ultimately destroy our life and the life of the universe. The *tsaddik* or adept task is to work with these forms so that they transform, which in one sense means the descent into the hells that we considered in the previous chapter and, in another, dealing with the forms that emerge and seek to dominate our psyche.

As we encounter these obsessing energies within us, therefore, our first task is to hold them steady in the beam of our attention and surround them with awareness so that they cannot slip away. As we do so, and as we connect with the roots of our soul, the sense of judgment arises as we see truly into the heart of the form. As our clarity and desire for union and order connects with the core of will at the heart of the form, we discover the tension of opposites. For example, the desire to be at peace and the desire to possess another. As we hold this tension and offer it up to the divine in an act of prayer and surrender, we return to the non-dual place of beginning in which both our will and love are renewed and set free and the locked-up energy returns into the heart of the universe. Ultimately this is a practice of stillness and relaxation. Much as we find the initiate seated on her serpent throne and holding the shining star in her hand, so, as the forms arise, we simply sit securely with them and let the light shine through until all are freed. This is how idols become icons; their opacity clears as the light of awareness penetrates all the layers of the idol or, to put it another way, the obscuring adhesions that bind things inappropriately dissolve and the spark of light within the lost form is seen and, in the act of being seen, returns home.

We will recall that in the initiatory books of ancient Egypt, Apep is not destroyed or driven out but restrained or pinned down so that he cannot move; the principle of Maat and judgment is invoked, there is a conjunction of opposites, and then a return to the primeval waters of the Nun that are called "the waters of the first time"—Zep Tepi. In this process the serpent sheds its skin, is made new and fresh again, and becomes the uraeus guardian that opens the road for Ra. As we hold the "strange thought" in our attention we pin it down, and as we work with the conjunction of energies that sustain it and bring it increasingly into our heart, we break apart the adhesions that maintain its shape, which then dissolves into the primal waters of life just as the serpent sheds its skin. So, for example, the desire for a person becomes simply the desire for love and connection, and the aspects of will and love that were bound within the form are freed so that the Apep serpent that kept us bound becomes the protective serpent that guides and brings us into new life as we become more open to the energies of love in life.

CHAPTER 19

The collective dybbuk—the egregore

Having worked with the Qliphoth deep in the underworld and within ourselves we now turn our attention to the world around us and to collective experience. It is the nature of qliphothic forms that they are unstable and, because they are separated from the flow of the universe, they function in a parasitic way, attracting and binding the free energy of the universe into the closed loops and cul-de-sacs of their nature. The Tree of Death, like the ancient Egyptian serpent Apep, is dedicated to entropy. This functions in collective experience by fostering a regressive, backward-looking view of life, making links to old angers and resentments and establishing them as central. We have already looked at this in relation to Serbia and the Bosnian war, but it is ubiquitous. To use another example, the invasion of Iraq by the western powers to topple Saddam Hussein in 2003 created enormous instability in the Middle East and was seen by some as a replaying of the dynamics of the crusades. Tony Blair, the United Kingdom Prime Minister who was pivotal to this invasion, in his 2010 memoir, says this about the way in which his experiences changed him:

> The difference between the TB [Tony Blair] of 1997 and the TB of 2007 was this: faced with this opposition across such a broad

spectrum in 1997, I would have tacked to get the wind back behind me. Now I was not doing it. I was prepared to go full into it if I thought it was the only way to get to my destination. "Being in touch" with opinion was no longer the lodestar. "Doing what was right" had replaced it. (Blair, 2011, p. 659)

His conviction of righteousness and the belief that his moral certainty overruled the need for consensus and even for proof that Saddam Hussein possessed weapons of mass destruction was echoed by President George Bush's rhetoric of Saddam Hussein being part of an "axis of evil". Both men had strong Christian beliefs and, while it is unlikely that they consciously saw themselves as crusaders, the belief that has the Christian West being morally superior to the Islamic East is deeply rooted in generations of thinking about the Muslim as the dangerous and alien other. In response, much of the Muslim world explicitly made a link between this invasion and the crusades and, in the chaos that followed the breakdown of Iraq, one of the unforeseen consequences was the establishment of the organisation called the Islamic State of Syria and the Levant, ISIL, which proclaimed itself as renewing the Caliphate of Islam against the crusaders of the West. In both cases, we see the image or *eidolon* of ancestral righteousness establishing itself as a dominant form in the minds and hearts of those who align with it, legitimising terrible acts. It is the nature of qliphothic forms to seduce and convince and to produce acts that increase entropy and despair. They are truly the children of Samael, the poisonous liar, and Lilith the mother of death.

Collective forms like this are deeply connected to ancestral consciousness and represent the unresolved strange thoughts of collective experience, and we work with them much as we have done with the strange thoughts that arise in our psyche although, of course, the scale of disturbance is much greater. One way to think of these strange collective thoughts is to see them as a form of ancestral dybbuk whose nature it is to cling to and adhere to that which gives it life. Most if not all these forms are based around old fear and rage that remains unresolved, and they attach themselves to any person or group that also has that sense of fear and rage and is sympathetic to the genesis of the dybbuk in question. Such forms can be very powerful, particularly when groups are gathered and act to bring the unresolved past into the present. When I was learning Welsh as a child, in the classroom was a banner put there by the Welsh teacher which said "Treachery 1284". This was the date when Edward I annexed Wales, and the point of the banner was to remind us that all that English people were inherently treacherous and had done a great wrong to Wales. The teacher concerned would speak vividly of the pernicious presence of Edward I, producing in his listeners a sense of rage and desire for justice and a wish to throw off the yoke of the English oppressors. Whatever the political issues surrounding this statement, what was being evoked here was an ancestral dybbuk given life and agency by the consent of our wills. Guesting of the dybbuk within our hearts turned us into people who sought justice for our ancestors and in its crudest form this justice manifested as a desire to harm and even kill the English. The dangerous aspect of these forms is their capacity to glue things together without reason or perspective so that righteous vengeance becomes the primary motivation for present-day actions. In Wales at that time (the 1970s) it led to the blowing up of pipelines and the burning down of holiday cottages. Across the water however, in Northern Ireland, the Troubles were in full swing and ancestral dybbuks were causing enormous pain and damage.

The collective dybbuk is an aspect of what in the nineteenth and early twentieth century was termed an *egregor*. The term is derived from the Greek word *egregoros*, meaning "a watcher". Mouni Sadhu, an early twentieth century Polish occultist who wrote a significant text simply called *The Tarot* defines an egregore as:

> a collective entity, such as a nation, state, religion, sects and their adherents and even minor human organisations. The structure of an egregore is similar to that of human beings. They have physical bodies (that is collectively the physical bodies of all who belong to the particular egregor) and also astral and mental ones; the egregor being the sum total of these components. (Sadhu, 1968, p. 24)

The egregor is an example of the creative power of the human mind to generate icons and idols, but here the process is a collective one having the potency, presence, and will generated by collective intention and then, like any empowered image, forming a feedback loop with those who generate it. As we have seen, images that function as icons raise human consciousness to deeper levels of clarity and compassion, but idols dominate and enchain the human heart and will.

Egregors can be quite consciously generated, as in the case of modern occult groups or the ancient Egyptian art of bringing god images into being, but mostly in modern life they are unconsciously brought into being. They come into existence wherever there is collective human intention and action combined with a continuing sense of identity, which is why they are so prevalent in ethnic and tribal identities. We can see this process in the egregor that watches over a football team; around the physical team a sense of identity and history constellates as supporters gather. Indeed, it is the supporters that constitute the body of the egregore as they remain consistently faithful to the watching spirit, more so than a professional footballer who will move from team to team as his or her career dictates. The dedication and devotional acts of the supporters, such as attending matches, wearing clothing modelled after the team colours, painting their faces in the team colours, and above all performing acts of collective devotion such as chanting and shouting in support of the team all empower the egregore, which in return bestows a sense of belonging and a feeling of life and competitive power upon those who participate. Depending upon the fortunes of the team, supporters experience ecstasy and despair, all of which feeds into the life of the egregor and back into the individual lives of those who are committed to it. In the case of a football team, the egregor in balanced form and linked to a sense of fair play and sportsmanship is a positive and innocent force for all involved. As with all forms, it can develop in an unbalanced way so that, for example, the idea of winning at all costs comes to dominate, perhaps combined with commercial implications as (these days) football clubs are large businesses. It is this unbalanced development, combined with the rejection of deeper principles, that leads to the egregor acting as a form of dybbuk which, instead of bringing about the sense of connection and co-operation we find from the Tree of Life, enters into the separating and alienating dynamics of the Tree of Death.

Working with these dynamics to bind their qliphothic nature and enhance their angelic nature is an important part of this work, and reminds us of the importance of the art of mirroring and the realignment shown in the bone teachings. This requires us to be able both to take into ourselves the disturbed and vengeful energy, hold it in our heart, and enable it to return to the essence or "bone" from which it derives, bringing it back into the Tree of Life so that it finds balance once again and can function as a source of support for human life rather than being a parasitic growth.

This practice is very much an everyday practice of being aware of the energies and presences that pass through the collective field of the world. This involves both our sense of personal location and our position in the web of connections of space and time.

At its simplest level, this involves our home and our local environment. Many of us as children will have undertaken the exercise of writing our name followed by our street address, then the town or village we live in then, followed by the county or province, followed by the country we are part of, then the continent, then the Earth, the solar system, the Milky Way, and finally the universe. This is one set of connections from near to far but, if we include the dimension of time, then a whole other set of connections comes into being; we connect to the place we were born, and the maternal and paternal ancestral lines that brought us into being. If we add to this the sense of our travels to different places and peoples, and what we might call the sense of "affinity with" or "empathy for" places and peoples, another set of connections will arise.

In my case, for instance, I live now near Glastonbury in Somerset, UK, and am Welsh. I have travelled a great deal in my life, and have a particular interest and affinity for the Middle East. For nearly twenty years I worked regularly in Jerusalem, which has given me a very particular relationship with that sacred and problematic city. My own contemplation of egregores, both in balanced and unbalanced forms, has caused me to contemplate the roots of national identity in relation to Welshness, the roots of the Qabalah and Abrahamic religion in relation to connections with both Egypt and Jerusalem, and current aspects of esoteric spirituality in relationship to Glastonbury and the beliefs and people who live in and around the town. I have, of course, been affected and influenced by many other egregoric forms, but the main thrust of my life's work in the practice of the Qabalah has meant that the major forms I have both been attached to and worked with arise out of these connections. My focus, in terms of collective forms, has been the collective consciousness of Britain but also the connections between Britain and the Middle East that arise from my connection with the tradition of the Qabalah.

For eighteen years I visited Jerusalem regularly to teach Qabalah and psycho-spiritual psychotherapy. When not teaching, I spent much of my time wandering around the old city of Jerusalem, visiting the various holy sites but mostly just walking around this city that exists on so many different levels. It is, at one level, a place where people live; it is politically and culturally contested between Israelis and Palestinians and between the Abrahamic religions who all exercise some claim on it, and it is also a great archetypal form in the collective consciousness. It is the root archetype of the Holy Mountain, Holy City, Holy Temple, and Holy of Holies, patterns we find in the eighty-seventh psalm, and thus whenever I have visited, my sense of that psalm, the sanctum sanctorum, and the root traditions of the Qabalah are strengthened and vivified. Like all holy places, however, it has a strong shadow side. It is a city of violence, conflict, and polarisation, and these shadow aspects need binding and gathering into the light. In my case, therefore, a good deal of my work has been involved in working with this ancient egregor.

There have been two aspects of this work: temple work and field work.

Temple work involves building the form of the sanctum sanctorum and inviting the spirit of the egregore to enter the Holy of Holies. The sanctum is the mediating form between ourselves and the wider universe. As we work within it, held by the divine pressure that it houses, we will be aware of the way in which our particular nature and experience fits us to pay attention to particular aspects of the egregor that need balancing. In my case, as a British qabalist, my connection to the spirit of Jerusalem through my link to the Qabalah is fundamental, but also my Britishness provides another link that incorporates ancestral encounters, such as the crusades, the British mandate in Palestine, and so on. My personal involvement with it through repeated visits and the relationships I have built up there provides another link. This comes together in a sense of Jerusalem as an actual place, here and now, as an entity that exists through time and as both local and individual for those who live there, and as a universal image within the human collective. As I contemplate these links, I become present to the depth and complexity of the form and life of Jerusalem, being aware of its potency and power, but also aware of its pain, grief, and disturbance. I then link with the divine presence in the sanctum, bringing the sense of Jerusalem into the divine presence and becoming a channel that links them together. After a period of time, there is a sense of completion for now and then the forms are dissolved. This practice can be undertaken with any egregor we are connected to or come across; it is work that is carried out regularly as part of our daily office of prayer.

Field work applies to being physically in a place and encountering the spirit of the place in some form or another. For example, in my wanderings around Jerusalem I would sometimes be aware of the history of that place or might be aware of presences or feelings particular to that place that need attention. On one occasion I was near an old church in the Greek Orthodox quarter and was suddenly aware of the crusades, a graphic experience of slaughter and feelings of pain and rage that seemed to repeat itself on a loop. My response was to align myself with the name *YHShVH*, to repeat the name and to bring the pain and rage and images into the presence of the name within my heart. On another occasion I was in the Armenian cathedral and was aware of many Armenian dead, and of grieving, which linked me to the sense of Armenian genocide in the early twentieth century. Again, I aligned with the name and brought the sense of grief and lostness into the name within my heart. In fieldwork there is an immediacy as we are physically present to whatever is manifesting, and in that immediacy we find ourselves responding to the perceived need. This is normally an essentialised practice in which we relate to the root of our own spirituality and bring that into relationship with whatever is manifesting.

CHAPTER 20

Exorcising places and persons, the living and the dead

As we become more involved in this path of alchemical blessing we will encounter people and places that have become trapped in or contaminated by aspects of the Qliphoth, either as a result of the dybbuk phenomenon or through choices made that align place or person or both with the energy of entropy and separation. The experience I began the book with was an example of a contaminated place that had at its heart a living soul who had become lost to the Qliphoth and was continuing to generate disturbance. These very dramatic events are rare but, when encountered, they are important opportunities to bring about healing and release and deepen our capacity to work with the Qliphoth.

The Qabalah speaks of the mystery of the overshadowing of souls and suggests that we can either be overshadowed by those who are transmitters of light and blessing—who bring us to the state of *devekut*, cleaving to the divine presence—or else we can be overshadowed by beings who are committed to darkness and bring us increasingly into the place of isolation, rage, despair, and all the qualities that we have been contemplating in the hells of the Qliphoth. If we cleave to the light, we find ourselves inhabiting a heaven world and conveying that quality into our surroundings. If we adhere to shadow, we inhabit a hell and embed that quality in our surroundings.

Energy states are contagious; if we spend time sitting with somebody who is very depressed, unless we have taken care to ensure we maintain our own connection to life and happiness we can quickly start to feel that life is not worth living. When that energy state is linked to the Tree of Death and the archetypes of entropy, then that sense of depression or rage or envy or bitterness is amplified a thousandfold. Such a condition does not alter when the person who has generated it leaves the place or dies; the generative power of human beings is such that the physical environment becomes saturated with and aligned to the qualities that have been brooded on. It can also be the case that when someone who has developed this condition dies, they remain attached to the place and simply do not leave. In the case of the soul I encountered in the small country church, he remained attached to his body and his consciousness remained where it was in the crypt of the church, continuing to generate the Qliphoth. In the inner levels there is a timelessness which means that such a being can remain in what is, to them, a present moment that in outer time extends for vast periods. That present moment is maintained by our wish and will to remain contained within our own sense of what is real and to avoid the new circumstances we have found ourselves in. The malleable conditions of the inner planes mean that we surround ourselves with a field of images that prevents us from experiencing the transition of death; we are, as the corrupted elders of Jerusalem in the book of Ezekiel, trapped within our own chambers of imagery.

In order to help free someone who has become trapped in this way, an incarnate person is necessary to disrupt the bond with matter and make the deeper link with those on the inner who can help the deceased soul. In the experience of the country church I was overshadowed by an inner-place helper who assisted me, first of all, to work with the corrupted energy atmosphere of the church itself, and then to engage with the lost soul that was the source of the disturbance. This involved the capacity to link with the light and with the pain, rage, and fear of the lost one, and to hold the link long enough for something new to happen. Another example of this was when I visited Gallipoli in Turkey, the scene of a terrible First World War battle. I was wandering in what is now a green and peaceful scene when I became aware of a small group of Turkish soldiers who seemed to be crouching in a foxhole. They were too frightened to even look outside it and had no sense that they were dead. Once again, there was a sense of linking with the light and mediating that light to them. I found myself repeating the phrase *Bismallah ir Rachman ir Rachmin*, "In the Name of God, the All Merciful, the All Compassionate", one of the fundamental statements of Islam, feeling the divine love and mercy flowing to them. At a certain point they were just gone, leaving behind a sense of fragrance and peace. This was a much gentler experience than that of the country church as there was not an active, oppositional will tied into a qliphothic form; it was simply fear.

Central to this work is a principle developed in the early medieval Qabalah, *sod ha ibbur*, which means "the mystery of impregnation" or "the mystery of transition". It refers to the way in which energies, ideas, beliefs, are transmitted from person to person and generation to generation, and focuses around the word *debak*, the root both of the word *dybbuk*, "the possessing soul", and *devekut*, "the union with the divine". This takes us into the heart of the mystery of the Tree of Life and Death and the nature of the mutual mirroring in which we come into resonance with that which we contemplate, and which contemplates us. If we enter into communion with the divine and experience a version of *devekut* as we then contemplate another, this other is drawn also into communion with the divine. If we lose that deeper communion and simply commune with the disturbed soul, then we enter into the mutual mirroring of disturbance that leads into imprisonment within the convolutions of the Tree of Death. This process is fundamental to the dynamic between icons and idols that we keep returning to in this work. The nature of iconic images is their translucent quality: they point always into the roots of the Tree of Life and towards the experience of *devekut*. Idols are solid, impermeable forms that prevent the egress of light and cast shadow and, like dybbuks, adhere to and restrict and confine our capacity to will and our capacity to love. The idol or dybbuk seals our will to itself and devours love, whereas the icon enables love and will to cooperate freely and without hindrance.

Working with overshadowed souls in this way requires us to enter into this field of restriction, like the blind heavenly serpent of the *Treatise on the Left Emanation*, so that we are part of it but without losing our connection to the divine. Guided by the aligned will and by being open to the other through love, the dynamic of imprisonment generated by the idol or dybbuk becomes disrupted and new options become available. In occult novels, such experiences of release are described as immediate acts but, in practice, this freeing of the soul is a process that can take a great deal of time and, just as a psychotherapist may sit with human pain for long periods, so too the work of qabalistic prayer may need to be pursued day by day until the entrapped dynamic can free itself. Preparation is important in that we must connect strongly to our own source of light and life and let it fill us—although not entirely, for there must be part of our awareness that is open to receive the pain and disturbance and hold it within our heart, making it our own but not being overwhelmed by it. The image of the blind heavenly serpent is very accurate here, because this is a work of feeling into and of visceral digestion rather than seeing from a distance. We, being one with the source, must become one with the other and one with the possessing idol. The work is founded on our capacity to work with the "strange thoughts" we have found within ourselves.

A particular contemplation that arises out of the *Treatise on the Left Emanation* that is central here is the nature of boundary. We are told that the energies of creation derive from a single emanation that arises out of the principle of repentance, which acts as a dividing screen separating holiness from impurity. Rabbi Isaac tells us that it was the teaching of the sages of Beziers that, from this dividing screen, forms of good and evil, beauty and horribleness manifested. The angelic presence who presided over the act of dividing and separation is called Masukhi'el; his name is derived from the word *masakh* מסך, which is the name given to the curtain that hangs at the entrance to the tabernacle denoting the difference between secular and sacred space. When the evil emanations become too dominant, Masukhi'el is asked to gather them and to destroy them, returning them to their original state using the image of the destruction of a candleflame by immersing the wick in the oil that is its ground and sustainer. This process arises out of the principle of repentance, or *teshuva* תשובה, which means "to return" and is the experience of *devekut*, "uniting with the divine". What is required here is for us to return to the divine and to contemplate the doorway to the temple or sanctuary. In its simplest form, *masakh* is the body and the senses so, as we encounter people and places that are overwhelmed by the Qliphoth, our first consideration is to bring awareness into *masakh*, into the physical sense of our body, and to embody the quality of Masukhi'el coming into relationship with the way in which boundary separates and contains but also enables touch and contact. As we encounter the place or person who is overshadowed by the poisonous image, our capacity to be Masukhi'el and hence both container and doorway into the sacred is important, as is our openness to be overshadowed by Gabriel and Michael (or other such forms and beings), the personifications of will and love. This enables us to begin the process of *teshuvah* and the act of return that enables us to absorb and consume the poisonous forms of Yesod, which keep the place or person aligned with the Qliphoth. From here we lift up the person and their condition into the Holy of Holies, the cloud of unknowing of Da'ath.

In this mystery of *sod ha ibbur* we are one and many. We are simply ourselves encountering another in pain and struggle; we are overshadowed by the divine manifesting through Masukhi'el, through the mystery of the barrier that is the door; and we are in turn overshadowed by Gabriel and Michael even as we overshadow the one who is in pain and who is themselves overshadowed by the qliphothic form or dybbuk. Through this mystery of mirroring, the separated form acting out of rage, fear, and opposition is itself quenched by returning into the divine ground. Rabbi Isaac reminds us that *sod ha ibbur* is the deepest of mysteries, hidden even from the angels, and each time we perform it we gain another glimpse of its nature: the mystery of division and union, creation and destruction, and the enacting of the identity of "One is the spirit of the Living God" אחת רוח אלהים חיים with *Olam Ha Qliphoth* עולם הקליפות, "the World of Shells".

As in the previous chapter, this work can be carried out in the sanctum or with the person. If we are working in the sanctum then we would, having entered the sanctum and aligned with the divine, visualise the person with us and, extending our clarity and compassion to them, join with them, letting their pain, rage, fear, and whatever is adhering to them come into our heart. We then simply align with the sense of presence in the sanctum and act as a vessel and transmitter of that uncreated light. If we are working in the presence of the person, we would normally perform the qabalistic cross and invite the presence of the archangels to hold both of us, and we would chant the name *YHShVH* before again reaching out energetically to the person and surrendering to the divine presence that works through us. This may be a work performed simply in silence, or we may speak a blessing or make some gesture of connection and release as a spontaneous gesture. Neither Ernest Butler nor Tom Oloman nor I have ever performed a conventional exorcism on a person, and I would counsel against any such attempts. Ours is a work of love and silence and anything that smacks of driving out demons has no place here.

In working with places this normally involves working directly in the place. We might use the ritual invocation of the sanctum sanctorum to overlay the place with its energies, or we might simply invite the presence of light into the space. Often what happens is that we will be overshadowed by our connection to the Tree of Life and a spontaneous action, such as the cleansing of the country church. The particular approach will depend upon the history of the place and the conditions that have created the disturbance.

For example, in some places in Jerusalem there have been powerful old memories caused by violence having happened there. These are, in a sense, hot spots in which it is very easy to feel rage and fear. Sometimes these places are quite public and so it is not possible to carry out obvious ritual actions. In those cases I have simply spent some time sitting in the place, as if I were just being a tourist, whilst aligning with the name *YHShVH* and drawing the memories into my heart and into the heart of the name. The transformation has not always been immediate, so I subsequently have worked with the place from a distance using the body of light to gradually dissolve the embedded forms. It is possible to work distantly with places and situations that we have not visited in the body as we become more skilled in working with the body of light, but if we have been able to visit the place our connection will be stronger.

CHAPTER 21

Radical innocence—becoming Simple Simon

> We shall not cease from exploration
> And the end of all our exploring
> Will be to arrive where we started
> And know the place for the first time. (Eliot, 2001, p. 43)

As we come to the end of his book, I am reminded by T.S. Eliot that the end of exploration is to arrive at our starting point and to know it for the first time. In my case, it takes me back to getting out of a taxi in the spring of 1973 to meet a mild-seeming primary school teacher. I did not know then that this was going to be one of the most important relationships of my life and would continue until his death twenty-two years later. Tom Oloman embodied a radical simplicity in his life and inner practice; he took the ideas and practices of the Tree of Life and Death and, through patient daily work, entered into the heart of all that has been described here. I remember clearly him deciding that he would study the tarot from scratch again—this, after some sixty years of qabalistic study, practice, and teaching, and in what was to be one of his last and enduring lessons to me: his revelation that the tarot trump he most identified with and that would be his major focus in the years ahead was the Devil. He used the Rider-Waite-Smith pack and the image of the devil there is of a big-bellied, goat-headed, bat-winged satyr seated on an altar with chained male and female figures standing beneath him who have themselves become similar to the major figure.

Surmounting the figure is a reversed pentagram, and the overall tone of the card is blackness. There is a way in which this card sums up all that has been said here about the Qliphoth. Its keynote image is the reversed pentagram, upholding the principle of division without union. The devil here is a solid form, which obstructs the light and casts shadows and converts those who are dominated by it into versions of itself. If we compare it to the card the Lovers from the same pack, we will see some interesting correspondences.

In the Lovers is a similar triangular arrangement, though here the central figure is an angel extending its hands in blessing and the background of the figure is a radiant sun. The three figures are in relationship, the man looking at the woman, the woman looking at the angel, the angel looking down on both of them. In contrast, the figures in the Devil card all look outwards and the background is darkness and shadow. A subtle detail is that the tails of both human figures in the Devil card replicate the images of the trees in front of which the human figures in the Lovers card stand. The Lovers card shows us the method of the icon, which unites opposites and allows the divine light to shine through form. These two cards therefore show us the essence of the Tree of Life and the Tree of Death; they can be seen as mirrors of each other and as a summation of this entire territory.

It is this simplicity we see in Crowley's fictional figure of Simon Iff who, as well as appearing in the novel *Moonchild*, is also the hero of a series of detective stories in which he solves cases through the use of paradox and the application of the way of the Tao. Each story begins with an absurd and impossible-seeming situation that he places himself within and through applying the way of the Tao resolves in unexpected ways. Crowley translated the *Tao Te Ching* and the following verses about the appearance of true nature show us this way in action.

1. The adepts of past ages were subtle and keen to apprehend this Mystery, and their profundity was obscurity unto men. Since then they were not known, let me declare their nature.
2. To all seeming, they were fearful as men that cross a torrent in winter flood; they were hesitating like a man in apprehension of them that are about him; they were full of awe like a guest in a great house; they were ready to disappear like ice in thaw; they were unassuming like unworked wood; they were empty as a valley; and dull as the waters of a marsh.
3. Who can clear muddy water? Stillness will accomplish this. Who can obtain rest? Let motion continue equably, and it will itself be peace.
4. The adepts of the Tao, conserving its way, seek not to be actively self-conscious. By their emptiness of Self they have no need to show their youth and perfection; to appear old and imperfect is their privilege. (Crowley, 1995, pp. 30–1)

This way of the Tao, which we might also call the way of the empty hand, is the path that unfolds when we are established as the living icon, the mirror that enables complete opposites to completely align. This is the basis of the 0 = 2 equation that underlies the dynamic of the Tree of Life and of life itself; the place where the tarot cards of the Devil and the Lovers are one in their difference: +1 the Lovers, −1 the Devil.

The qualities that Crowley identifies here as belonging to the ancient adepts of the Tao are worth considering. He begins by telling us that their profundity is not seen by men; that they like the Tao itself are wrapped in darkness. Their activity is not at all dramatic, they are careful like men crossing a winter torrent or apprehensive or awed by things around them; they are like melting ice, unworked wood, an empty valley, and as dull as a marsh. We learn that they work with stillness and motion and are content to be old and imperfect. This was very much the way of Tom Oloman, which I am still learning and that takes us to the centre of this book and this work—the capacity to enter the roots of the Tree of Life and to allow those roots to shape us and all we come across. The sense of presence required to maintain this is very much like the presence you would need not to be swept away by a torrent, or to be safe in hostile surroundings, or a guest in a great house. More deeply, to be as melting ice is to continually dissolve rigidity and frozenness and to embrace flow, just as to be unworked wood is to allow our shape to grow naturally. To be empty and dull is to create space for the emergence of new life, and to be old and imperfect frees us to be quite simply ourselves. The spontaneous gesture of the empty hand, which invites, creates boundary, and touches all in a thousand ways becomes the heart of the practice. The contemplation of the 0 = 2 equation, combined with the unity of the Lovers and the Devil, contains all we have been speaking of here and more. Tom's image of the white-robed monk is an image whose whiteness contains all shades of all colours, and his mirror for a face means that all faces are his own. The central blessing that Tom practised was "face beholds face", which brings the angel and the demon, the saint and the sinner, the dybbuk and the *tzaddik* into the mysterious union and cleaving of *devekut*, which has no separation and is the place where +1 and −1 unite into 0 and, in the next moment, delights in the separation and contraries of +1 and −1.

To be Simple Simon we must be simple as Kether is simple; to rest in the singularity of our bodies and senses in an open and undefended way, trusting in the mirroring of the Tree of Life and treating all we come across with the curiosity of Alice, who passes to and from Wonderland, and who works on both sides of the mirror. From this place we enter into dialogue and union with all we encounter, resting in the rootedness of the Eloquent Peasant, the compassion of the Good Shepherd, and the silence of the *Geru Maa*.

In the final verse of his translation of the *Tao Te Ching*, Aleister Crowley speaks of simplicity:

1. True speech is not elegant; elaborate speech is not truth. Those who know do not argue; the argumentative are without knowledge. Those who have assimilated are not learned; those who are gross with learning have not assimilated.
2. The Wise Man doth not hoard. The more he giveth, the more he hath; the more he watereth, the more is he watered himself.
3. The Tao of Heaven is like an Arrow, yet it woundeth not; and the Wise Man, in all his Works, maketh no contention. (Crowley, 1995, p. 99)

As we assimilate this work, learning and complication passes away. We more and more enter into the flow of life and are supported by it, trusting in the precision of the Tao that is as focused as the arrow that always hits its mark but never wounds. We do not contend, because our fundamental gesture is that of welcoming the guest and offering safety, nourishment, and the peace that passes all understanding. In being this we are all the living Tree of Life, standing in the midst of the garden. We are all the source of the spring that irrigates all worlds at all times. There is just one tree and it is us.

REFERENCES

Addis, S., & Lombardo, S. (1993). *Tao Te Ching*. Indianapolis, IN: Hackett.
Apuleius, L. (2011). *The Golden Ass*. New Haven, CT: Yale University.
Blair, T. (2011). *A Journey*. London: Arrow.
Buber, M. (2013). *I and Thou*. London: Bloomsbury Academic.
Buber, M. (2015). *Hasidism and Modern Man*. New Jersey: Princeton University.
Butler, W.E. (1959). *The Magician, His Power and Work*. London: Harper Collins.
Butler, W.E. (1971). *Magic: Its Ritual, Power and Purpose*. Wellingborough: Aquarian.
Butler, W.E. (1972). *Apprenticed to Magic*. Wellingborough: Aquarian.
Butler, W.E. (1978). *Magic and the Qabalah*. London: Harper Collins.
Butler, W.E. (2004). *Lords of Light*. Vermont: Destiny.
Butler, W.E. (2022). What we are. https://tinyurl.com/2p87au9m (servantsofthelight.org). Accessed January 2022.
Crowley, A. (1971). *Moonchild*. Newburyport, MA: Weiser.
Crowley, A. (1973). *Magick Without Tears*. Minnesota: Llewelyn.
Crowley, A. (1973). *The Qabalah of Aleister Crowley*. Newburyport, MA: Weiser.
Crowley, A. (1974). *Magical and Philosophical Commentaries on the Book of the Law*. Montreal: 93.

REFERENCES

Crowley, A. (1983). *Confessions of Aleister Crowley.* London: Routledge, Kegan & Paul.
Crowley, A. (1988). *Gems from the Equinox.* Minnesota: Llewelyn.
Crowley, A. (1995). *Tao Te Ching.* Newburyport, MA: Weiser.
Crowley, A. (2015). *The Holy Books of Thelema.* Berkeley: Conjoined Creation.
Dan, J. (1986). *The Early Kabbalah.* Mahwah, NJ: Paulist.
Dehn, G. (2015). *The Book of Abramelin.* Florida: Ibis.
Eliot, T.S. (1944). *Four Quartets.* London: Faber.
Fortune, D. (2018). *The Mystical Qabalah.* Newburyport, MA: Weiser.
Fortune, D. (1970). *Psychic Self Defence.* London: Aquarian.
Idel, M. (2020). *Primeval Evil in Kabbalah.* Jerusalem: Ktav.
Iranaeus of Lyon (2012). *Against Heresies.* Jackson, MI: CreateSpace.
Kaplan, A. (1971). *Sefer Yetzirah.* Newburyport, MA: Weiser.
Kaplan, A. (1977). *The Bahir.* Maryland: Aronson.
Karenga, M. (2012). *Maat the Moral Ideal in Ancient Egypt.* London: Routledge.
Kipling, R. (1909). The rabbi's song. https://tinyurl.com/yvtrmf7p (poetryloverspage.com). Accessed January 2022.
Kipling, R. (1994). *Collected Stories.* London: Everyman.
Lévy, C. (2018). Philo of Alexandria. https://tinyurl.com/mry6b5td (stanford.edu). Accessed January 2022.
MacGregor Mathers, S.L. (1970). *The Kabbalah Unveiled.* London: Routledge Kegan & Paul.
Matt, D.C., et al., (2018). *Zohar,* Pritzker Edition (12 vols). Redwood City: Stanford University.
Plutarch (1936). *Moralia,* vol. 5. Cambridge, MA: Harvard University.
Prescott-Steed, D. (2019). *Tracing Invisible Lines.* Anderson, SC: Parlor.
Qafih, Y., ed. (1972). *Sefer Yetzirah Hashalem.* Jerusalem: Committee for Publishing the Books of Rabbi Saadia Gaon.
Rautenbach, N. (2010). *YHWH Loves the Gates of Zion.* Pretoria: VDM.
Regardie, I. (1964). *The Art of True Healing.* Cheltenham: Helios.
Regardie, I. (1998). *The Middle Pillar.* Minnesota: Llewellyn.
Sadhu, M. (1968). *The Tarot.* London George, Allen & Unwin.
Salaman, C. (2004). *The Way of Hermes.* Vermont: Inner Traditions.
Simpson, W.K. (2003). *The Literature of Ancient Egypt.* New Haven: Yale University.
Stang, C.M. (1986). *Our Divine Double.* Cambridge MA: Harvard University.
Tishby, I. (1991). *The Wisdom of the Zohar,* 3 vols. Liverpool: Littman Library of Jewish Civilisation.
Tompkins, J.M.S. (1959). *The Art of Rudyard Kipling.* London: Methuen.
Wilkinson, T. (2016). *Writings from Ancient Egypt.* London: Penguin.

INDEX

Abaddon, 191
"abyss, the", 39, 44, 177–178
    Choronzon, 178
    dwellers of, 179
    falling into, 135
    oath of, 138
act
    of elevation, 200
    of possession, 199
    of scribing, 97
Adam Kadmon. See inner—golem
Addis, S., 143
adept (*tsaddik*), 12
Adept of *The Book of Gates*, 201–202
alchemical vessel, 161
alchemy, 37
Alexandria, 23
    Christian era, 24
    hermetic literature, 25–28
    Philo of Alexandria, 24, 28
    underground worship and practice, 24–25
"a man and a man", 127–129

Amen, 116
ancestral dybbuks, 207. *See also* collective dybbuk
angel, descent of the, 37
ankh, 13
Ankh af na Khonsu, 165–166
Anubis, 5
Apep, 14, 34, 203, 205. *See also* Egyptian myths
Apostle John, 102–103, 162
Apuleius, L., 145
archangel
    holy living creatures and, 172
    and letters of name, 173
archetypal temple, 169–170. *See also* sanctum sanctorum
Ark of the Covenant, 170
art of mirroring, 149–158
    body and senses, 156
    bone, 157
    bones of the matter, 157–158
    bone teachings and Ezekiel's vision, 154–155, 157

228 INDEX

"Christoslavism", 157
Colette Aboulker Muscat, 152–153
divine will, 155
exorcism, 152
experience of body as living image of divine, 156
Ezekiel, 154–155
internal qliphothic forms, 151
parasitism, 151
process of creation, 154, 156–157
process of manifestation of will, 153–154
sephiroth replication, 150
supernal triangle, 151
"Thing in the Garden", 150
Yehi, 152
astral projection, 133. *See also* body of light
Ateh, 116
Augiel, 136, 183
Auriel, 55

Baal Shem, 95
baptising demons, 187–193
Bar Shachath, 190–191
ba soul, 112
Binah, 40, 49, 169–170
    Chockmah, 75–76
    Geburah, 73
    Tiphareth, 73–74
Blair, T., 206
blessing formula of priesthood, 97–98
body and senses, 156
body as living image of divine, 156
body of light, 101, 130. *See also* image
    Apostle John, 102–103
    astral projection, 133
    blessing and purifying, 102–103
    expanding body of light, 132–133
    inner golem, 101
    Jesus' true form, 102
    manifesting body, 130–132
    mummification, 101
    PRDS meditative process, 101–102
    redemption of all worlds, 102
    splitting moon and stepping forward, 132
    steps to open, 159
bone, 157
    bones of the matter, 157–158
    teachings, 154–155, 157
Book of Ezekiel, 31, 87. *See also* Ezekiel
Book of Gates, The, 201
Book of Genesis, 81
Book of Thoth, The, 26
breathing exercise, 110–112. *See also* Eloquent Peasant
Buber, M., 128
Buddhist formula from Heart Sutra, 143
Butler, W. E., 3, 4, 81, 145
    contact of power, the, 117
    "dissolving and reforming", 85
    human capacity to generate life, 7–9
    magical personality, the, 4
    Robert King, 4–6
    root of the inner work, 109
    sanctum, 174
    symbolism of light, 10
    teachers of, 4
    training method, 4
    Tree of Life, 31
    Yesod and Da'ath, 84

Caliphate of Islam vs. crusaders of the West, 205–206
catacombs of Kom El Shofaqa, 25
Chesed, qliphoth of, 184
Chockmah, 40, 48, 136
    Gedulah, 74
    Tiphareth, 75
Choronzon, 178, 191
Christian Hermetic Qabalah, xii
Christomorph, 162
"Christoslavism", 157
Church architecture, 170–171. *See also* sanctum sanctorum
circulation of light, 117–121. *See also* Eloquent Peasant

"cities of the plains, the", 177
Colette Aboulker Muscat, 152–153
collective dybbuk, 205
  ancestral dybbuks, 207
  Caliphate of Islam vs. crusaders of the West, 205–206
  connections from near to far, 209
  egregor, 207
  factors empowering egregore, 208
  field work, 211
  invasion of Iraq, 205
  qliphothic forms, 205
  sanctum, 210
  seeking justice for ancestors, 207
  temple work, 210
congealing and fragmenting, 182
contemplation of paths of Tree of Life and Death, 122–123. *See also* Eloquent Peasant
contemplative awareness, 81–82
Corpus Hermeticum, 132
cosmology of Hermopolis, 25–26
Covenant, Ark of the, 170
creation, 154, 156–157
creation, process of, 154
  of qliphotic forms in collective, 156–157
cross
  extended qabalistic, 175
  qabalistic, 115–116
Crowley, A., xv–xvi, 135, 137
  aligning with verse from Thelemic holy book, 164–165
  appearance of true nature, 222–223
  becoming Simple Simon, 219–224
  Choronzon, 178
  Egyptianized form of Qabalah, xv
  Liber Liberi vel Lapidus Lazuli, 144
  magical working in Tunisian desert, 178
  "magical memory, the", 142
  Moonchild, xv–xvi, 137, 143
  oath of the abyss, 138
  Silent Sage, 166
  Simon Iff, 222
  simplicity, 224
  soul and God, 139–140
  Taoist teachings, 143–144
  Tao Te Ching, 222–223, 224
  way of Simon Iff, 164–167
  0 = 2 equation, 45, 223

Da'ath, 38–42, 50, 83–84
  enterting, 40
daleth, 100
Dan, J., 179, 180, 182
debak, 215
demons, baptising, 187–193
descent of the angel, 37
"desert path, the", 39
Devil, 220–221
Devil Rides Out, The, 93
Dialogue of the Man and his Ba Soul, The, 126
"dissolving and reforming", 85
"dividing screen, the", 180
divine breath, 163
divine double, 126–127
Divine Double, The, 127
Divine Presence, 89, 188
divine will, 155
driving out. *See* sense of exile
dwellers of the abyss, 179
dybbuks, 215. *See also* collective dybbuk

Edom, 91
Edomite kings, 91
egregor, 207
egregore, 205–211. *See also* collective dybbuk
  factors empowering, 208
Egyptianized form of Qabalah, xv, 14–22, 23
Egyptian myths, 14, 25–26, 110
  ancient garden, 19
  Apep, 14
  Book of Amenope, The, 19
  Book of Thoth, The, 26
  Corpus Hermeticum, 27

Esna, 14
geru maa, 19, 22
heart as centre of awareness, 20–21
Hermes Trismegistus, 25, 26
Hermetica, 26
Instructions for Merikare, The, 19
internalisation of presentation of Maat ritual, 19–20
Ished Tree, 14, 18
Maat, 13, 15, 17
Maat-infused human being, 22
maat kheru, 16
New Kingdom books of the netherworld, 14
Nuit, 21
Pharaoh as incarnate divine being, 16–18
Poimandres, 26
Ra, 14, 17
Ra Horakhty, 21
sacred king, 18
scarab of Amenophis, 16
Tale of the Eloquent Peasant, The, 15–16
Thoth and Maat, 25–26
Egyptian temples, 170. *See also* sanctum sanctorum
Eliot, T. S., 33, 219
Eloquent Peasant, 33–36, 106, 107, 156, 187
 Amen, 116
 Ateh, 116
 ba soul, 112
 beginning exercises, 107
 breathing exercise, 110–112
 circulation of light, 117–121
 contemplation of paths of tree of life and death, 122–123
 effects of training practices, 107–108
 eternal circulation of life and energy, 119
 Geburah, 116
 Gedulah, 116
 interwoven light, 117
 ka soul, 111
 Maat, 107
 magical imagination, 112–114
 magical voice, 116
 Malkuth, 116
 Orphic prayer, 120
 Osirian myth, 109, 110
 PRDS meditations, 121–122
 qabalistic cross, 115–116
 relaxation exercise, 108–110
 root of the inner work, 109
 salutes of the Sun, 114–115
energy states, 214
Enoch, 47
Esna, 14
Esoteric Christian, 162–164
eternal circulation of life and energy, 119
evening exercise, 130
evil, 79–85
 contemplative awareness, 81–82
 Da'ath, 83–84
 degrees or levels of sin, 80
 "dissolving and reforming", 85
 "house of the soul", 84–85
 inner sea, 84
 nature of, x
 sin, 80
 steps in creation of qliphothic forms, 80
 Yesod, 83–84
exorcism, 152, 213
 debak, 215
 dybbuks, 215
 energy states, 214
 freeing of the soul, 215–216
 hot spots, 218
 icons and idols, 215
 masakh, 216
 Masukhi'el, 216
 "mystery of impregnation, the", 215
 sanctum, 217–218
 sod ha ibbur, 217
 "strange thoughts", 216
extended qabalistic cross, 175
Ezekiel, 87, 154–155
 barriers, 87
 bone teachings and Ezekiel's vision, 154–155, 157

Book of Ezekiel, 87
Divine Presence, 89
Edomite kings, 91
"iniquity", 88–89
likeness and appearance, 88
Qliphoth within Jerusalem, 90
restoration of energies of the
 garden, 92
"speaking silence, the", 88
sword, 90
transforming Qliphoth, 87
visions, 89, 91, 154–155, 157
Ezekiel, Book of, 31, 87. See also Ezekiel

field work, 211
figure of Christ, 102
Firth, V. See Fortune, D.
Fortune, D., xiii, 81
freeing of the soul, 215–216
freeing prisoners, 187–193

Gabriel, 58, 179
Gamaliel, 59, 184
Gamchicoth, 184
garden, 41
 return to the, 40
Gates of Zion, 95–96
Geburah, 51–52, 116
 Gedulah, 72–73
 hell of, 190–191
 Hod, 70
 qliphoth of, 184
 Tiphareth, 70–71
Gedulah, 50–51, 116
 hell of, 191
 Netzach, 71
 Tiphareth, 72
Genesis, Book of, 81
Geru Maa, 19, 22, 106, 131, 135, 156,
 166, 187. See also Egyptian
 myths; Maat
 Buddhist formula from Heart
 Sutra, 143
 falling into the abyss, 135
 interlocking dimensions, 144
 Kether, 136

knowledge and conversation of
 Holy Guardian Angel, 140
"magical memory, the", 142
Moonchild, 137, 143
oath of the abyss, 138
Pharaoh Iuput as Horus the
 Child, 141
piercing veil of temple, 136
principle of universalising, 140–141
process of becoming, 136
silent child, 141–142
soul and God, 139–140
Taoist teachings, 143–144
will and love, 144–145
gnosis, 28
gnostic teachings, 28
 Christianity and Islam, 29
 Sefer Bahir, 29–30
 Sefer Yetzirah, 28, 29
Golachab, 184
Good Shepherd, 36–38, 106, 143–144,
 156, 187
 "a man and a man", 127–129
 body of light, 130–133
 *Dialogue of the Man and his Ba Soul,
 The*, 126
 Divine Double, The, 127
 evening exercise, 130
 human personality and divine
 double, 126–127
 morning meditation, 129–130
 psyche within Holy Mountain, 127
 *Sacred Magic of Abra-Melin the Mage,
 The*, 129
 tomb image, 125
 tselem, 128
 work of, 125–133
Gospel of John, images in, 164
grade of the Hermit, 135. See also
 Geru Maa
Grey, C., 137
Guardian Angel, 140

Hagia Sophia in Istanbul, 171. See also
 sanctum sanctorum
ha Kohen, I., 179–180, 198, 216

232   INDEX

Healing Name, ix
    practice of, 160–162
heaven, 188
    of Hod Reqia, 189
    seven hells and seven heavens,
        180–181
hell, 188
    of Geburah, 190–191
    of Gedulah, 191
    of Netzach, 190
    seven hells and seven heavens,
        180–181
    of Tiphareth, 190
Hermes Trismegistus, 25, 26
Hermetica, 26
hermetic literature, 25
    Book of Thoth, The, 26
    Corpus Hermeticum, 27
    Hermes Trismegistus, 25, 26
    Hermetica, 26
    Poimandres, 26
    Thoth and Maat, 25–26
Hod, 35, 56–57
    Netzach, 67
    qliphoth of, 184
    Yesod, 65–66
holiness and impurity, 179
Holy City, 96
Holy Mountain, 94–95
    foundations of psyche within, 127
Holy of Holies, 97. *See* sanctum
        sanctorum
Holy Temple, 96
"house of the soul", 84–85
"House Surgeon, The", 9
human capacity to generate life, 7–9
human personality and divine double,
        126–127

icon, 99
idols, 215
image, 99–100. *See also* body of light
    daleth, 100
    experience of body as living image
        of divine, 156
    figure of Christ, 102
    in Gospel of John, 164
    icon, 99, 102
    lamed, 100
    qoph, 100
    tsaddik, 100
    tselem, 99
imagination, magical, 112–114
"impregnation, the mystery of", 215
"infinite light, the", 44
infinite, the, 169
"iniquity", 88–89. *See also* Ezekiel
inner. *See also* sanctum sanctorum
    dialogue, 35
    golem, 101
    sanctuary, 171
    sea, 84
inner work, root of, 109
innocence, radical, 219–224
interwoven light, 117
invasion of Iraq, 205
Iranaeus of Lyon
Ished Tree, 14, 18, 97. *See also*
        Tree of Life
ISIL. *See* Islamic State of Syria
        and the Levant
Islamic State of Syria and the Levant
        (ISIL), 206
Iyyun circle of mystics, 182

Jesus' true form, 102
Jewish mysticism. *See* throne mysticism
Jewish temples, 170. *See also* sanctum
        sanctorum
John, Apostle, 102–103, 162
John, images in Gospel of, 164

Karadzic, R., 156
Karenga, M., 17, 19
ka soul, 111
Kether, 46–47, 136, 183
    Binah, 76–77
    Chockmah, 77–78
    sphere, 44
    Tiphareth, 76
Khamael, 52
King, R., 4–6

Kipling, R., 8
Korahite psalms, 94

lamed, 100
Leviathan, 199
Lévy, C., 28
life generation, 7–9
light, interwoven, 117
Lilith, 61, 179, 180, 184, 188–193
linen-clad priest. *See* Ezekiel
Lombardo, S., 143
Lovers, 221–222

Maat, 13, 15, 17, 26, 107. *See also* Egyptian myths; *Geru Maa*
    -infused human being, 22
    internalisation of presentation of Maat ritual, 19–20
    Maat-infused human being, 22
    maat kheru, 16
    principle of, 13
    ritual internalisation, 19–20
    Thoth and, 25–26
Mabinogion, 93
MacGregor Mathers, S. L., 183
magical. *See also* Eloquent Peasant
    imagination, 112–114
    voice, 116
"magical memory, the", 142
Malkuth, 34, 59–60, 116
    Hod, 65
    Netzach, 66
    qliphoth of, 184
    Yesod, 34, 64
manifestation of will, 153–154
man or woman of earth, 33–36
Man or Woman of Silence, 106
masakh, 216
Master of the Temple, 135. *See also Geru Maa*
Masukhiel, 180, 216
meditation
    morning, 129–130
    PRDS, 121–122
Mehen, 201
Merlin, 7

Metatron, 47, 160
Michael, 53, 179
"minor adept, the", 36–38
mirroring, art of. *See* art of mirroring
Moonchild, xv–xvi, 137, 143
    Simon Iff, xv, 21, 137, 143, 222
    way of Simon Iff, 164–167
morning meditation, 129–130
mummification, 101
"mystery of impregnation, the", 215
"mystery of transition, the", 215

neo-platonic philosophers, 24
Netzach, 35, 54–55
    hell of, 190
    qliphoth of, 184
New Kingdom Netherworld books, 14, 142
Nuit, 21

Oloman, T., 3, 4, 11, 145, 219
    golden cross and rose, 12
    radical simplicity, 219
    sanctum, 174
    training method, 4
    Zen Qabalah of, 167
Oreb Zereq, 184
Orphic prayer, 120
Osirian myth, 109, 110

parallelism of holiness and impurity, 179
parasitism, 151
Paroketh, 35
"path of the lover, the", 36–38
paths of light and shadow, 61
    Binah—Chockmah, 75–76
    Binah—Geburah, 73
    Binah—Tiphareth, 73–74
    Chockmah—Gedulah, 74
    Chockmah—Tiphareth, 75
    Geburah—Gedulah, 72–73
    Geburah—Hod, 70
    Geburah—Tiphareth, 70–71
    Gedulah—Netzach, 71
    Gedulah—Tiphareth, 72

Hod—Netzach, 67
Hod—Yesod, 65–66
Kether—Binah, 76–77
Kether—Chockmah, 77–78
Kether—Tiphareth, 76
Malkuth—Hod, 65
Malkuth—Netzach, 66
Malkuth—Yesod, 64
Tiphareth—Hod, 68
Tiphareth—Netzach, 69–70
Tiphareth—Yesod, 68–69
Yesod—Netzach, 66–67
Peniel, 55
Pharaoh Iuput as Horus the Child, 141
Philo of Alexandria, 24, 28
Plutarch, 14
Poimandres, 26
possession, act of, 199
prayer, Orphic, 120
PRDS, 30, 81, 101, 107, 121–122. *See also* Eloquent Peasant
Prescott-Steed, D., 138
pre-Socratic philosophers, 23
primordial sanctum, 169. *See also* sanctum sanctorum
principal practice, 159
  alchemical vessel, 161
  Ankh af na Khonsu, 165–166
  Apostle John, 162
  Christomorph, 162
  divine breath, 163
  Esoteric Christian, 162–164
  images in Gospel of John, 164
  practice of healing name, 160–162
  practice of the name *YHShVH*, 160
  Sandalphon and Metatron, 160
  Silent Sage, 166
  steps to open body of light, 159
  way of Simon Iff, 164–167
  Zen Qabalah of Tom Oloman, 167
principle of universalising, 140–141
process of congealing and fragmenting, 182
process of manifestation, 182
Proclus, 24
psalm, 98

psyche within Holy Mountain, 127
Psychic Self-Defence, xiii

Qabalah, xi, 149, 151, 213
  abyss, the, 177
  adept, xii, xiv
  beginning of, 28–29
  contemplative awareness, 81–82
  cosmology of, 81
  creation of magical personality, 101
  Egyptianized form of, xv, 14–22
  Firth, Violet, xiii
  four worlds of, 88
  Iyyun circle of mystics, 182
  Metatron, 47
  "mystery of impregnation, the", 215
  paradise and levels of contemplation, 30–31
  paradoxes in, xi
  practice of extended qabalistic cross, 175
  "return to the garden, the", xii
  Stele of Revealing, The, xv
  Tree of Death, xii
  Tree of Life, xi
  tselem, xii
  Zen Qabalah, 167
qabalistic cross, 115–116. *See also* Eloquent Peasant
  extended, 175
Qafih, Y., 28
Qliphoth, xii, 30, 31, 33, 79, 149, 177–185. *See also* evil
  "abyss, the", 177–178
  blessing and purifying, 102–103
  of Chesed, 184
  Choronzon, 178
  "cities of the plains, the", 177
  congealing and fragmenting, 182
  creation of qliphotic forms in collective, 156–157
  "dividing screen, the", 180
  dwellers of the abyss, 179
  Ezekiel, 87
  Gamali'el, 184

Gamchicoth, 184
of Geburah, 184
Golachab, 184
heaven and hell, 181, 188–193
of Hod, 184
holiness and impurity, 179
icons of deeper worlds, 181
images of inner sea, 84
internal qliphothic forms, 151
Iyyun circle of mystics, 182
within Jerusalem, 90
Lilith, 184
of Malkuth, 184
manifestation, 182
of Netzach, 184
"ravens of dispersion, the", 184
Samael, 184
Samael and Lilith, 179, 180, 183, 188–193
serpent, 179
seven hells and seven heavens, 180–181
steps in creation of qliphothic forms, 80
Thagriron, 184
of Tifaret, 184
transforming, 87
of Yesod, 184
qliphothic forms, 202, 205. *See also* strange thought
creation of, 80
Qliphoth, transforming, 87
qoph, 100
Queen. *See* Good Shepherd

Ra, 14. *See also* Egyptian myths
Rabbi's Song, The, 7, 8
radical innocence, 219–224
Ra Horakhty, 21
Raphael, 56–57
Ratziel, 48
Rautenbach, N., 94
"ravens of dispersion, the", 184
Regardie, I., 183
relaxation exercise, 108–110. *See also* Eloquent Peasant

"return to the garden, the", xii, 40
Rider-Waite-Smith pack, 220
Devil, 220–221
Lovers, 221–222
root of inner work, 109

Sacred Magic of Abra-Melin the Mage, The, 129
Sadhu, M., 207
Salaman, C., 27, 133
salutes of the Sun, 114–115. *See also* Eloquent Peasant
Samael, 57, 179, 180, 184, 188–193
sanctum, 210, 217–218
primordial, 169
sanctum sanctorum, 169–175, 188
archangels and letters of name, 173
archetypal temple, 169–170
Ark of the Covenant, 170
balancing universe, 173–174
Binah, 169–170
in Christianity, 170–171
Egyptian temples, 170
feature of, 175
Hagia Sophia in Istanbul, 171
holy living creatures and archangel, 172
infinite, the, 169
inner sanctuary, 171
Jewish temples, 170
practice of extended qabalistic cross, 175
primordial sanctum, 169
principal function, 175
style of practice and adaptation of, 174
ways of approaching, 171–172
Sandalphon, 160
Satariel, 49, 183
Sathariel, 136
scribing, act of, 97
seeking justice for ancestors, 207. *See also* collective dybbuk
Sefer Bahir, 29–30
Sefer Yetzirah, 28, 29
sense of balancing of opposites, 26

sense of exile, xi
sephiroth, 43
    "abyss, the", 44
    Binah, 49
    Chockmah, 48
    Da'ath, 50
    Geburah, 51–52
    Gedulah, 50–51
    Hod, 56–57
    "infinite light, the", 44
    Kether, 46–47
    levels, 45–46
    Malkuth, 59–60
    Netzach, 54–55
    roots of, 43
    sense of balance, 44
    shadow, 192
    sphere Kether, 44
    Tiphareth, 52–53
    vices of, 79
    Yesod, 57–59
    zero, the, 45
serpent, 179
    energy, 201
"serpent is the savior, the", 187, 197–203
seven hells and seven heavens, 180–181
Shaare Mazvoth, 190
Sheol, 191
Shepherd King. *See* Good Shepherd
silent child, 141–142
Silent Sage. See *Geru Maa*
Simon Iff, 222
    way of, 164–167
simplicity, radical, 219
Simpson, W. K., 15–16, 20
sin, 80
sin, degrees of, 80
Society of the Inner Light, xiii
sod ha ibbur, 217
sons of Korah, 94
soul
    freeing of the, 215–216
    and God, 139–140
    house of the, 84–85
"speaking silence, the", 88

sphere Kether, 44
Stang, C. M., 127
Stele of Revealing, The, xv
stillness, wheel of, 38
"strange thought", 198, 216
    act of elevation, 200
    act of possession, 199
    Adept of *The Book of Gates*, 201–202
    art of transformation, 200
    "elevation of strange thoughts", 197–198
    Mehen, 201
    serpent energy, 201
    thought of desire concerning person, 198–199
    Yesod, 202
Sun, salutes of the, 114–115
supernal
    sephiroth, 41
    triangle, 151
symbolism of light, 10

Tale of the Eloquent Peasant, The, 15–16
Tao, 144
Taoist teachings, 143–144
Tao Te Ching, 143, 222
temple
    Egyptian, 170
    priesthood, 97
    work, 210
Thagriron, 53, 184
Thaumiel, 136, 183
"Thing in the Garden", 150
Thoth, 25–26
throne mysticism, 28
    seven hells and seven heavens, 180–181
Tifaret, qliphoth of, 184
Tiphareth, 37, 52–53
    hell of, 190
    Hod, 68
    Netzach, 69–70
    Yesod, 68–69
Tit ha Yeven, 190
tomb image, 125

Tompkins, J. M. S., 9, 10
training, 106. *See also* Eloquent Peasant
  effect of, 149
Tree of Death, xii, 33, 205, 215
Tree of Life structures, 33
  abyss, 39
  Apep, 34
  Binah, 40
  Chockmah, 40
  Da'ath, 38–42
  descent of the angel, 37
  "desert path, the", 39
  Eloquent Peasant, 33–36
  enterting Da'ath, 40
  garden, 41
  Hod, 35
  inner dialogue, 35
  Malkuth to Yesod, 34
  man or woman of earth, 33–36
  "minor adept, the", 36–38
  Netzach, 35
  Paroketh, 35
  "path of the lover, the", 36–38
  Queen, 36–38
  return to the garden, 40
  Shepherd King, 36–38
  supernal sephiroth, 41
  Tiphareth, 37
  triumvirate of Tiphareth, Geburah,
    and Gedulah, 38
  underworld path, the, 34
  wheel of stillness, 38
  Yesod, 34
Tree of Life, xi, 32, 63, 95, 149
  Book of Ezekiel, 31
  Butler, 31
  creation of, 33
  engaging with, 33–42
  Ished Tree, 14, 18

  lower spheres of, 101
  Sefer Bahir, 29–30
  sephiroth, 32
  triumvirate of Tiphareth, Geburah,
    and Gedulah, 38
tsaddik, 100
tselem, 99, 128
"Tunnels of Set, the", 192
Tzadkiel, 50
Tzal Maveth, 189
Tzaphkiel, 49

underground worship, 24–25
underworld path, the, 34
universalising principle, 140–141

voice, magical, 116

Wheatley, D., 94
wheel of stillness, 38
Wilkinson, T., 126
will
  divine, 155
  and love, 144–145
  manifestation of, 153–154
worship, underground, 24–25

Yehi, 152
Yesod, 34, 57–59, 83–84, 202
  Netzach, 66–67
  qliphoth of, 184
  Yesod and Da'ath, 84
YHShVH, ix
YHVH, 95

Zen Qabalah, 167
Zep Tepi, 14, 203
0 = 2 equation, 45, 79, 223
Zion, 96–97

CPSIA information can be obtained
at www.ICGtesting.com
Printed in the USA
JSHW031950311022
32390JS00003B/9

9 781801 520065